YOU CANNOT ESCAPE FROM GOD

On 20th June 2018 wed afternoon

A Primer on Evangelism

Dennis J. Prutow

WEM

Westminster Evangelistic Ministries
Pittsburgh, PA

COPYRIGHT 1987, 1988, 1989, 1994, 1996, 1997, 2014 by Dennis J. Prutow
All Rights Reserved.

Unless otherwise indicated, the Scripture quotations are from
the NEW AMERICAN STANDARD BIBLE,
Copyright © 1960, 1962, 1963, 1968, 1971, 1972, 1973, 1975, 1977, 1995
by The Lockman Foundation. Used by Permission.

No part of this publication may be reproduced, stored in a retrieval system or transmitted, in any form, or by any means, electronic, mechanical, photocopying, recording or otherwise, without the prior permission of the author.

ISBN Paperback: 978-0-9885215-7-5

ISBN eBook: 978-0-9885215-8-2

Library of Congress Control Number: 2014911831

Printed in the United States of America
at McNaughton & Gunn, Inc., Michigan

Cover Art: Nicora Gangi
Cover and Book Design: Eileen Bechtold

To Russ Ryherd:
A Son-in-law, Student, and Friend
He encouraged the publication of what follows.

Table of Contents

Foreword	v
Preface to the Book	xi

Section One: You Cannot Escape From God

Preface to Section One	3

Part One: Approaching Unbelievers

Part One Introduction	13
1. Point A: You Were Created by God and You Are Therefore Responsible to Him	15
2. Point B: You Often Break God's Law and You Are a Sinner	21
3. Point C: You Will Be Judged and You Face Eternal Punishment for Your Sin	29
4. Confirmation of the Methodology	33
Part One Conclusion	39

Part Two: Presenting the Gospel

Part Two Introduction	43
1. Point A: Forgiveness of Sin and Freedom From Guilt Are Obtained Through Repentance of Sin and Faith in the Lord Jesus Christ	47
2. Point B: The Gift of Eternal Life and Access to Heaven are Obtained through Faith in the Lord Jesus Christ	67
3. The Gospel is Not a Sales Pitch	79

Section Two: Going About the Town

1. Going About the Town	103
2. Talking With Unbelievers	115

3. Recognizing the Harvest	129
4. Presenting Your Faith: Relating Your Hope, Part One	137
5. Presenting Your Faith: Relating Your Hope, Part Two	149
6. Presenting Your Faith: Relating Your Hope, Part Three	161
7. God Must Exist to Play Basketball	173
8. Seek the Lord	177
9. Scripture's Example: Paul's Conversion	185
10. The Conviction of Sin and the Word of God	197
11. The Conviction of Sin: Providence and the Fear of God	209
12. Conviction: God's Means to Promote Seeking	221
Appendix A: Tract for You Cannot Escape From God	233
Appendix B: Suggested Timeline for the Conversion of Paul	241
Appendix C: God's Means of Drawing Sinners to Himself	242
Bibliography	245
Index of Persons	261
Index of Scripture References	263
Index of Subjects	269

Foreword

WE LIVE IN A DAY AND AGE when evangelical Christianity emphasizes personal evangelism, calling all believers to share their faith in their respective circles of influence. While good fruit has certainly resulted from such an emphasis, there has been a void in the broader church in communicating a Biblically Reformed vision for local, church-based evangelism. This void is the very need that Dr. Dennis Prutow's *You Cannot Escape From God* seeks to address, and helpfully resolves. Para-church organizations and the privatization of Christianity have removed various ministries from within the work of the church itself, and individualized those ministries and isolated them from the larger body of Christ. As Reformed Christians, who believe ministry belongs to the Church, particularly local ministries belong to the local church, then what does that look like in the case of evangelism? How would we go about executing church-based evangelistic, and outreach oriented ministries? How would we go about equipping and training the saints to actively and accurately engage in this portion of the ministry? Dr. Prutow supplies a Biblical answer to those questions in this long-awaited volume.

As a student of Dr. Prutow's, at the Reformed Presbyterian Theological Seminary, in his Care and Administration of the Local Church course, I was presented with this material for the first time. Considering the fact that I was not raised in the context of Reformed ecclesiology, but instead was raised in a more broadly, and loosely, evangelical background, these ideas were rather novel and revolutionary for my thinking. I was immediately convinced that evangelism belongs primarily rooted in the ministries of the local congregation, and since then the material found within this now newly printed volume has become the basis for my evangelistic and outreach ministries as a pastor in my home congregation. My prayers, vision, teaching, and training have been affected by the foundational principles in this book; and my discipling and equipping congregants for evangelism and outreach has been saturated with the practical truths of this volume.

While much can be said about the overarching principle of church-centered evangelism and outreach, one of the greatest strengths is the practical how-to portions of this work. For instance, Dr. Prutow's treatment of the apostle Paul's testimony, its structure and breakdown, has been the basis for several teaching opportunities, workshops, and training sessions on "how to prepare your testimony," which I have led. These have all been met with great responses from the congregants in attendance.

Another example of the useful, practical content contained within these pages, is the reformed tract itself, "You Cannot Escape from God." See Appendix A. Nearly every pastor or congregation committed to regular evangelistic interactions with unbelievers has had the disheartening, labor-intensive effort of trying to find an adequately Biblical tract they feel comfortable giving to non-Christians. We have all read well-intentioned tracts that introduce unbelievers to erroneous interpretations of John 3:16, or tragic applications of Revelation 3:20, or harmful understandings of 2 Peter 3:9. But where are the simple gospel presentations in short, booklet form that not only demonstrate an earnest desire for the conversion of sinners, but present such content in a thoroughly Biblical way? Thankfully, such a tract is presented herein. Additionally, it is less than adequate to simply provide would-be evangelists with a tract and then release them on their unsuspecting non-Christian friends, loved ones, and acquaintances; equipping the saints to employ such materials and confidently and cogently present the gospel is essential! The text you presently hold in your hand provides both: a reformed tract and the explanation, theology, and practice behind it.

I have personally used the tract in pastoral evangelism; however, it is not the tract's primary intention and design to be distributed as a standalone (though of course it can be used as such), but Dr. Prutow intends for it to serve as a foundational document. Certainly, a student of this book could take it upon him or herself to craft their own tract from the principles contained in this volume; however, that too is seemingly not the *primary* intention of the author. What Pastor Prutow accomplishes with the tract is establishing the Biblical methodology and structure upon which to hang the proper elements of a clear gospel presentation. I cannot stress the value of such a structure enough.

I pastor in a college town, with a major university but a few miles from the front door of the church. I have the privilege of doing evangelism on campus alongside of students who are members in our congregation; trained and equipped for such evangelistic ministry; and overseen by our Session as they are sent out. It is immensely encouraging to see those students simply and easily share the contents of the Good News, according to the same methodology outlined in "You Cannot Escape From God" because of how clearly the message comes across. And at the same time, it is not canned. It is not rote-memorization. Students grasp the logical construction of the Biblical gospel message, and then naturally speak to the unconverted about its essential truths.

I was encouraging a young brother in Christ one day after on-campus evangelism. I had the chance to observe this man present the gospel to some of his fellow students, and was pleased by the simple clarity with which he did so. His response was humble, but direct. He said, "Once you grasp the progression of the gospel message, it's rather easy to explain." Maybe this is obvious, but this is the power of boiling down a Biblical methodology to its most basic structure, as Prutow does in this book. It provides the ease with which we may share the hope that we have within us.

These are but a few of the highlights of *You Cannot Escape From God*. More could be said of the value of Dr. Dennis Prutow's volume;

however, it is best if you read it for yourself. You will be blessed for having done so. And may we all be doers, as well as hearers of the rich contents within.

Rev. Keith Evans
Associate Pastor
Reformed Presbyterian Church
Lafayette, IN

Preface to the Book

THE MATERIALS THAT FOLLOW were first assembled as a syllabus for an evangelism class taught at Sangre de Cristo Seminary in Westcliffe, Colorado. My first son-in-law was a member of one of those early classes and has encouraged me to publish the material. Since the material was already assembled, my class in the Care and Administration of the Local Church taught at Reformed Presbyterian Theological Seminary also received the syllabus with appreciation. Because of these encouragements, the same material is presented in these pages. The concepts set forth in what follows were forged in the heat of active evangelistic ministry seeking to renew a crippled, discouraged, and distraught congregation. Here is part of the story.

The congregation began with families from a local mainline church considered too liberal for the people involved. They associated with a more conservative Presbyterian denomination holding to the Westminster Confession of Faith, Larger and Shorter Catechisms. As the new pastor, one of my objectives was to see the church properly organized with an active Session, board of elders, and active deaconate. Attendance slowly improved and weekly worship saw seventy-five to a hundred people gathering to sing God's praise and to hear the weekly sermons.

However, there was a problem. The core families were committed dispensationalists. The men in this core group had been elected as elders but they declined to stand for ordination. They could not, in good conscience, subscribe to the denominational Standards. They would not take the vows requiring them to submit to and uphold the Westminster Confession and Catechisms.

To my way of thinking, the solution was simple. If these men would step aside, then the congregation could elect other men as elders and deacons and move ahead. When asked to step aside for the betterment of the congregation, all but one refused. The church was at loggerheads. What to do? Again, to my way of thinking, the men in question stood in violation of the vows of church membership requiring them to submit to the government and discipline of the church. What to do? The difficult and gut-wrenching course of church discipline seemed to be the only answer. This church discipline led to two full-length church trials at the local level. The families involved also sought to have the Presbytery remove me as pastor of the congregation. In God's providence, when the course of discipline was completed, the families involved left the congregation. The church was spared but not without suffering great loss.

When I looked out over the congregation one Lord's Day morning, after our ecclesiastical nightmare was over, there were nineteen people, including my own family, remaining from the church of seventy-five to a hundred strong. It was a day of reckoning for me. I thought to myself, "Denny, you had better get busy or there will be no congregation here to serve."

As a result, we began several avenues of community outreach and evangelism. Since our church property was close to an elementary school and the children often crossed our churchyard on their way to and from school, we began to recruit them for an afternoon Bible club. Our objective was to connect with neighborhood families. We did bulk mailings inviting people to come to church and offering a Bible correspondence course. We placed weekly devotional columns in the local newspaper to raise church visibility. We put up signs on strategic corners to direct people to the church's building. The church also sponsored special meetings for evangelism, missions, and Biblical counseling.

In addition, I developed an evangelistic tract with which I was comfortable, "You Cannot Escape from God," which went through various editions and printings. The pages of the tracts are displayed in Appendix A. Section One of what follows was developed as background information for and to help people use the tract.

The primary use of "You Cannot Escape from God" was in door-to-door calling. I personally committed myself to regular community calling. When we were able, we had the help of seminary interns. My procedure was simple. With tracts in hand along with church calling cards, I went from house to house. When a door was answered, I introduced myself, invited these neighbors to worship with us, and gave them the gospel tract and the calling card. The card had a little map showing the church's location.

During the course of this calling I began to notice that some people stood at their doors waiting for me to say more, to talk to them more, to give them something more. It was during this period that, in God's providence, Matthew 9:35-36 popped out at me:

> Jesus was going through all the cities and villages, teaching in their synagogues and proclaiming the gospel of the kingdom, and healing every kind of disease and every kind of sickness. Seeing the people, He felt compassion for them, because they were distressed and dispirited like sheep without a shepherd.

When this text came home to me, I realized that many of the people we encountered in our calling were "distressed and dispirited like sheep without a shepherd." As a result, our calling became more focused. We began looking for people who were like sheep without a shepherd. We focused on them, remembered them, and sought to arrange further discussions with them. Chapters 1, "Going About the Town" and 3, "Recognizing the Harvest," of Section Two, unpack Matthew 9:35-36, and explore what we learned about door-to-door visitation.

One of the problems attending this kind of personal work is fear. My preaching in First Peter during this period once again proved providential. Peter addresses the problem of fear forthrightly:

> But even if you should suffer for the sake of righteousness, you are blessed. AND DO NOT FEAR THEIR INTIMIDATION, AND DO NOT BE TROUBLED, but sanctify Christ as Lord in your hearts, always *being* ready to make a defense to everyone who asks you to give an account for the hope that is in you, yet with gentleness and reverence; and keep a good conscience so that in the thing in which you are slandered, those who revile your good behavior in Christ will be put to shame (1 Pet. 3:14-16).

Chapters 4, and 5 of Section Two, laying out aspects of "Presenting Your Faith: Relating Your Hope," unpack 1 Peter 3:14-15. Chapter 6 of Section Two gives an outlined for giving a short testimony based on 1 Peter 3:15 and derived from the apostle Paul.

Part of the mix is not only overcoming fear but also having confidence to approach unbelievers. Chapters in both Section One and Section Two devote space to our point of contact with those outside of Christ. Recognizing God's means for converting sinners will also give us confidence in approaching and talking with unbelievers. The chapters outlining Paul's Conversion and discussing Conviction of Sin offer help in these areas. See also Appendix C. Finally, knowing that the Sovereign God of the universe is the Master at converting men and women, we must learn to present the gospel to those in need and to trust God to do the work that He alone can do and that He does best. Hence the chapters titled, "The Gospel is Not a Sales Pitch," and "Seek the Lord."

Many hands were involved in the preparation of this volume. In addition to the basic cover and book design, Eileen Bechtold patiently did the edits on several iterations of the manuscript. Thank you for your faithful work, Eileen. Nicora Gangi has a special gift from God. Her cover art beautifully captures the message of Matthew 9:36. Thank you, Nicora. Professor Tom Reid, RPTS Librarian, compiled the indices. Tom's work is always careful and precise. Thank you, Tom. As expressed in his Foreword, Keith Evans implemented in the congregation what is taught in this short book. Thank you, Keith, for adding your hand to this project with your Foreword. This book is dedicated to my son-in-law, Russ Ryherd. He too was a patient student. His encouragement kept this project alive. Thank you, Russ. Errors in the final manuscript are my own.

Finally, I am grateful to God for His saving grace, for the patience and love of my dear wife, for my family who bears the testimony of Christ, and for God's people who listened and learned the truths set forth in the following pages.

Dennis J. Prutow

SECTION ONE:
YOU CANNOT ESCAPE FROM GOD

Preface to Section One

The following presentation is an effort to help individuals and churches in the task of taking the gospel to their neighbors. The study will also be found helpful for those who are interested in using the gospel tract printed by the writer called "You Cannot Escape from God." You can see the layout of the tract in Appendix A.

The main points in what follows are not only an effort to set forth the way of salvation, they are an outline setting forth a particular methodology. And it is this very basic methodology, along with the gospel of saving grace, which I am eager to communicate. Let me hasten to say that my eagerness is based on the fact that I am persuaded that the methodology I set forth is not only Biblical but it is also the one followed by the Lord Jesus Christ and the apostle Paul. This methodology is not meant to be a canned gospel presentation that drives toward a decision. Far from it! Nor are the main points to be viewed as rigid steps through which prospective converts must be pushed. Rather, the methodology is intended to reveal the basic form and the basic content of the message to be presented. Where circumstances vary, the message varies. But both the approach to unbelievers and the primary thrust of the message remain the same.

In brief, the methodology I set forth is quite simple. On one side, I point to inescapable truth. Those who refuse the authority of God over them deny this truth, unavoidable as it is. Yet this same truth, when acknowledged, betrays the fallen and sinful condition of men and women before God.

On the other side, I present the only alternative to this sinful condition: full and free salvation through Christ. A major portion of what follows is devoted to an exposition of this Good News.

But understanding the methodology requires that we give some attention to the starting point. As to this starting point, my mentors are the apostle Paul and men who have followed him such as John Calvin, Abraham Kuyper, Herman Bavinck and Cornelius Van Til. I go back to Calvin and his instruction:

> There is within the human mind, and indeed by natural instinct, an awareness of Divinity. This we take to be beyond controversy. To prevent anyone from taking refuge in the pretense of ignorance, God Himself has implanted in all men a certain understanding of His Divine Majesty ... Since, therefore, men one and all perceive that there is a God and that He is their Maker, they are condemned by their own testimony because they have failed to honor Him and to consecrate their lives to His will.[1]

Here is the point of contact we have with unbelievers; the inescapable knowledge of God that they, though they may deny it, if they are honest with themselves, will admit. The methodology I propose relies on this point of contact. And I begin my presentation with expositions of Romans 1:18 and 19 and Romans 2:14 and 15. These texts show that Calvin is correct in his assessment that the unbelieving human heart possesses a certain implanted knowledge of God. Speaking of this implanted knowledge, Abraham Kuyper said:

> Calvin called this the seed of religion (*semen religionis*), by which he indicated that this innate knowledge of God is an ineradicable property of human nature, a spiritual eye in us, the lens of which may be dimmed, but always so that the lens, and consequently the eye, remains.[2]

In following both Calvin and Kuyper, Herman Bavinck carries us forward as he defines the terms "implanted" and "innate."

---

1. John Calvin, *Institutes of the Christian Religion*, trans. F. L. Battles, ed. J. T. McNeill (Philadelphia: Westminster Press, 1965), 43.
2. Abraham Kuyper, *Sacred Theology* (Wilmington: Associated Publishers and Authors, n.d.), 104.

Preface to Section One

> Accordingly, the words "implanted, inborn, innate," do not indicate "that wherewith a man is born," but merely state that the knowledge of God is obtained in a natural manner, without intellectual argumentation (reasoning): that it is inherent in the structure of the human soul itself ... Indeed, man himself constitutes the most important object of God-revealing nature. Moreover, from the entire realm of nature (both within him and exterior to him) man receives impressions and perceptions, which, prior to all argumentation and discussion, imbue his consciousness with the idea of a Highest Being. It is God Himself who does not leave any man without witness.[3]

You see, God reveals Himself as the Creator in and through the consciousness of every human being. And no human being can escape such revelation. Men and women may suppress and deny the truth welling up within them, but they cannot escape it. And so we have a vital point of contact with the unbeliever. In the words of Cornelius Van Til: "The point of contact for the gospel, then, must be sought within the natural man. Deep down in his mind every man knows that he is the creature of God and responsible to God."[4] And again:

> The natural man at bottom knows that he is the creature of God. He knows also that he is responsible to God. He knows that he should live to the glory of God. He knows that in all that he does he should stress that the field of reality which he investigates has the stamp of God's ownership upon it. But he suppresses his knowledge of himself as he truly is. He is the man with the iron mask. A true method of apologetics [and preaching] must seek to tear off that iron mask.[5]

And this is my aim: to tear off that mask and cause unbelievers

---

3. Herman Bavink, *The Doctrine of God*, trans. William Hendricksen (Edinburg: Banner of Truth, 1977), 58-59.
4. Cornelius Van Til, *The Defense of the Faith* (Philadelphia: Presbyterian and Reformed, 1972), 94.
5. Ibid., 101.

to face the truth about themselves. For once they squarely face this truth, the Good News of God's grace in Christ will make sense.

But there is more. Van Til goes on to stress that every human being knows and seeks to suppress at least three related facts.

He knows he is a creature of God; he has been simply seeking to cover up this fact to himself. He knows that he has broken the law of God; he has again covered up this fact to himself. He knows that he is therefore guilty and is subject to punishment forever; this fact too he will not look in the face.[6]

And so I make these three truths my starting point. And I come to those who reject the Christ of the Bible with this inescapable truth. I present these three facts at the outset:

A. You were created by God and you are therefore responsible to Him (Gen. 1:27 and Rom. 1:20).

B. You often break God's Law and you are a sinner (1 John 3:4, Jas. 4:17, and Rom. 3:22-23).

C. You will be judged and you face eternal punishment for your sin (Heb. 9:27 and Matt. 25:41).

As is often the case, the bad news precedes the good news. But without an acknowledgement of these three points, the bad news, the good news of God's grace in Jesus Christ will not be viewed as truly Good News.

Will those confronted with this truth accept and acknowledge the truth as it is presented? Allow me to answer by again quoting Van Til.

> As for the question whether the natural man will accept the truth of such an argument, we answer that he will if God pleases by His Spirit to take the scales from his eyes and the mask from his face. It is upon the power of the Holy Spirit that the Reformed preacher relies when he tells men that they are lost in sin and in need of a savior. The Reformed preacher does not

---

6. Cornelius Van Til, *Apologetics* (Philadelphia: Westminster Theological Seminary, n.d.), 98.

tone down his message in order that it may find acceptance with the natural man. He does not say that his message is less certainly true because of its non-acceptance by the natural man. The natural man is, by virtue of his creation in the image of God, always accessible to the truth, accessible to the penetration of the truth by the Spirit of God.[7]

And so, you see my starting point and point of contact with the unbelievers. My purpose in what follows is to display that the methodology based upon this starting point and point of contact is derived from Scripture. I also hope to display that the apostle Paul utilized this methodology. Not only so, I am anxious to encourage you to follow the apostle Paul in your personal approach to unbelievers. And I am convinced, that once seeing the basis for the methodology of the apostle Paul, and once understanding how Paul puts this methodology into practice, you will have a new confidence to follow Paul. You will speak the truth in love. You will urge those who have rejected Christ to accept the truth about them. You will present Christ to unbelievers. And you will urge them to flee to Christ for refuge. He is the only alternative to facing certain judgment for sin. Further discussion of these points is in Part I, which follows.

Having briefly set forth the bad news, I come to the Good News and "The Presentation of the Gospel." Again, the presentation set forth in what follows will help those interested embellish the outline given in the tract, "You Cannot Escape from God." The alternative to sin and judgment, the good news of the gospel, gives answer to the inescapable truth within every unbeliever.

   A. Forgiveness of sin and freedom from guilt are obtained through repentance of sin and faith in the Lord Jesus Christ (Rom. 5:6; Acts 3:19, 16:31).

   B. The gift of eternal life and access to heaven are obtained through faith in the Lord Jesus Christ (Rom. 6:23; John 17:3; Matt. 25:34).

---

7. Van Til, *The Defense of the Faith*, 104.

C. The Lord Jesus Christ freely offers Himself to you saying: *"Come to Me, all who are weary and heavy-laden, and I will give you rest"* (Matt. 11:28).

First, there is the matter of freedom from guilt for sin. The death of Christ as a sacrifice for sin must be pressed on the unbeliever. Not only so, the perfect life of Christ must also be displayed as the only acceptable ground for entrance into heaven. In theological terms, men and women must come to terms with the passive and active obedience of Christ. Second, cleansing from sin is not enough. We must be clothed with the perfect righteousness of Christ. Justification includes both. This is the rationale behind the first two major points in this section. They coincide with the points given in the first section of the tract.

Of course it is my desire to set forth the work of Christ through the points just related. Not only so, it is my desire to describe true conversion through these two points. As a result, it is my desire to call men and women to repent of sin and to place saving faith in Christ. And so, I will discuss these matters in Part II of what follows.

I also plan to emphasize further the need to present Christ as Lord to those seeking Him. We must not make the mistake of encouraging men and women to come to Christ as savior while being ignorant of His demand to serve Him as Lord. It is always to the Lord Jesus Christ that men and women must turn. The basic Christian confession is, "Jesus is Lord" (Rom. 10:9; 1 Cor. 12:3). And so, men and women must bow before Christ as Lord. They must pledge themselves to follow Him as His servants. This emphasis in the gospel upon the Lordship of Christ must also be explored in an expansion of Part II.

The answer to facing judgment is to accept the invitation of Christ. This is neither my invitation nor your invitation. It is Christ's invitation. He issues the call. We are ambassadors for Christ. And as an ambassador for Christ, you must invite men and women to turn to Christ. I will discuss the import of this invitation and the need to issue it in an expansion of Part III of what follows. I call this section

"The Gospel is not a Sales Pitch." My plan is to discuss the free offer of the gospel as seen in Scripture.

In all of this, the work of the Holy Spirit is of utmost importance. We must learn to understand the convicting work of the Holy Spirit. And we must become discerning. We must come to the place of recognizing the outward manifestations of this convicting work. And as we grow in our discernment, we will grow in our ability to recognize God's harvest. We will not go too fast in pressing the claims of Christ upon men and women but we will recognize when they are "sheep without a shepherd" (Matt. 9:36) and when the Chief Shepherd is bringing the work of conviction to fruition. My plan is to explore these matters in Section Two of this discussion. May God help us all to present the truth of the claims of Christ to those so much in need!

You Cannot Escape From God

PART ONE:
Approaching Unbelievers

Introduction

*We have obtained our introduction by faith into this grace
in which we stand.* ~Rom. 5:2

ONE LORD'S DAY AFTER EVENING WORSHIP I was asked the question, "Do you really think the apostle Paul had a specific methodology in mind when he presented the gospel to unbelievers?" The question was in response to a presentation of the material that follows. I sought to show that there is a specific Biblical rationale for the first three points in my tract, "You Cannot Escape from God." And my answer to the above question was and is a resounding "Yes!" I am persuaded that Paul, although he did not follow specific points in a ritualistic manner, did indeed hold to specific principles that molded his presentations of the gospel.

It must be noted that we are concentrating on Paul's approach to unbelievers who did not have the Scriptures and who were totally unfamiliar with the content of the Scriptures. Paul's approach to his fellow Jews who were members of the synagogue and who were familiar with the Old Testament prophecies is not in view. Paul's approach to Jewish people was dramatically different than his approach to the Gentiles. Of course we face a situation today similar to the one faced by the apostle Paul in his day. There is a deplorable lack of interest in and knowledge of the Bible among unbelievers. And so Paul's methodology should be of utmost interest to us. Not only so, if, in the providence of God and through the inspiration of the Holy Spirit, we are given a model by the apostle, we are given that model, not only by Paul but we are given that model by God Himself. This makes it all the more critical that we understand the approach of the apostle to the unbelieving world of his generation.

The discussion that follows is given in outline form in my tract, "You Cannot Escape from God." A cursory review of this tract shows the three points that compose the core of Paul's approach to unbelievers. What follows, is an attempt to show that Paul did use these basic points, along with the Biblical reasons behind his thinking. Part Two of our discussion will also follow the outline of the tract that sets forth a presentation of Christ as the answer to Part One. The first three points for discussion are:

A. You were created by God and you are therefore responsible to Him.

B. You often break God's law and you are a sinner.

C. You will be judged and you face eternal punishment for your sin.

I will attempt to show from Scripture that every unbelieving human being knows these three points to be true. Not only so, every unbelieving human being knows these three points to be true about himself or herself. Although they may outwardly deny the validity of these three truths, in the hidden recesses of their hearts, they cannot deny them.

Secondly, the fact that every unbelieving human being knows the truth, while denying it, makes it imperative that the truth be simply presented. This also comports with the specific work of the Holy Spirit outlined for us by Christ Himself. And so, we should make every effort to implement the methodology that Christ promises will be blessed by the work of the Holy Spirit. And third, if we are on the right track, we should see the apostle Paul not only bolster the methodology in a theoretical fashion, but we should see the apostle implement this methodology in very practical situations. I will attempt to show that the apostle does this in very astonishing ways. Having said all of this, let's move on.

1

POINT A:
YOU WERE CREATED BY GOD AND YOU ARE THEREFORE RESPONSIBLE TO HIM

> *For the wrath of God is revealed from heaven against all ungodliness and unrighteousness of men, who suppress the truth in unrighteousness, because that which is known about God is evident within them; for God made it evident to them.* ~ROM. 1:18-19

THE HOLY SPIRIT IS TELLING US through the apostle Paul that God has made certain things known about Himself to every human being. This text speaks specifically of unbelievers. It speaks of those against whom the wrath of God is being revealed. And it tells us that God has placed certain knowledge of Himself within these unbelievers. Verse 21 gives us the same slant on unbelieving human nature. "For even though they knew God, they did not honor Him as God." In other words, unbelievers know God. They obviously do not know God in a saving way because they do not properly honor God. They do not honor Him as their God. But this does not obviate the fact that certain knowledge of God is resident within them.

What is the content of this knowledge concerning God that all unbelievers possess? Romans 1:20 answers: "For since the creation of the world His invisible attributes, His eternal power and divine nature have been clearly seen, being understood through what has been made, so that they are without excuse."

Here Paul tells us that the invisible attributes of God can be clearly understood. These invisible attributes include, on one side, God's eternal power, and on the other side, God's divine nature. On one side, the great creative power of God can be and is clearly seen by all. On the other side, the divine nature of God, the fact that He is God over all, is also clearly seen by all. Putting it another way, the knowledge that God is God and the knowledge that God is the Creator, is present within every human being, including those human beings who do not properly honor God.

Paul also tells us how we all, including unbelievers, obtain this knowledge of God. This knowledge of God, this understanding of God, is obtained "through what has been made." We rightly point to this text to undergird the teaching of general revelation. God reveals Himself through His creation. "The heavens are telling of the glory of God; and their expanse is declaring the work of His hands" (Ps. 19:1). Yes, when we look into the heavens and view the stars hung in their places in the arch of heaven we can give glory to God for His handiwork. Creation does display the "eternal power and divine nature" of God.

We ought not to neglect the fact that *we* are a part of God's creation. In fact, we are God's creation. God created our hearts, minds, and consciences. Our very minds function the way they do because God created them. As such, God's eternal power and divine nature are revealed in and through our hearts and minds. They are a part of God's creation. And because we are creatures of God made in His image, the fact that God is God and the fact that God is our Creator is imbedded within the very fabric of our being. No human beings can avoid these truths, which are revealed through their own hearts and minds, because they are a part of the creation of God. To put it in terms the apostle uses, God's "eternal power and divine nature" are "clearly seen" because they are "understood through what has been made." And God made your heart and mind and my heart and mind. Therefore every human being knows God because he or she is the creation of God.

Artists working in various media readily understand what Paul is teaching. Any artwork in oils, in watercolors, in stone or clay, or in some musical form, carries the signature of the artist on that work. I do not refer to the initials in the corner of the painting or on the bottom of the sculpted work. These initials are really only a small part of the artist's signature. When those who know an artist see a painting or hear composition, they recognize that artist immediately. The artist is recognized by his or her work. So it is with God. God is recognized by and in His work, by what He has made. God's character and personality are all over and within His handiwork. God's signature is all over and within you and me.

And so, Paul affirms that unbelievers know God to be God. And in addition, they know God to be their Creator. It is impossible for unbelievers to escape this knowledge of God. God has placed it in them. Hence the title, "You Cannot Escape from God.

But what is the reaction of unbelievers to this knowledge of God that God has placed within them. Romans 1:18 answers. "They suppress the truth in unrighteousness." In other words, unbelievers push down the truth of God that bubbles up within them. They push it down, repress it, and deny it. If you have ever had a water pipe burst in your home, you know how fast you act to cover up the flow of water through the hole in the pipe. You get your hands around that gush of water and wrap it with rags. And you shout for help to get someone to turn off the water. So it is with unbelievers. They will do almost anything to cover up and to plug up the spring of truth that bubbles up within them. However, no matter how the truth is denied, as with the teaching of evolution, the truth still exists. And when all the smoke is blown away, the implanted truth that God is God and that He is the Creator is there within every unbeliever.

And so how should this teaching of Paul be applied in our evangelism? Very simply, we should present the truth. We should realize that although the unbeliever may deny the truth, deep down he or she really knows the truth. And so we should say with love and concern,

"You were created by God and you are therefore responsible to Him." And although you know that your unbelieving friend may laugh, you also know that his laugh is really a denial of himself. Why? Because in the end, your unbelieving friend cannot escape from God. God speaks to him out of the inner recesses of his own being and reveals Himself as the Creator. Your prayer is that the Holy Spirit will be pleased to regenerate the hostile heart of this unbeliever and cause him to acknowledge openly what he really already knows but denies and suppresses.

The witness of the apostle Paul confirms this methodology. In Acts 14:8-18 we see Paul and Barnabas encounter the Greeks at Lystra.

> And at Lystra there was sitting a certain man, without strength in his feet, lame from his mother's womb, who had never walked. This man was listening to Paul as he spoke, who, when he had fixed his gaze upon him, and had seen that he had faith to be made well, said with a loud voice, "Stand upright on your feet." And he leaped up and began to walk. And when the multitude saw what Paul had done, they raised their voice, saying in the Lycaonian language, "The gods have become like men and have come down to us." And they began calling Barnabas Zeus, and Paul, Hermes, because he was the chief speaker. And the priest of Zeus, whose temple was just outside the city, brought oxen and garlands to the gates, and wanted to offer sacrifice with the crowds. But when the apostles, Barnabas and Paul, heard of it, they tore their robes and rushed out into the crowd, crying out and saying, "Men, why are you doing these things? We are men as the same nature as you, and preach the gospel to you in order that you should turn from these vain things to a living God, WHO MADE THE HEAVEN AND THE EARTH AND THE SEA, AND ALL THAT IS IN THEM. And in the generation gone by he permitted all the nations to go their own ways; and yet He did not leave himself without witness, in that He did good and gave you rains from heaven and fruitful seasons, satisfying your hearts with food and gladness."

> And even saying these things, they with difficulty restrained the crowds from offering sacrifice to them.

It was a dramatic situation. By the grace of God a lame man was healed. A crowd gathered. The local priests wanted to lead the crowd in a sacrifice to honor Paul and Barnabas. In restraining the crowd, Paul preaches to these pagans. And what does he do but direct their attention to the "living God" (v. 14). And Paul proceeds to describe this living God. He is the creator. He is the One who "made the heaven and earth" (v. 14). In other words, Paul directs the attention of these people of Lystra to the God who made them. And he emphasizes the fact that God has not left himself without a witness to them. "He did good and gave you rains from heaven and fruitful seasons" (v. 17).

In terms of the above discussion, Paul appeals to the knowledge of God within these people as he presents the Creator to them. And he points to general revelation around these people of Lystra saying that God has spoken to them through all of His creation.

We should do no less. The point is not to engage in debates over the existence of God. The methodology of Paul demands that we begin with God. We present Him as the Creator. We appeal to the knowledge of God placed within every unbeliever by God Himself. And we pray that God by His grace will see fit to convict the unbeliever of this truth. We want the unbeliever to desist from his or her denials and suppression of the truth and step forward in full confession of the truth. And so our task is plain.

To reiterate, in approaching unbelievers in our day, we should direct their attention to their Creator. We should do this unashamedly. We have a vital point of contact with every unbeliever. God has placed certain knowledge of Himself in every unbelieving heart. We simply appeal to that inescapable knowledge of God by presenting the truth. Of course, acceptance of God as your Creator carries with it the corollary that you are responsible to God. There is no escaping this second step. The one follows the other. Hence Point A: "You were created by God and you are therefore responsible to Him."

2

Point B:
You Often Break God's Law and You Are A Sinner

For when Gentiles who do not have the Law do instinctively the things of the Law, these not having the Law, are a law to themselves, in that they show the work of the Law written in their hearts, their conscience bearing witness, and their thoughts alternately accusing or else defending them. ~Rom. 2:14-15

Romans 2:14-15, as quoted above, guides our thinking at this point. The Holy Spirit speaking through the apostle Paul is directing our attention to "Gentiles," that is, to all of humanity outside the race of the Jews. And so Paul is again telling us something about all human beings including the unbeliever. First of all, he refers to them as those who "do not have the Law." They do not have the Law of God written as the Jewish nation has the Law of God written. God gave the Ten Commandments to Israel in tablets of stone written with His own finger. The Gentiles had no such written table of commandments by which they were to guide their lives.

But although these Gentiles do not have access to the written commandments, Paul tells us they "do instinctively the things of the Law." The point is that even unbelievers have a certain morality. Because God is a moral being and because men and women are made in God's image, they too are moral beings. And so even unbelievers "do instinctively the things of the Law." The word "instinctively" means "by nature." A bird instinctively builds her nest and a beaver instinctively builds his den. That is, because of the nature of the bird's being, the bird builds her nest. She is in a sense programmed by God to function in this way.

In the beginning, God created Adam and Eve with the moral "Law written in their hearts." We can conceive of these Ten Commandments as the fingerprints of God. These fingerprints were all over and in Adam and Eve. Looking at it another way, Adam and Eve were created in God's image. And God's moral Law is a picture of God's righteous character and righteous character was implanted in Adam and Eve. Paul puts it this way, "The Law [was] written in their hearts."

Now when Adam and Eve sinned against God, the image of God within them was not totally obliterated. The image of God in man was damaged. But it was not erased. And so the apostle tells us that even those who do not possess a written copy of the Ten Commandments "do instinctively the things of the Law." Paul does not mean that unbelievers keep God's commandments. It is impossible for them to do so. But every unbeliever's life is affected by God's commandments. He cannot escape them. For example, the unbelieving businessman who commits adultery does not announce the fact to his wife. He knows the adultery is contrary to his marriage vows. He cannot escape this sense of morality or immorality. It has also been said that there is honor among thieves. A group of thieves may steal from the bank. But woe be it to the one who steals from the thief. Even for a thief, theft is wrong, under these circumstances. This sense of morality is inescapable. In this way unbelievers "show the work of the Law written in their hearts."

Notice that Paul says that unbelievers "show the work of the Law written in their hearts." What Paul means is that the moral requirements of the Law are present within the very fabric of every unbeliever's being. The unbeliever cannot escape the requirements of God's moral Law. Paul is careful in his use of language when he speaks of "the works of the Law." Paul does not say that the Law itself is written on their hearts. This is the promise of the new covenant. "After those days, says the Lord: I will put my Laws into their minds, and I will write them upon their hearts" (Heb. 8:10; Jer. 31:33).

What Paul says in Romans 2:15 is that although the image of God in man is greatly damaged due to the fall, the moral requirements of God remain a part of every human being. They are God's fingerprints all over them and in them. The result is that no unbeliever can escape God's moral Law. God's requirements for living "bubble up" within them. Yes, they do "suppress the truth in unrighteousness" (Rom. 1:18). But unbelievers cannot completely cover the spring of God's morality present within them. As a result, "these not having the Law, are a law to themselves" (Rom. 2:14). That is, they continually present the law to themselves. They cannot escape it.

To confirm what he says, Paul first points to the human conscience. The conscience exists because men and women are moral beings. Right and wrong are always before them. In whatever people do, the conscience bears witness. It says 'yes' or 'no' with regard to every action. It feels good or bad subsequent to every action. This response proves that there is a standard resident within every person, including the unbeliever, against which the conscience makes its judgments. And so, Paul speaks of "their conscience bearing witness" to their actions, that is, saying 'yes' or 'no' with regard to their respective actions.

Then too, Paul affirms this truth by the fact that the thoughts of unbelievers are "alternately accusing or else defending them." This internal conflict is something we have all experienced. For example, say it is raining quite hard. You are in the grocery store. As you depart, there is an elderly lady struggling with a large package. You set your groceries down, take the lady's groceries, and help her to her car. You feel pretty good about helping this woman. You go back to claim your grocery bag only to find that the rain has almost totally disintegrated it. So you must go back in the store for a new bag. By this time you are soaked through. You are wondering, "Why in the world did I help that woman? Look at me. I'm soaked!" Then you feel guilty for having these thoughts. After all, the woman did need your help. And so the internal debate continues.

But the point is simply this; you are like those of whom Paul speaks, "Their thoughts [are] alternately accusing or else defending them." And Paul rightly maintains that this internal debate proves that there is in fact a standard of right and wrong resident within you and resident within every human being. An internal debate such as the one described above could not even be started if there were no such standard. And so all of this proves the basic premise that the Gentiles "show the work of the Law written in their hearts." And this being the case, we have evidence of the fact that no unbeliever can escape from God. He knows God to be God. He knows God to be His creator. And he knows that God has a standard by which He expects everyone to live.

How does Paul's teaching about the Law of God affect our evangelism? The answer is again quite simple. We are obligated to present the truth of God's moral standard, the Ten Commandments, to the unbeliever. Yes, we should be straightforward and say, "You often break God's law and you are a sinner." And we should properly define sin. "Sin is the transgression of the law" (1 John 3:4, KJV).

We may even have the opportunity to speak to specific sins. If adultery is the problem faced in the unbeliever's life, we should, with all love and compassion, remind the unbeliever that God says, "You shall not commit adultery" (Exod. 20:14). We should not be bashful about this. In most cases there will be an admission that the adultery is sin even if there is no repentance. On the other hand, if the unbeliever denies the written word, you know that the very same moral requirement is present within the unbeliever confronting the unbeliever from within. And so, you should not be ashamed to point out the truth. You have a vital point of contact with unbelievers to whom you preach or to whom you witness. That point of contact is "the work of the Law written in their hearts."

Let me give you one example of how I have experienced this. In doing door-to-door calling, I have often commented to people after inviting them to worship, "You know you should be in church on Sunday." The response has invariably been, "Yes, I know that's true." Now why would a total stranger and an unbeliever respond in this way? Well, there is only one reason. God's moral law includes the requirement that one day in seven be set aside as a special day of worship. This is the requirement of the Fourth Commandment, "Remember the Sabbath day, to keep it holy" (Exod. 20:8). And this requirement speaks loud and clear from within the heart of the unbeliever. And so the response is one that can be expected. As a result, an opportunity exists to speak about how Christ died in payment for sin and how He rose again from the dead on the first day of the week. And so, Christians worship on the first day of the week in celebration of the resurrection. You see, God's moral Law opens the door to speak about Christ.

Pursuing the point a step further, note what Jesus says concerning the work, the very first work, of the Holy Spirit. "And He, when He comes, will convict the world concerning sin" (John 16:8). The Holy Spirit comes to those who are in the world and His initial work is to convict of sin. As a result, we can pray for the convicting work of the Holy Spirit when we say to an unbeliever, "You often break God's law and you are a sinner." And we can be confident that we are praying in accordance with God's will. A primary work of the Holy Spirit is to convict of sin.

And so, I maintain that we should, in a positive way, stand in the path of the work of the Holy Spirit. We can do this by simply being forthright with the truth. With reverence before God and with compassion for the unbeliever we can say to him or her, "You often break God's law and you are a sinner."

That the apostle Paul follows this path in his approach to Gentile unbelievers can be seen from his contact with Felix, the Roman governor of Judea. Paul had been arrested and he subsequently made his defense before Felix. But Felix had Paul imprisoned. Acts 24:24-25 relates the following:

> But some days later, Felix arrived with Drusilla, his wife who was a Jewess, and sent for Paul and heard him speak about faith in Christ Jesus. And as he was discussing righteousness, self-control and the judgment to come, Felix became frightened and said, "Go away for the present, and when I find time, I will summon you."

What was Paul's approach to this Roman governor? Paul spoke of righteousness. And how would we assume the apostle would speak of righteousness? Let Paul speak for himself. "So then, the Law is holy, and the commandment is holy and righteous and good" (Rom. 7:12). If Paul spoke of righteousness, it was in terms of the moral Law of God. The commandments of God are righteous and give to us the true standard of righteousness. Now, lest we get the idea that we are heading down the path of legalism, look at how Paul sees the place of God's Law.

> Therefore, did that which is good become a cause of death to me? May it never be! Rather it was sin, in order that it might be shown to be sin by effecting my death through that which is good, that through the commandment sin might become utterly sinful. For we know that the Law is spiritual; but I am of the flesh, sold in bondage to sin (Rom. 7:13-14).

You see the moral Law of God is a concrete standard of righteousness. It is good! It is spiritual! And it is used by God to show the utter sinfulness of sin. Again we can see the connection with the work of the Holy Spirit outlined above, the work of bringing conviction of sin.

Now Paul also discussed self-control with Felix. Self-control is a fruit of the Spirit. It is a requirement for Christian living. And one of the places it comes to the fore is in the problem of discontent. When we are discontent with the lot in life given to us by God, our fleshly appetites tend to dominate us. We covet our neighbor's wife or house or other possessions. And if we fail to rein in these appetites, we find ourselves caught in adultery or caught in theft. We are obviously speaking in terms of the Ten Commandments here. And Paul experienced the same thing. Look at what he says,

> What shall we say then? Is the Law sin? May it never be! On the contrary, I would not have come to know sin except through the Law; for I would not have known about coveting if the law had not said, "You shall not covet" (Rom. 7:7).

The point is that Paul understood the need to rein in discontent. He goes so far as to say, "I buffet my body and make it my slave, lest possibly, after I have preached to others, I myself should be disqualified" (1 Cor. 9:27). In other words, Paul learned the need for self-control. Without it, all sorts of other sins would follow. And Paul learned this lesson through the application of the Tenth Commandment to his own life by the Holy Spirit.

And so how would Paul have approached the subject of self-control? In all likelihood, he would have applied what God had taught him about God's own moral standards found in the Ten Commandments.

You will note that Paul finally discussed the judgment to come with Felix. We will discuss the judgment to come under Point C, "You will be judged and you face eternal punishment for your sin." And we will see how this point fits into Paul's preaching. At present, suffice it to say that Paul discusses the judgment to come forthrightly.

The response of the governor to Paul's discussions is also important. "Felix became frightened." The Word of God accomplished its task (Isa. 55:11). Yes it was rejected. And Paul was sent back to prison. But this is a lesson for us. We should not be afraid of a negative reaction to the presentation of the truth. And we should not be afraid that the message we bring might cause fear or might cause anger. As the apostle Peter says, "Do not fear their intimidation [fear] and do not be troubled" (1 Pet. 3:14). And so the example of Paul once again teaches us to act in reverence before God, with prayer for the blessing of the Holy Spirit, and compassionately urge: "You often break God's law and you are a sinner."

3

Point C:
You will be Judged and You face Eternal Punishment for your Sin

And He, when He comes, will convict the world concerning sin and righteousness and judgment.
~John 16:8

One of the proof texts given for Point C is Hebrews 9:27, "It is appointed for men to die once, and after this comes judgment." We laugh when tax season is on the horizon saying, "There are two things we cannot escape, death and taxes." But the Bible takes a little different slant saying we cannot escape death and judgment. And the fact of the matter is that every human being knows just this. As all unbelievers know God as God and as their Creator; as all unbelievers know they stand before the moral standards by which God desires all men to live; so all unbelievers know that after death comes judgment. Taking Hebrews 9:27 and 28 together, this is exactly what we learn.

> And inasmuch as it is appointed for men to die once, and after this comes judgment; so Christ also, having been offered once to bear the sins of many, shall appear a second time, not to bear sin, to those who eagerly await Him, for salvation.

You see, the writer to the Hebrews is desirous of confirming that Christ will come a second time in glory. He wants us to have great assurance regarding the second coming of Christ. And so, in order to build this assurance, the writer to the Hebrews compares the second coming of Christ to events we all know are certain. These events are death and judgment. Here is his argument. "You know that death and judgment are sure," he says. "You know that one day you will die and face God in judgment." This is his starting point. The writer to the Hebrews assumes the knowledge of death and judgment is common to all people everywhere. And so he says, "Inasmuch as it is appointed for men to die once, and after this comes judgment; so Christ also ... shall appear a second time ... " In other words, just as death and judgment are certain to be experienced by everyone, so also the second coming of Christ is certain. And since you know that you will one day die and face judgment, you can be just as confident with regard to the coming of Christ a second time.

The argument is quite simple. The thing to grasp is that it is based upon the common knowledge possessed by men that death and judgment are certain. Is this truth born out in our daily experience? Yes it is. Although many unbelievers joke about it, the fact of judgment does not escape their conversation. "God will get you for that," they say, after something is done to them. It may be a joke. But it is based on the common knowledge of judgment to come. More than one unbeliever has also spoken of hell in terms like this: "All my friends will be there. Why shouldn't I join them?" The problem is that there is no terror of judgment within the unbeliever. But this lack of fear before God obviates neither the fact of judgment nor the knowledge of this fact. Rather, the jokes betray anxiety underlying this knowledge.

Now, let's turn again to the words of Christ concerning the work of the Holy Spirit. Jesus promised, "And He, when He comes, will convict the world concerning sin, and righteousness, and judgment" (John 16:8). We have mentioned conviction of sin in the above discussion. We should also briefly mention conviction concerning righteousness since Paul spoke to Felix concerning righteousness. Since this righteousness has to do with the great standard of God's moral Law, conviction in this area is a two edged sword. On one side, there is the conviction that we have not attained the standard and are guilty before God. On the other side, there is the conviction that we need perfect righteousness to be acceptable before God. We see Christ as the one who has met the standards for us. And we see our need to be clothed with the righteousness of Christ. To bring unbelievers to the point of understanding their need of Christ's righteousness, it is necessary to discuss righteousness and it is necessary to pray for the conviction of the Spirit concerning righteousness.

But then, the Holy Spirit also convicts concerning the judgment to come. The Holy Spirit blows the smoke of deception away from the unbeliever's heart and convicts of the truth already known by the unbeliever. The Holy Spirit leads the unbeliever to the point of confessing the truth that is known by him and is being presented by us. This means that we can pray specifically for this conviction to be brought upon the unbelievers to whom we speak.

The applicability to our evangelism of what has been said can be readily seen. Our obligation is to speak the truth in love to the unbeliever. Again, with reverence before God and with compassion for the unbeliever, we issue a warning such as this, "You will be judged and you face eternal punishment for your sin." We know that we have a vital point of contact with the unbeliever. The point of contact is the knowledge that he or she one day will face judgment before God. This knowledge is part of the fabric of the unbeliever's being. It is inescapable knowledge.

As we set forth the truth, we also pray. We ask God to send His Spirit to this unbeliever and convict him or her of the truth. Because we know that this unbeliever knows the truth, we want him or her to desist from suppressing the truth. We want to see him or her acknowledge the truth. And so we pray for the conviction of the Holy Spirit.

This is the methodology of the apostle Paul as confirmed by his discussions with Felix, the Roman governor. Paul discussed "righteousness, self control, and the judgment to come" (Acts 24:25). And we should do no less than follow Paul in our approach to unbelievers whether in preaching or in personal witness. We should set the truth of the judgment to come before the unbeliever and say, "You will be judged and you face eternal punishment for your sin."

4

Confirmation of the Methodology

For men swear by one greater than themselves, and with them an oath given as confirmation is an end of every dispute. ~Heb. 6:16

My effort has been to show that all men and women possess certain knowledge of God, certain knowledge of His moral requirements, and certain knowledge of the judgment to come. My position is that Paul understood that this certain and inescapable knowledge of God is resident within every human being. Further, my position is that the apostle Paul guided his evangelistic efforts among the Gentiles by a methodology based upon this inescapable knowledge. He saw this knowledge of God as a point of contact placed by God in every unbeliever.

Therefore, I maintain that a proper approach to unbelievers involves a loving confrontation including at least the substance of the three points discussed above. These three points directly answer the point of contact we have with the unbeliever.

    A. You were created by God and you are therefore responsible to Him.

    B. You often break God's law and you are a sinner.

    C. You will be judged and you face eternal punishment for your sin.

We have seen two examples of Paul's witness to unbelievers, which appear to confirm the methodology. However, these examples point to only a portion of the supposed methodology. Is there not an example of Paul's preaching where the full-blown methodology can be seen? Yes there is. Paul's sermon to the elite among the Athenian intellects is an excellent example. Look again at what Paul has to say in Acts 17:22-31. Allow me to break the sermon down into its main points.

> INTRODUCTION: Men of Athens, I observe that you are very religious in all respects. For while I was passing through and examining the objects of your worship, I also found an altar with this inscription, "TO AN UNKNOWN GOD." What therefore you worship in ignorance, this I proclaim to you.

> POINT A. The God who made the world and all things in it, since He is Lord of heaven and earth, does not dwell in temples made with hands; neither is He served by human hands, as though He needed anything, since He Himself gives to all life and breath and all things; and He made from one, every nation of mankind to live on all the face of the earth, having determined their appointed times and the boundaries of their habitation, that they should seek God, if perhaps they might grope for Him and find Him, though He is not far from each one of us; for in Him we live and move and exist, as even some of your own poets have said, "For we also are His offspring."

> POINT B. Being then the offspring of God, we ought not to think that the Divine Nature is like gold or silver or stone, an image formed by the art and thought of man.

> POINT C. Therefore having overlooked the times of ignorance, God is now declaring to men that all everywhere should repent, because He has fixed a day—in which He will judge the world in righteousness through a Man whom He has appointed, having furnished proof to all men by raising Him from the dead.

Having Paul's words before us in outline form, what does he say? First, Paul's introduction points to the fact that these men of Athens are "very religious." They have an altar inscribed, "TO AN UNKNOWN GOD," which God they worship in ignorance. Paul jabs the Athenians here, accusing them of worshipping the agnostic's god. At any rate, the fact that these educated men are at base religious is emphasized by the fact that they worship a god which they either do not know or in which they do not believe. Most commentators agree that Paul uses this altar "TO AN UNKNOWN GOD" as a starting point for his remarks that follow.

And where does Paul begin in the body of his remarks? First of all, Paul directs the attention of his educated listeners to the "God who made the world and all things in it." In other words, Paul begins by pointing to God the Creator. And Paul emphasizes that He is "Lord of heaven and earth." He further emphasizes that God created every human being on the face of the earth. "He made from one, every nation of mankind to live on the face of the earth." Not only so, God appointed the time every family and nation would exist on the earth. And He also appointed the specific boundaries within which these families and nations would live upon the earth. The clear implication is that the Athenians occupied the land they did when they did by the plan and appointment of God.

Now Paul confirms to these Greek philosophers that they are creatures of God. He tells these educated men that God is quite near. In fact, "In Him we live and move and exist." Do these pagan philosophers know they are creatures of God and exist by His power? The answer is, "Yes." And Paul knows they know. And so he presses the issue by pointing out to his listeners that some of their own poets have confessed this truth. Then Paul quotes one of their poets, "For we also are His offspring."

HERE IS PAUL'S FIRST POINT. He confronts the Stoic and Epicurean philosophers of Athens with the truth that they are creatures of the living

God. In summary we might say that Paul challenges these men of Athens with the simple truth, "You were created by God and you are responsible to Him."

The second part of Paul's sermon is short and to the point. Since the Athenians know they are the "offspring of God," they know better than to engage in idolatry. One form of idolatry is the worship of gods in forms of silver, gold, or stone. Paul says these people know better.

Two things should be noted at this point. First, these men of Athens know the "Divine nature" (Acts 17:29). Compare Romans 1:20 where Paul says the "divine nature" of God is "understood through what has been made." Second, since these Athenians recognize the divine nature of God, they also know that idolatry is wrong. What Paul is referring to is a violation of the Second Commandment, "You shall not make for yourself and idol" (Exod. 20:4). In an indirect way, Paul refers to God's moral Law.

HERE THEN IS PAUL'S SECOND POINT. After confronting the Athenians with the fact that they are creatures of the living God, he points out their sin of idolatry. He points to their living in violation to the Second Commandment. In so many words, Paul challenges each of them with the truth, "You often break God's law and you are a sinner."

The third point of Paul's sermon follows logically. "God is now declaring to men that all everywhere should repent." That is, God is calling people like you to turn from your sin of idolatry to worship and serve the living God. Why? The answer is simple. Judgment is coming. God "has fixed a day in which He will judge the world." Yes, judgment day is coming and you will all have to face the living God to give an account for your lives.

HERE IS PAUL'S THIRD POINT. Men of Athens, you know God, the Creator: You know you are His offspring. You therefore know that it is sin to worship this great God by making idols. Turn from your sin!

Why? Judgment is coming. The message is very straightforward and clear. Again, in so many words, Paul says, "You will be judged and you face eternal punishment for your sin."

Now, note a couple of additional points. First, it is only after presenting a careful argument, outlining the three points we have discussed at length, that Paul begins to speak about Christ. Christ, His work on the cross, and His resurrection, have little or no meaning unless there is conviction of sin, conviction of the need of Christ's righteousness, and conviction concerning the judgment to come. So in his witness to the Gentiles, Paul follows a methodology designed to foster such conviction when blessed of the Holy Spirit. It is only then that he speaks of Christ.

Second, and quite significant in understanding Paul's methodology, is the fact that objections arose among the Athenians only when Paul mentions the resurrection of Christ. "Now when they heard of the resurrection of the dead, some began to sneer" (Acts 17:32). You should notice this. These philosophers and teachers in Athens did not openly voice objections to Paul's three main points. They did not counter him when he said they were creatures of the living God. They did not counter him when he said they knew better than to make idols. They did not counter him when he spoke of the judgment to come. These truths are self-evident. Every human being knows them. They may and often do "suppress the truth in unrighteousness" (Rom. 1:18). But the fact is that God placed these truths within the heart and being of everyone. And so it was difficult at best for these educated pagan philosophers to openly deny what Paul was saying.

Part One Conclusion

The conclusion, when all has been heard ...
~Eccles. 12:13

In conclusion, we see that the apostle Paul had a specific methodology undergirding his approach to the unbelieving world of his day. It was a methodology based upon the knowledge placed by God in every human being. Paul did not follow this methodology in a rigid fashion. But he did, in one way or another, make the major points of the methodology plain to those Gentiles to whom he spoke.

This methodology underlies the three points we have discussed. And in a general fashion, these points represent the major thrust of Paul's approach to unbelievers.

A. You were created by God and you are therefore responsible to him.

B. You often break God's law and you are a sinner.

C. You will be judged and you face eternal punishment for your sin.

Because of the truth of these points, and because of the work of the Holy Spirit promised by Christ, which corresponds to these points, you can be confident in your approach to unbelievers in your community. You can be confident in saying to them, "You cannot escape from God." And you can be confident as you show them why.

You Cannot Escape From God

PART TWO:

Presenting the Gospel

Introduction

*Come to Me, all who are weary and heavy-laden, and
I will give you rest.* ~Matt. 11:28

The three main points discussed in Part One, "Approaching Unbelievers," present the inescapable knowledge of God, which is within every human heart. The three main points discussed in what follows answer the three points of Part One. They present the alternative to eternal punishment for sin and are as follows:

A. Forgiveness of sin and freedom from guilt are obtained through repentance of sin and faith in the Lord Jesus Christ.

B. The gift of eternal life and access to heaven are obtained through faith in the Lord Jesus Christ.

C. The Lord Jesus Christ freely offers Himself to you saying: *"Come to Me, all who are weary and heavy-laden, and I will give you rest"* (Matt. 11:28).

If men and women come to the place of confessing the truths discussed in Part One, they must of necessity begin to see their need of salvation from the consequences of sin and judgment. In other words, they will be brought to the place of seeking the alternative to facing judgment for sin.

And what is salvation unless it is salvation from the consequences of sin? Salvation does not simply lift human beings to new and higher ground upon which they may enjoy new pleasures in this life and in the life to come. Salvation is exactly what the word implies. It is salvation. Someone who has fallen into a well or who has been trapped in a mine does not need encouraging words exhorting him to live a better life with God's help. This person needs someone else to dig him out of his predicament and to save him from the certain death that will follow, if he is not saved. Note how I put this! The trapped individual must "be saved." Those trapped in a mine disaster do not save themselves. They must be saved.

Similarly, those who are "dead in trespasses and sins" (Eph. 2:1) and those who are "slaves to sin" (Rom. 6:6), must "be saved" from their sin and its consequences. The apostle Peter emphasized this on the day of Pentecost when he told the multitude, "Be saved from this perverse generation" (Acts 2:40). Peter knew his listeners could not save themselves. He knew they must be saved. And the only One who was and is able to save sinful human beings is God.

And so, the whole thrust of the gospel is the requirement to turn from self to God. This is the only answer to human sin. As Paul puts it in Romans 1:21 through 25,

> For even though they knew God, they did not honor Him as God, or give thanks; but they became futile in their speculations, and their foolish heart was darkened. Professing to be wise, they became fools, and exchanged the glory of the incorruptible God for an image in the form of corruptible man and of birds and four-footed animals and crawling creatures. Therefore God gave them over in the lusts of their hearts to impurity, that their bodies might be dishonored among them. For they exchanged the truth of God for the lie, and worshipped the creature rather than the Creator, who is blessed forever. Amen.

Men and women must turn from self-centeredness, self-indulgence, self-sufficiency, and self-interest. They must turn back to God. And in the process, they must realize that simple moral change or reformation is not enough. They must come to see the mercy of God in Christ. They must come to see the work of Christ on the cross in relationship to their personal sin. And they must cast themselves upon the mercy of God seeking shelter from His wrath against sin by trusting in the sacrifice of Christ. This is radical conversion.

It cannot be overemphasized that salvation is not simply a step in a new direction in which a person decides to enhance his or her life by following God. God cannot be used as a ladder to achieve success in living. Salvation involves radical conversion. In the literal sense of the word, we are converted by the grace of God from following sin and Satan to following Christ. We are saved. Again, as the apostle Paul puts it, converted people have this testimony: "He delivered us from the domain of darkness, and transferred us to the kingdom of His beloved Son" (Col. 1:13). This is the work of God. It is the saving work of God. And so the gospel message informs men of the work of God in bringing about salvation. And the call of the gospel is an exhortation given to men and women to stop trusting themselves. Rather, men and women must be urged to trust in God to save them from the shambles they have made of their lives. To relate anything less is to deceive unbelievers and to lull them into further complacency.

To this end, the three points introduced above can be used to direct the unbeliever to the mercy of God in Christ. In Point A, the unbeliever is shown the work of Christ on the cross and the necessity of radical conversion. This point answers the problem of guilt before God because of sin. Then, in Point B, the unbeliever is shown that the only way to heaven is on the basis of faith in Christ. This point answers the problem of the unbeliever's inability to please God and assure a place in heaven. Finally, in Point C, the unbeliever is issued the invitation given by Christ, "Come to Me" (Matt. 11:28). How important it is for men and women to accept this invitation and accept Christ for who He is, Lord and Savior.

Again, these three points compose a presentation of the gospel that can be used in following up on the conviction brought by the Holy Spirit when Paul's approach to unbelievers is utilized. They represent a plan for presenting the gospel that is first of all simple. But these points also bring out the important aspects of the gospel that must be both presented and grasped. Finally, the unbeliever is called to place faith in the only savior, the Lord Jesus Christ. The discussion that follows is an attempt to present the Biblical content of the gospel, along with the background for each of the points, in order that they may be confidently and easily presented.

Having set the stage, we move on to a discussion of Point A: Forgiveness of sin and freedom from guilt are obtained through repentance of sin and faith in the Lord Jesus Christ.

Point A:
Forgiveness of sin and Freedom from Guilt are Obtained through Repentance of Sin and Faith in the Lord Jesus Christ

Therefore repent and return, so that your sins may be wiped away. ~Acts 3:19

THREE BASIC POINTS must be covered under this heading. First, we must discuss some elements of the gospel. Then we must discuss the proper response to the gospel: men and women must be converted. And what is conversion? True conversion consists of repentance on one side and faith on the other. And so both repentance and faith must be explored. Then too, these basic points must be seen in their proper context. They must be seen as integral parts of our witness to the grace of God.

1. ELEMENTS OF THE GOSPEL
The gospel is given, in part, in the proof text for our first point: "While we were still helpless, at the right time, Christ died for the ungodly" (Rom. 5:6). There are a number of important points in this text. First of all, Paul speaks of "while we were still helpless." Contrary to popular opinion, unbelievers are helpless. They are unable to save themselves. This must be emphasized. In addition, Paul tells us that Christ died for the "ungodly." Yes, unbelievers must see themselves

as ungodly. Again, we are thrown back to part one, "Approaching Unbelievers." Conviction of sin by the Holy Spirit along with conviction concerning judgment drive men and women to view themselves as helpless and ungodly. And so Romans 5:6 applies to them.

Paul also emphasizes the fact that Christ died "at the right time." Christ died at the right time because He died in accordance with God's plan. In like manner, Paul says, "When the fullness of time came, God sent forth His son, born of a woman, born under the Law" (Gal. 4:4). When the proper time had come, in accordance with God's plan, Christ was born. He grew to manhood and was "tempted in all things like we are, yet without sin" (Heb. 4:15). And He was crucified. He is the "Lamb slain from the foundation of the world" (Rev. 13:8, KJV). In other words, God's eternal plan was brought to fruition and Christ was "delivered up by the predetermined plan and foreknowledge of God" (Acts 2:23). To understand the nature of God's plan and for the individual to link God's plan to his own salvation can have a profound effect upon later assurance of salvation.

But the centerpiece of this text is the death of Christ. Why did Christ die? Paul answers, "for the ungodly." Paul's words have at least two emphases. On one side, Christ died on behalf of the ungodly. That is, Christ took upon Himself the burden of unbelievers. This would be similar to a benevolent neighbor paying the fine imposed upon you by a judge because of your violation of the law. On the other side, Christ died in the place of the ungodly. Christ was and is the sinner's personal substitute. He stood in the place of unbelievers. This would be similar to the neighbor who was willing to stand in your place and go to jail for you or go to the electric chair for you to pay the penalty you owe for a crime committed. Why was this necessary?

Let's get it straight. Men and women must "be reconciled to God" (2 Cor. 5:20). The import of this cannot be overemphasized. If unbelievers must "be reconciled to God," the problem is that the unbeliever offends God. We can see this by looking at Matthew 5:23 and 24.

"If therefore you are presenting your offering at the altar, and there remember that your brother has something against you, leave your offering there before the altar, and go your way; first be reconciled to your brother, and then come and present your offering."

Here we are exhorted by Christ to "be reconciled" to our brother. These are the same words used with reference to the unbeliever and God. What is the problem? The problem is "that your brother has something against you." In other words, your brother has been offended by your conduct. Have you sinned against him? Perhaps. But in any event, a problem exists between the two of you. He has something against you. This is the point to grasp. In the same way, God has something against the unbeliever. Has the unbeliever sinned against God? Yes! And as a result, God's wrath is directed against the unbeliever.

The apostle John confirms this. "In this is love, not that we loved God, but that He loved us and sent His Son to be the propitiation for our sins" (1 John 4:10). The word "propitiation" presupposes the wrath of God. Propitiation is a sacrifice that satisfies wrath. Christ, the propitiation for our sins, stands between God and us. He stands in the place of sinners. And He takes upon Himself the full force of God's wrath against sin.

This is done on the cross. Christ experiences the full force of God's wrath against sin. One of the ways Scripture defines judgment is as separation from God. "And these will pay the penalty of eternal destruction away from the presence of the Lord and the glory of His power" (2 Thess. 1:9). This is final judgment, eternal separation from the grace and mercy of God.

But Christ also experiences the fury of God's judgment. Darkness fell upon the land at mid-afternoon and Christ felt such agony because of the sins of His people imputed to Him. He cried out, "My God, My God, why hast Thou forsaken Me?" (Matt. 27:46). It was as though the Father had turned His back on the Son in full fury because of sin. This is what the cross is all about.

And so, it is on the basis of God's gift in Christ that men and women are reconciled to God. "For it was the Father's good pleasure for all the fullness to dwell in Him, and through Him to reconcile all things to Himself, having made peace through the blood of His cross" (Col. 1:19-20). Yes, reconciliation is achieved by Christ who suffers and dies on the cross to pay the penalty due for the sins of people like you and me. God has been offended. Christ has satisfied his wrath. The apostle Paul sums it up:

> But God demonstrates His own love toward us, in that while we were yet sinners, Christ died for us. Much more then, having now been justified by His blood, we shall be saved from the wrath of God through Him. For while we were enemies, we were reconciled to God through the death of His Son (Rom. 5:8-10).

This is Good News. Unworthy sinners, those who merit only the wrath of God because of their sin, are spared and delivered from the wrath to come because of the death of Christ. In this way, these same unworthy sinners, who were formerly enemies of God, are reconciled to God. This is truly Good News. And it is summed up for us in this text, "While we were still helpless, at the right time, Christ died for the ungodly" (Rom. 5:6).

As you may note, this gospel message begins to answer the irrefutable knowledge of God placed by God within every unbeliever and already expounded in the first part of our discussion. It is this gospel message that must be set lovingly, yet forcefully, before the unbeliever. And it must be set before the unbeliever from the Scriptures. That is, the message of the Scriptures must be explained. Our own ideas and thoughts must not be substituted for the message of the Scriptures. This message must not be muted or diluted. The messenger must confess with the apostle Paul, "I am not ashamed of the gospel, for it is the power of God for salvation to everyone who believes" (Rom. 1:16). This is the reason the three points in the gospel presentation I propose are simple and straightforward. The gospel is simple and straightforward. And the gospel must be presented in a simple and straightforward fashion.

2. REPENTANCE:

> *Repent therefore and return, that your sins may be wiped away* (Acts 3:19)

This text brings us to the only proper response to the gospel message of Christ's death on the cross on behalf of sinners. And what is the only proper response? It is the response that God desires, not only so, demands, if sinful men and women are going to escape the due reward for their sins. The apostle Paul points us in the right direction when he tells the elders from the church at Ephesus, "I did not shrink from declaring to you anything that was profitable, and teaching you publicly and from house to house, solemnly testifying to both Jews and Greeks of repentance toward God and faith in our Lord Jesus Christ" (Acts 20:20-21).

Note the burden of Paul's message. It contained two main elements: "Repentance toward God and faith in our Lord Jesus Christ." Here are the two sides of genuine conversion: repentance and faith. Men and women must repent of sin and trust in the Lord Jesus Christ as the only adequate payment for their sin. This is the response to the gospel which must be presented to unbelievers and which must be elicited from unbelievers. Nothing less than this will do. Let's begin looking into this response by examining repentance.

Literally, repentance means a change in mind. People start thinking differently. That is, they begin to think differently about God and about sin. They change their mind about sin and begin to think about sin the way God thinks about sin. And they begin to think about God in the way the Bible presents God.

This again gets back to Part One, "Approaching Unbelievers." Men and women must face God as their Creator. They must see themselves as sinners. And they must acknowledge the solemn fact of judgment and their unworthiness to face judgment. Unbelievers must acknowledge and accept these truths about themselves. Not only so, having come to grips with the facts of sin and judgment, unbelievers must turn from their sin.

This is what repentance is all about. Listen again to the apostle Paul in 2 Corinthians 7: 9-10,

> I now rejoice, not that you were made sorrowful, but that you were made sorrowful to the point of repentance; for you were made sorrowful according to the will of God, in order that you might not suffer loss in anything through us. For sorrow that is according to the will of God produces a repentance without regret leading to salvation, but the sorrow of the world produces death.

You see, when the Holy Spirit brings real conviction upon individuals regarding their sins, there is sorrow. There is not sorrow for being caught. There is a sorrow before God for offending Him. In other words, convicted persons begin to view their sins the way God does. A change in thinking results in a change in conduct. When a person comes to believe that his conduct is repugnant to God and is deeply convicted before God, he changes that conduct. This is a sorrow according to the will of God that produces repentance.

Good examples of what I am talking about can be found in the Gospels and in the book of Acts. On one side, when John was baptizing outside of Jerusalem, many came to him including the Pharisees and Sadducees. "But when he saw the Pharisees and Sadducees coming for baptism, he said to them, 'You brood of vipers, who warned you to flee from the wrath to come? Therefore bring forth fruit in keeping with your repentance'" (Matt. 3:7-8).

John chastised the Pharisees and Sadducees. They knew that God would one day judge them. But they did not manifest any sorrow for their sin. Neither did they manifest any repentance. How so? Their conduct displayed the fact that they did not think at all differently about their sin. Rather, they were clinging to their sin. And so John called them "vipers" and exhorted them to change their behavior and bring it in line with the profession of repentance. From a negative perspective then, we see that repentance means a change in thinking, which results in a change in conduct.

On the positive side, we see conviction brought by the Holy Spirit upon the people in Jerusalem on the Day of Pentecost. Peter had been preaching. Acts 2:37-38 gives the response: "Now when they heard this, they were pierced to the heart, and said to Peter and the rest of the apostles, 'Brethren, what shall we do?' And Peter said to them, 'Repent, and let each of you be baptized for the forgiveness of your sins.'"

The reaction of the people to Peter's sermon is quite clear. The Word of God is "sharper than any two edged sword" (Heb. 4:12). The word, borne by the Holy Spirit, cut Peter's listeners to the core. They cried in misery before God and had to know, "What shall we do?" This was not idle conversation. There was urgent need and the cry of wounded souls. These people were ready to take action. God called their conduct into question and the Holy Spirit convicted them of evil. They were on the threshold of a change. Peter answered and cried, "Repent!"

Again, we see that repentance involves not only what a person thinks. It involves what a person does. He or she must change. He or she must turn from following self, sin, and Satan and turn to the living God.

And this is what the apostle Paul had in mind when he spoke of "repentance toward God" (Acts 20:21). This is repentance "with reference to God." Many men and women engage in what has been called reformation. Because their conduct is displeasing to their family or business associates, they change. And their family and friends are pleased that they "clean up their act." But repentance with reference to family or business partners is not what Paul is talking about. He is concerned about repentance with reference to God.

A good example is Paul's words to the Thessalonians. He reminds these Christians, "You turned to God from idols to serve the living God" (1 Thess. 1:9). Here is the repentance Paul is after. These people "turned to God from idols." They did not simply turn to God and bring along all their idols. They forsook their idol worship. So too, contemporary unbelievers must look at God. They must see their own sin. They must be convicted of that sin before God. They must understand that they will never be able to stand before God in judgment. And so they must repent. They must turn away from their sin. This is why Point A in our gospel presentation simply states, "Forgiveness of sin and freedom from guilt are obtained through repentance of sin ... " Repentance is one side of Biblical conversion. We must all be prepared to call men and women to repentance. This is a vital part of the gospel message.

We have already seen Paul and Peter speak of the need of repentance. Where else do we find this emphasis? "John the Baptist came, preaching in the wilderness of Judea, saying, 'Repent, for the kingdom of heaven is at hand'" (Matt. 3:1-2). Again, "John the Baptist appeared in the wilderness preaching a baptism of repentance for the forgiveness of sins" (Mark 1:4). Later, "Jesus came into Galilee, preaching the gospel of God, and saying, 'The time is fulfilled, and the kingdom of God is at hand; repent and believe the gospel'" (Mark 1:14-15). The emphasis is plain. There is a continual call for repentance. And for this reason, respond to the conviction of the unbeliever by saying, "Forgiveness of sin and freedom from guilt are obtained through repentance ... " The proof text given is in the words of Peter, "Repent therefore and return, that your sins may be wiped away" (Acts 3:19).

Two additional comments are in order. First, it should be noted that both John the Baptist and Peter link repentance with the forgiveness of sins. John came "preaching a baptism of repentance for the forgiveness of sins" (Mark 1:4). And as just quoted, Peter said, "Repent therefore and return, that your sins may be wiped away" (Acts 3:19). Why is this connection made so clear? The answer is simple.

There can be no real forgiveness without repentance. Paul puts it another way when he asks, "What shall we say then? Are we to continue in sin that grace might abound?" He answers, "May it never be!" (Rom. 6:1-2). It is totally inconsistent for someone to continue to live a sinful life and at the same time claim the name of Christ and declare he is forgiven. "If we say that we have fellowship with Him and yet walk in darkness, we lie and do not practice the truth" (1 John 1:6). The word of God is clear. The prostitute must give up her prostitution. The adulterer must give up his adultery. Not only so, anger, hatred, pride, lying, cheating, stealing must be abandoned on every level. Repentance is a must. It is a vital part of conversion. And there can be no forgiveness without it. As a result, Point A of our gospel presentation must be proclaimed, "Forgiveness of sin and freedom from guilt are obtained through repentance of sin ... "

Second, the questions must be asked, where does an individual get the capability to turn away from sin to God? Is repentance an ability of the unregenerate human heart? Let's allow the Scriptures to answer these questions. First of all, Romans 8:7-8 tells us, "The mind set on the flesh is hostile toward God; for it does not subject itself to the law of God, for it is not even able to do so; and those who are in the flesh cannot please God." Here is the astounding truth. Men and women who are "slaves to sin" (Rom. 6:6) are incapable of turning to God and pleasing God. The whole point is that such men and women must "be converted." God must change them from the inside out. And because repentance is one side of conversion, those who "are converted" must receive repentance as a gift, a gift from God. The Scriptures bear out the point. When Peter reported to the disciples in Jerusalem concerning the conversion of the Gentiles in the house of Cornelius, the response was immediate. Acts 11:18 tells us, "And when they heard this, they quieted down, and glorified God saying, 'God has granted to the Gentiles also the repentance that leads to life'" (Acts 11:19). You see, repentance was recognized as a gift from God. And so it is today.

Since repentance is a gift of God, the messenger is totally reliant upon the grace of God working in the hearts of those to whom he is speaking. The messenger will never change the sinner's heart. Only the Holy Spirit is capable of working this miracle. And so, the messenger must pray. The one who witnesses to the grace of God in Christ must pray that this very grace will be made manifest in the listener's heart. To put it simply, we must pray for the outpouring of the Holy Spirit upon the individual to whom we speak. We pray that the Father will draw this person away from sin and to Christ so that the words of Jesus are fulfilled, "No one can come to Me, unless the Father who sent Me draws him" (John 6:44).

3. FAITH IN THE LORD JESUS CHRIST:

Believe in the Lord Jesus, and you shall be saved (Acts 16:31)

But repentance does not stand alone. The apostle Paul taught "repentance toward God and faith in our Lord Jesus Christ" (Acts 20:21). Faith in Jesus Christ is the other side of the coin of true conversion. When an individual turns away from a life of sin, he must turn to something else or someone else. In true conversion, the repentant sinner turns away from living in sin to living for Jesus Christ. Again, the apostle Paul reminded the Thessalonians: "You turned to God from idols to serve the living God" (1 Thess. 1:9). Note the emphasis. The Thessalonians turned to God. And they turned to God for a specific purpose. The purpose was not another brick in the wall of self-centeredness. There was a turning from self for the purpose of "serving the living God." More must be said about this under the heading of the Lordship of Christ. For now, suffice it to say, men and women must turn from self to God.

Jesus puts it this way, "Repent and believe the gospel" (Mark 1:15). Again, here are the two sides of true conversion, repentance and faith. And Mark tells us that when Jesus went about calling people to "repent and believe the gospel," He was "preaching the gospel of God" (Mark 1:14). And so, men and women must turn to God by believing the gospel.

But what is faith? Here is a pretty concrete definition: "Now faith is the assurance of things hoped for, the conviction of things not seen" (Heb. 11:1). But what does it mean? Well, let's key in on two words. First of all, we have already spoken of conviction in connection with the words of Jesus in John 16:8 regarding the work of the Holy Spirit, "And He, when He comes, will convict the world concerning sin, and righteousness, and judgment." Hebrews 11:1 uses the same root word found in John 16:8. In the former case, we have a predicate nominative and in the latter case we have the verb form. The word is conviction. Jesus promised that the Holy Spirit would bring conviction concerning sin, righteousness, and judgment. Faith is also a form of conviction. In other words, men and women become convinced that their sins outrage God. In the same way they become convinced that Jesus Christ shields them from the wrath of God against sin. They trust in Christ. They trust in the sacrifice of Christ. And it is the Holy Spirit who convinces them. He takes the written Word of God and convinces them of the truth of the gospel. And as Hebrews says, they are convinced of that which they do not see. It is this conviction with regard to the truth that is characterized as faith. The apostle Peter puts it this way, "And though you have not seen Him, you love Him, and though you do not see Him now, but believe in Him, you greatly rejoice with joy inexpressible and full of glory, obtaining as the outcome of your faith the salvation of your souls (1 Pet. 1:8-9).

The unbeliever comes to the place of casting himself or herself upon the gift of God in Christ. He or she trusts in that which they cannot see, the sacrifice of Christ. They trust in that sacrifice as the only adequate payment for their sins. They do this because they are convinced of the truth of the gospel. This is faith.

Yes, our obligation is to set the truth before unbelievers. We must act as the apostle Paul did. Acts 28:23 tells us, "He was explaining to them by solemnly testifying about the kingdom of God, and trying to persuade them concerning Jesus." And so we must present the truth with the objective of persuading men and women of their need of Christ. "Therefore knowing the fear of the Lord, we persuade men" (2 Cor. 5:11). At the same time, we must realize that the Holy Spirit is the One who will convince men and women of their need of Christ and compel them to turn in faith to Him. It is this conviction with regard to the truth that characterizes faith.

The other word in Hebrews 11:1 on which we should key is the word "hope." "Now faith is the assurance of things hoped for." The apostle Paul lays this hope before us in Romans 5:1-5.

> Therefore having been justified by faith, we have peace with God through our Lord Jesus Christ, through whom also we have obtained our introduction by faith into this grace in which we stand; and we exult in hope of the glory of God. And not only this, but we also exult in tribulations, knowing that tribulation brings about perseverance; and perseverance, proven character; and proven character, hope; and hope does not disappoint, because the love of God has been poured out within our hearts through the Holy Spirit who was given to us.

"We exult in hope of the glory of God," says Paul. This is the hope that "the creation itself also will be set free from its slavery to corruption into the freedom of the glory of the children of God" (Rom. 8:21). And Paul says, "I consider that the sufferings of this present time are not worthy to be compared with the glory that is to be revealed to us" (Rom. 8:18). Is this hope a vapor that may disappear in a moment? Is it hope against hope? Not at all! This is hope born of the Holy Spirit. "Hope does not disappoint, because the love of God has been poured out within our hearts through the Holy Spirit who has been given to us" (Rom. 5:5). Children hope to get certain toys from their parents and are disappointed. Parents hope their children will achieve certain goals in life and are disappointed. But this is not the type of hope about which the Bible speaks. The hope concerning which the Bible speaks "does not disappoint." Why? Christians, by the grace of

God, receive a down payment on the glory that is to come. This down payment is the Holy Spirit Himself. The Holy Spirit is "given to us." The Holy Spirit "is given as a pledge of our inheritance" (Eph. 1:14). And He becomes the down payment, literally the substance, of things hoped for. And when a person, by the grace of God, is reborn by the power of the Holy Spirit, the Holy Spirit brings hope into that person's life. And this hope, as the substance of things hoped for, is faith.

Not only so, the word "assurance" in Hebrews 11:1 may also be translated "conviction." That is, the Holy Spirit also brings conviction concerning the truth of the hope which God sets before men and women. And this conviction, which rests in the power of the Holy Spirit, is also characterized as faith. The point again being that faith is not a work of the intellect. It is not something that is developed through rational argumentation. This faith is born of the Spirit of God. Like repentance, it is a gift of God. It is a denial of self that rests in the truth of God. And it expresses itself by trusting in and resting upon the gospel of God, the message of salvation.

Now let's put this requirement for faith in perspective. We hear much these days about receiving Christ. What does it mean to receive Christ? The Gospel of John talks about receiving Christ. "But as many as receive Him, to them He gave the right to become children of God, even to those who believe in His name, who were born not of blood, nor of the will of the flesh, nor of the will of man, but of God" (John 1:12-13). First of all, the apostle John equates receiving Christ with believing in Him. This needs to be understood. John describes the "as many as receive Him" as "those who believe in His name." In other words, to receive Christ is to receive Him for who He is. He is the very Son of God who was conceived by the power of the Holy Spirit in the womb of the Virgin Mary and was born of her yet without sin. This same Son of God died on the cross in payment for the sins of others. And to receive Christ is to simply believe in Him and cast yourself upon Him as your savior from sin.

Secondly, those who receive Christ and believe in Him are described as those who have been born again. Note how the apostle explains what happens. Those who receive Christ were not born of blood. They were not born as a result of the will of the flesh. And they were not born as a result of the will of man. They were born of God. And there are two tremendous implications. First of all, John connects faith in Jesus Christ with being born again of God. And John gives us some specifics with regard the new birth. He tells us that the new birth is not a result of three things. First, those who are born again are not "born not of blood." That is, the new birth is not a result of ordinary human generation. Second, the new birth does not come about through "the will of the flesh," that is, through the "desire that arises out of man's bodily constitution."[1] Third, the new birth does not come about through the exercise "of the will of man." The word "man" can be translated "husband" and the text may refer to "the procreative urge of the male."[2]

Another interpretation of the third negative is plausible. John declares that the new birth does not come about by an act of the human will, "by the will of man." The apostle Peter has something quite similar to say about how Scripture came into being. "But know this first of all, that no prophecy of Scripture is a matter of one's own interpretation, for no prophecy was ever made by an act of human will (2 Pet. 1:20-21).[3] Bible believing Christians never deny that the Bible came into existence as a result of God's initiative. No human being, by an act of his will, initiated the writing of Scripture. God did use human instruments. The question is, who determined that Scripture should be written; who initiated the action to produce Scripture? The answer is God. In the same way, we could ask the questions: Who determined that men and women should be born again? Who initiated

---

1. Leon Morris, *The Gospel According to John* (Grand Rapids: Eerdmans, 1973), 101.
2. William Hendriksen, *Exposition of the Gospel According to John* (Grand Rapids: Baker, 1972), 1:83.
3. John 1:13 uses the Greek term andros denoting the male or the husband, ἐκ θελήματος ἀνδρὸς. On the other hand, 2 Peter 1:21 uses the generic term anthropos that refers to human beings, θελήματι ἀνθρώπου. However, anthropos can also refer to the male or the husband. The terminology overlaps.

the action that results in men and women being born again? Speaking of those who believe Christ, the apostle John states emphatically, they "were born not ... of the will of man, but of God." In other words, it is not by the exercise of their decision making power that men and women are born again. Quite to the contrary, "Blessed be the God and Father of our Lord Jesus Christ who has caused us to be born again" (1 Pet. 1:3). Who initiates the actions that result in men and women being born again? The answer is God.

The point is that saving faith is a gift from God. "For by grace you have been saved through faith; and that not of yourselves, it is the gift of God" (Eph. 2:8). And no unbeliever is able to trust in Christ unto salvation without a prior work of God granting the new birth and without God granting the gift of saving faith in and through the work of the new birth. This truth is a point of difficulty among Christians. Some liken it to the argument concerning the chicken and the egg. Which comes first? The Biblical answer is that regeneration logically precedes faith.

To help clear the air on this point we look at the apostle John. "Beloved, let us love one another, for love is from God; and everyone who loves is born of God and knows God" (1 John 4:7). Now few, if any, Bible believing Christians doubt John. Christians know that love is a fruit of the Spirit. It is a manifestation, a proof, if you will, of the new birth. A person cannot really love without first being born gain. The Scriptures are plain.

Amazingly enough, John uses the same concept in discussing faith and the new birth. "Whoever believes that Jesus is the Christ is born of God" (1 John 5:1). These words are exactly parallel to 1 John 4:7, "Everyone who loves is born of God." And the parallel should be clear. Just as a person cannot truly love in the Biblical sense without being born again, so a person cannot truly believe in Christ without being born again. In similar fashion, just as Biblical love is a manifestation of and fruit of the new birth, so true faith in Christ is also a manifestation of and fruit of the new birth.

It follows from all the above that the one who bears the message of salvation is absolutely dependent upon the work of the Holy Spirit in blessing the message and preparing the heart of the recipient. Again, as Jesus promised, "No one can come to Me, unless the Father who sent Me draws him" (John 6:44). As a result, the message of salvation must be set forth in purity in words similar to: "Forgiveness of sin and freedom from guilt are obtained through repentance of sin and faith in the Lord Jesus Christ." The Scriptures are clear, "Believe in the Lord Jesus, and you shall be saved" (Acts 16:31).

There is a second implication to John 1:12-13, in addition to the one outlined above. Men and women must be brought to the place of casting themselves on Christ. He is the savior. They must receive Him or believe in Him. Often the message is given in slightly different terms. Men and women are encouraged to "open their hearts" and allow Christ to enter their lives. To be sure, Christ must consume the believer's heart and life. But this is quite different than placing the unbeliever in the driver's seat. The gospel is not a sales pitch that is closed in a way similar to selling vacuum cleaners. Men and women do not save themselves. God must save them if they are to be saved at all. The message of the gospel is God's message to fallen humanity. Faithful ambassadors must deliver the message as God directs. There can then be full assurance that God will bless His Word. The prayer should be for the outpouring of the Holy Spirit to bring conviction and to bless the listener with a new heart.

An experience of the apostle Paul related in Acts 16:14-15 sets the record straight.

> And a certain woman named Lydia, from the city of Thyatira, a seller of purple fabrics, a worshiper of God, was listening; and the Lord opened her heart to respond to the things spoken by Paul. And when she and her household had been baptized, she urged us, saying, "If you have judged me to be faithful to the Lord, come into my house and stay." And she prevailed upon us.

The apostle Paul was preaching by the riverside in Philippi. Lydia, like so many in the church today, was sitting and listening. It is doubtful that she was really hearing at first. Jesus often warned, "He who has ears to hear, let him hear" (Matt. 11:15). Lydia was not really hearing as the narrative begins. How do we know this? Luke tells us very plainly, "The Lord opened her heart to respond to the things spoken by Paul." In other words, the Lord worked a miracle in Lydia's heart. He opened her heart. Why? So she could properly respond to the message Paul was preaching. Paul did not exhort Lydia to open her heart to the Lord. Quite the opposite took place. "The Lord [took action and] opened her heart."

This is astounding! It is also important. Men and women are born again, not by an act of human will but by the action of God. And because faith is a fruit of and manifestation of the new birth, saving faith is not a simple human decision made by an unbeliever as in responding to a carefully designed sales presentation. Saving faith is a denial of self in favor of God. It is a denial of the ability of self to please God in any way. It is recognition of the total inability of self to save and an admission of the total capability of Christ to save. Saving faith is a resting upon Christ alone for salvation.

The message of salvation therefore must not be cradled in terms that describe what men and women can do to be saved. God's grace in Jesus Christ must be set forth along with the exhortation to believe in and trust in the sacrifice of the Lord Jesus Christ. This is the message given to the apostles and transmitted by them. When the Philippian jailer cried, "Sirs, what must I do to be saved?" (Acts 16:30), the answer was simple. Men and women can do nothing to save themselves. They must trust in what God has done through Jesus Christ. This is what faith is all about. Men and women must stop seeking ways to save themselves. They must cast themselves upon the mercy of God in Christ. Thus Paul answered the Philippian jailer, "Believe in the Lord Jesus, and you shall be saved" (Acts 16:31). As a result, Point A of our gospel presentation states, "Forgiveness of sin and freedom from guilt are obtained through repentance of sin and faith in the Lord Jesus Christ."

4. SUMMARY

The first point of the second part of our gospel presentation provides an outline that may be embellished and presented to unbelievers who face the need of salvation. Unbelievers must be given this truth. They must come to grips with the gospel. They must repent of sin. They must trust in the sacrifice of Christ as the only adequate payment for their sin.

The truth must be presented in an uncompromising fashion. Perhaps this is done by reading through a tract such as "You Cannot Escape from God" with the unbeliever. Perhaps this is done by following the general outline of our discussion and setting the Scripture proofs before the unbeliever directly from the Bible. However the truth is presented, the methodology or outline represents a tool to assist you in your presentation of the gospel. And since you are using an outline, questions may be answered as needed and the basic outline may be embellished as needed. Under this first point in the gospel presentation, the various matters that are covered in the main point are supported in the proof texts and can be expanded as in the above discussion.

One caution should be noted. The task of evangelism does not demand that unbelievers come to grips with the rationale behind the points presented. That is, they should not be confronted with the fact that they cannot come to faith in Christ without being born again. Evangelism is not the place for theological discussion on points like this one. We do not see the apostles pressing such issues in their evangelism. Understanding the work of God in salvation comes later. An example is Paul's exposition for Christians in the first chapter of Ephesians.

My contention is that we should follow the apostles. It is of utmost importance to present the gospel and press home the points that are given in the Scripture proof texts.

> Forgiveness of sin and freedom from guilt are obtained through repentance of sin and faith in the Lord Jesus Christ.
>
> While we were still helpless, at the right time, Christ died for the ungodly (Rom. 5:6).
>
> Repent therefore and return, that your sins may wiped away (Acts 3:19).
>
> Believe in the Lord Jesus, and you shall be saved (Acts 16:31).

Here is the gospel, the Good News. And here are the requirements for repentance of sin and faith in Christ, the requirements for true conversion. This truth represents a portion of the truths that we must set before unbelievers. Should we be afraid of using a simple gospel such as the presentation outlined above? I think not. The use of such a presentation may be challenged saying, "But you do not know where the person may be spiritually." True. But God may have also brought the person to whom you are speaking to the very place where a simple, straightforward, presentation of the gospel will be effective. If not, so be it. The obligation of the Christian is to sow the Word of God. It is not the obligation of the Christian to regenerate the listener so that the word is effective. That is God's work.

2

Point B:
The Gift of Eternal Life and Access to Heaven are Obtained through Faith in the Lord Jesus Christ

The gift of God is eternal life through Jesus Christ our Lord. ~Rom. 6:23, KJV

1. CHRIST'S ACTIVE OBEDIENCE

The question has been asked of me more than once, "Why do you add this second point?" The answer is quite simple yet very important. This second point in the gospel presentation draws out a discussion of what the theologians call the "active obedience" of Christ.

What is this active obedience? Allow me to answer first in a negative way. We have just discussed why Christ went to the cross. At the cross, Christ satisfied the demands of the Law of God as a sacrifice for sin. Scripture is very clear, "The soul who sins will die" (Ezek. 18:4). "The wages of sin is death" (Rom. 6:23). The penalty imposed by God against the sinner is death, eternal death in hell. Jesus will one day pass sentence on the ungodly and say, "Depart from Me, accursed ones, into the eternal fire which has been prepared for the devil and his angels" (Matt. 25:41). The glory of the gospel is that Christ saves His people from their sins (Matt. 1:21). He takes upon Himself the penalty for sin due to others. In doing so, Christ obeys the Father. As Christ Himself says, "Behold I have come (In the roll of the book it is written of me) to do Your will, O God" (Heb. 10:7). This obedience is called the "passive obedience" of Christ because He willingly submitted to the penalty of the Law by going to the cross in the place of others.

On the other hand, the active obedience of Christ encompasses the whole life of Christ in contrast to His death on the cross. Christ led an active life. It was an active life of obedience. He was "tempted in all things as we are, yet without sin" (Heb. 4:15). This obedience fulfills the requirements of the Law to attain eternal life. "So you shall keep My statutes and My judgments, by which a man may live if he does them" (Lev. 18:5). The second point in the gospel presentation speaks to this side of the obedience of Christ on behalf of sinners. It answers the need of sinful human beings who are incapable of achieving eternal life through perfect obedience.

The apostle Paul puts Leviticus 18:5 in its proper context in Galatians 3:10-14,

> For as many as are of the works of the Law are under a curse; for it is written, "Cursed is every one who does not abide by all things written in the book of the Law, to perform them." Now that no one is justified by the Law before God is evident; for, "The righteous man shall live by faith." However, the Law is not of faith; on the contrary, "He who practices them shall live by them." Christ redeemed us from the curse of the Law, having become a curse for us—for it is written, "Cursed is everyone who hangs on a tree"—in order that in Christ Jesus the blessing of Abraham might come to the Gentiles, so that we might receive the promise of the Spirit through faith.

Here Paul is speaking about the wonderful work of Christ in sparing sinners the curse of death for sin. Paul contrasts faith and works. On one side, it is "evident," Paul says, "that no one is justified by the Law before God." Why? Paul answers by quoting Habakkuk 2:4, "The righteous man shall live by faith." Here is the crux of the gospel. Salvation, justification before God, is through faith. Now faith is contrary to works. As Paul puts it, "The Law is not of faith." There are two contrary approaches to God. They are the way of faith and the way of works, the works of law. The way of the Law is simply this, "He who practices them shall live by them" (Lev. 18:5). This is the way to eternal life by keeping the Law perfectly. But as Paul has said, no one has satisfied the demands of God and gained salvation through the works of the Law. "For all have sinned and fall short of the glory of God" (Rom. 3:23).

The point to grasp at this stage is that Paul understands Leviticus 18:5 to be speaking about the eternal life which Christians enjoy through the salvation of Christ. And Leviticus 18:5 therefore takes us back to the Garden of Eden and the covenant God made with Adam.

> Then the Lord God took the man and put him into the garden of Eden to cultivate it and keep it. And the Lord God commanded the man, saying, "From any tree of the garden you may eat freely; but from the tree of the knowledge of good and evil you shall not eat, for in the day that you eat from it you shall surely die" (Gen. 2:15-16).

God set before Adam the way of life and the way of death. The choice for Adam was clear: obey God and live; disobey God and die. This was a covenant that God made with Adam. And lest any of us doubt that it was a covenant, the prophet Hosea remembered it as a covenant. He spoke of the children of Israel in these terms, "But like Adam they have transgressed the covenant" (Hos. 6:7). Yes, Adam broke the covenant. As a result, sin and death came into this world. "Through one man sin entered the world, and death through sin, and so death spread to all men" (Rom. 5:12).

But when Christ entered the world in obedience to the will of His Father, He came as the second Adam. As Paul says, "The first man, Adam, became a living soul. The last Adam became a life giving spirit" (1 Cor. 15:45). Adam, as the first man, acted on behalf of mankind so that "through one transgression there resulted condemnation to all men" (Rom. 5:18). On the other hand, as the second or last Adam, Christ also acted on behalf of a new humanity. He stepped in where

Adam failed. Paul tells us that Christ was "born under the Law" (Gal. 4:4). And living under the Law, the writer to the Hebrews tells us He was "holy, innocent, undefiled, separated from sinners" (Heb. 7:26). This was so because He was "tempted in all things as we are, yet without sin" (Heb. 4:15). You see, Christ took upon Himself the obligations of the covenant and fulfilled the whole Law perfectly.

Again, this is the burden of Paul's teaching in Galatians 4:4 and 5 where he says, "But when the fullness of time came, God sent forth His Son, born of a woman, born under the Law, in order that He might redeem those who are under the Law, that we might receive the adoption as sons." Christ was born "under the Law" in order that He might personally fulfill all the requirements of the Law. And Paul tells us the purpose of this "active obedience." Christ's obedience was undertaken "in order that He might redeem those who were under the Law." To accomplish this redemption, Christ had to satisfy the requirements of the Law for those whom He was sent to redeem, in addition to satisfying the penalties of the Law. In other words, Christ had to fulfill the terms of the covenant Adam failed to fulfill. Christ did just that. He fulfilled Leviticus 18:5; "So you shall keep My statutes and My judgments, by which a man may live if he does them; I am the Lord."

Note the significance of this work of Christ. Christ did what you and I could not possibly do. He lived a perfect life. He lived that perfect life on behalf of sinners like you and me. He stood in the place of sinful men and women and lived a sinless life on their behalf. Thus He fulfilled the terms of the covenant with which Adam failed to comply. Adam plunged humanity into sin. Christ redeemed fallen humanity from the curse of the Law because of sin. Christ the Lord of Glory did not need redemption. He did not need to earn eternal life for Himself. Neither did He need to earn for Himself entrance into heaven. Rather, Christ took upon Himself the task of living a perfect life so that others might have life and others might gain entrance into heaven.

2. THE GIFT OF CHRIST'S RIGHTEOUSNESS

These questions now come to the fore: "Who may ascend into the hill of the Lord? And who may stand in His holy place? (Ps. 24:3). In other words, who is worthy to receive eternal life and stand before God in heaven? Who will hear these wonderful words on the Day of Judgment, "Come, you who are blessed of My Father, inherit the kingdom prepared for you from the foundation of the world" (Matt. 25:34)? The psalmist David answers with these simple words, "He who has clean hands and a pure heart" (Ps. 24:4). Two great requirements must be met if sinners are to stand before God in heaven. On one side, the hearts of men and women must be cleansed from sin. They must be cleansed through the blood of Christ. This cleansing comes through repentance of sin and faith in the sacrifice of Christ as discussed under Point A.

On the other side, men and women must come before God with clean hands. They must present a life of perfect righteousness to God. But how is this possible? No human being is absolutely righteous. Therefore, the righteousness with which men and women appear before God must be the righteousness of Christ. The glory of the gospel is that sinful men and women are clothed with the righteousness of Christ enabling them to stand in the very presence of God. This is the burden of Paul's teaching: "For as through the one man's disobedience many were made sinners, even so through the obedience of the One the many will be made righteous" (Rom. 5:19). "He made Him who knew no sin to be sin on our behalf, that we might become the righteousness of God in Him" (2 Cor. 5:21).

All of the above discussion stands behind Point B in the proposed gospel presentation. This point directs our attention to the work of Christ in procuring eternal life and access to heaven through the perfect life He lived on behalf of sinners. This great truth is an important aspect of the gospel. It relates directly to the justification of sinners. What is justification? Here is an excellent definition: "Justification is an act of God's free grace, wherein he pardoneth all our sins, and accepteth us as righteous in his sight, only for the righteousness of Christ imputed to us, and received by faith alone" (WSC, Q&A 33).

There are two significant sides to justification. First, men and women are forgiven of their sin. Second, men and women are clothed with the righteousness of Christ. Both are essential if sinful human beings are to find acceptance before a holy God. And so it is essential that both aspects of the gospel be defined for men and women.

3. BY FAITH ALONE

But how are men and women clothed with the righteousness of Christ and how do they thereby receive eternal life and access to heaven? The answer is faith in Christ. "The gift of God is eternal life through Jesus Christ our Lord" (Rom. 6:23, KJV). There is only one way to eternal life and heaven. Men and women must trust in the work of Jesus Christ on their behalf. "I am the way, and the truth, and the life; no one comes to the Father, but through Me," said Jesus (John 14:6). This truth is the burden of Point B in the gospel presentation. And this is exactly what must be pressed upon the unbeliever.

> The gift of eternal life and access to heaven are obtained through faith in the Lord Jesus Christ.
>
> The gift of God is eternal life through Jesus Christ our Lord (Romans 6:23, KJV).

Unbelievers must realize that it is only as they are clothed with the perfect righteousness of Christ that God will receive them in heaven. Only those who wear the robes of Christ's righteousness will hear these wonderful words on the Day of Judgment: "Come, you who are blessed of My Father, inherit the kingdom prepared for you from the foundation of the world (Matt. 25:34).

And so it is our obligation to simply state the beauty of the gospel. It is our duty to set the perfect life of Christ before unbelievers as a gift from God. This gift opens the door to heaven and procures eternal life. It is as simple as that. Once setting the truth before unbelievers, it is our obligation to urge them to trust in Christ by telling them, "The gift of eternal life and access to heaven are obtained through faith in the Lord Jesus Christ."

4. THE GIFT OF ETERNAL LIFE

The additional proof text under this point in the gospel presentation is John 17:3, "And this is eternal life, that they may know You the only true God, and Jesus Christ whom You have sent." Here Jesus equates eternal life with knowing God. This means that eternal life is something that may be experienced in the present and that is fulfilled in the future. But what does it mean to know God? Speaking to the Galatians on this subject, the apostle Paul says,

> When you did not know God, you were slaves to those who are by nature no gods. But now that you have come to know God, or rather to be known by God, how is it that you turn back again to the weak and worthless elemental things, to which you desire to be enslaved all over again? (Gal. 4:8-9).

In the negative, lack of a true knowledge of God involves slavery to sin. "You were slaves to those which are no gods," Paul says. In other words, there were idols in your life such as sex, power, money, property, etc. And you served these idols as though you were slaves to them. The point here is that the direct opposite of knowing God is serving the appetites of the flesh. You worship and serve the creature rather than the Creator (Rom. 1:25).

Now note the turn that Paul makes when he speaks in a positive sense about knowing God. He says, "But now that you have come to know God, or rather to be known by God." We might say that Paul made a mistake and is correcting himself. This seems unlikely. It is really the Holy Spirit who is speaking to us. Or we may say, Paul is speaking to us under the inspiration of the Holy Spirit. In either case, the text is inspired. The Holy Spirit is not correcting Himself. Going back to John 17:3, note that Christ also speaks in the active voice about knowing God. "And this is eternal life, that they may know You the only true God." Christ does not correct Himself by putting His statement in the passive voice and saying, "That they may be known by You the only true God." No, there is something else in the text.

What the Holy Spirit is really teaching us through the apostle Paul is that being known by God takes precedence over our active knowledge of God. Christ explains this fact when He reviews the awesome events to come on the Day of Judgment.

> Not every one who says to Me, "Lord, Lord," will enter the kingdom of heaven; but he who does the will of My Father who is in heaven. Many will say to Me on that day, "Lord, Lord, did we not prophesy in Your name, and in Your name cast out demons, and in your name perform many miracles?" And then I will declare to them, "I never knew you; depart from Me, you who practice lawlessness" (Matt. 7:21-23).

Here is an awesome statement, "I never knew you." It is not that Christ does not know all about every one. Christ is God. He knows all things. He does know all the facts, the intimate details, of your life and my life. Christ is not talking about knowing facts. He has something else in mind.

Very often, when the Scriptures use the word "know," the Scriptures are referring, at least in part, to "love." For example, when the Bible speaks of a husband knowing his wife, there is more involved than sexual relations. There is love involved. In fact, there is covenant love involved. The Bible describes the relationship between husband and wife in terms of a covenant. Malachi 2:14 says, "The Lord has been a witness between you and the wife of your youth, against whom you have dealt treacherously, though she is your companion and your wife by covenant." The point is that when a husband truly knows his wife, he is caught up in a love based upon a covenant relationship that has been established with her.

There can be little doubt that the marriage relationship pictures the relationship between God and believers. When Paul concludes his discussion of the marriage relationship in Ephesians, he says,

"This mystery is great; but I am speaking with reference to Christ and the church" (Eph. 5:32). This being the case, we are thrown back to the covenant relationship that God establishes with His people. This covenant relationship involves the display of His love in Christ. "But God demonstrates His own love toward us, in that while we were yet sinners, Christ died for us" (Rom. 5:8). And what is the blood of Christ poured out as a sacrifice for sinners? Christ tells us in the institution of the Lord's Supper. "This is My blood of the covenant, which is to be shed on behalf of many for the forgiveness of sins" (Matt. 26:28). The blood of Christ is the blood of the covenant.

But then, what does it mean to be known by God? The person who is known by God has been drawn into a covenant relationship with God. This person has his or her sins covered by the blood of Christ, the blood of the covenant. This person experiences the love of God. On one hand, this love is manifested in the death of Christ in payment for sins. The individual who experiences forgiveness is able to confess with the apostle Paul, "I have been crucified with Christ; and it is no longer I who live, but Christ lives in me; and the life which I now live in the flesh I live by faith in the Son of God, who loved me, and delivered Himself up for me" (Gal. 2:20).

On the other hand, the one who is known by God also experiences the love of God in a subjective way "because the love of God has been poured out within our hearts through the Holy Spirit who was given to us" (Rom. 5:5). In addition, God's Spirit is "the Holy Spirit of promise, who is given as a pledge of our inheritance" (Eph. 1:13-14). In other words, when the Holy Spirit is given to an individual, He is a down payment on the glorious life that is to come. And those who are known by God presently experience the eternal life of God through the presence of the Holy Spirit in their lives.

The negative statement of Christ then takes on quite awesome proportions. On the Day of Judgment, Christ will say to some, "I never knew you." He means, "I did not know you in eternity past when My Father's plan was being formulated. My special covenant love and the benefits of My death were not yours then. And I did not know you when you walked in the world and My benefits were not yours at that time either. And finally, I do not know you now. The benefits of My death are not yours as you now face Me in judgment. *I never knew you.*" These words are terrifying to say the least. They are also repugnant to natural human instincts.

But they cannot be dismissed because it is Christ who states that He will be brought to say, "I never knew you." And we dare not discard this statement. It dramatically amplifies the greatness of Christ's words in John 17:3, "And this is eternal life, that they may know You the only true God and Jesus Christ whom You have sent." Eternal life is to know God. This means you are drawn into a covenant relationship with God. The blood of Christ shed on the cross covers your sins. You receive the gift of the Holy Spirit as a down payment on the promise of eternal life in heaven with God. That is, you participate in the reality of eternal life here and now. In sum, you are known by God. This translates into the assurance that you will never hear those awesome and terrible words of Christ just discussed. It is impossible that those words should be in your future. Because Christ has known you through a covenant relationship of love, it is not possible for Him to say sometime in the future, "I never knew you." The reality is, you know God; or rather, you are known by God.

And so the additional proof text for Point B of the gospel presentation takes on significant meaning. It defines eternal life. It emphasizes the present reality of eternal life. We are not discussing a 'pie in the sky' gospel. The realities of the gospel are for here and now. And just as forgiveness and cleansing from sin are experienced in the present and must be, so eternal life must be understood and experienced in the present.

5. CONCLUSION

In summing up this point, it should be emphasized once again that sinful human beings cannot assure a place in heaven for themselves.

They must be given the perfect life of Christ, his righteousness, in order to be assured of heaven. This righteousness is a gift of God. It is obtained through faith in the Son of God, Jesus Christ. And this is a faith that trusts in and rests upon the perfect life of Christ, the only life that meets the requirements for entrance into heaven and eternal life. With this background in mind, you can place the wonders of the gospel before the unbeliever in these simple terms:

> The gift of eternal life and access to heaven are obtained through faith in the Lord Jesus Christ.
>
> The gift of God is eternal life through Jesus Christ our Lord (Rom. 6:23, KJV).
>
> And this is eternal life, that they may know Thee the only true God, and Jesus Christ whom Thou has sent (John 17:3).
>
> Come, you who are blessed of My Father, inherit the kingdom prepared for you from the foundation of the world (Matt. 25:34).

THE GOSPEL IS NOT A SALES PITCH

*And Jesus said to them,
"Follow Me, and I will make you become
fishers of men."* ~Mark 1:17

1. INTRODUCTION

Several years ago, being very much in need of a job after getting out of the army, I obtained work as a hearing aid salesman. The fellow who owned the business was a professing Christian and I was excited about the opportunity. But my excitement waned when my employer gave me the example of the use of the hard sell. If an elderly lady, who appeared to have the money, was hesitant about buying a hearing aid, my employer, in a rather crass fashion, would say, "Just remember lady, you can't take it with you." And he would then close the sale by pushing a contract in front of her nose and handing her a pen. In point of fact, these sales pitches disgusted me. They were examples of blatant manipulation. And I did not last long with this employer. Perhaps this example brings to mind a car salesman or a vacuum cleaner, encyclopedia or insurance sales person with whom you have dealt. Thankfully all those working in sales are not dedicated to the hard sell. But as anyone who has gone through training in sales knows, all sales presentations lead up to the all-important close. And it is true, if you don't close the sale, all your time is for naught.

After entering the pastorate, I was encouraged to take some training in evangelism. One of the members of the congregation generously paid the fee for the seminars and purchased the suggested materials. There was much to be gained in this training. But one overpowering emphasis pervaded what we were taught. The gospel of Jesus Christ was reduced to a sales pitch. As a man believing the great Bible doctrines of divine sovereignty and gracious election, I was repulsed by the notion that election meant our going out and choosing who would be saved by going through a prescribed outline on the doorstep of homes we chose. A neighborhood "survey" was used as a pretense to present the prescribed gospel outline. And the all-important close involved getting the person with whom we were talking to pray with us "now."

Although much good is done, and although people are brought to a saving knowledge of the Lord Jesus Christ by such means, the gospel of Jesus Christ is reduced to the level of a vacuum cleaner. And not only so, human beings, who may be the object of God's gracious election, are manipulated by the gospel presentation in order to extract the all-important prayer of decision.

To some, this may seem a bit too harsh. And perhaps a bit of hyperbole is used to emphasize the point. But at any rate, when such tactics are examined in the light of Scripture, they are found to be wanting. This is not to say that the use of tracts is bad, as long as these tracts are faithful to Scripture. Nor is it to criticize having a basic approach with the gospel to an unbelieving world. Quite to the contrary, I have labored to show that the apostle Paul used a very specific methodology. But that methodology was based squarely upon Biblical principles. And these Biblical principles in no way resemble modern sales techniques. As God's people, we are to follow Scripture and not the wiles of the world as outlined in modern sales procedures.

And so we have the question, where does prayer fit in our work of evangelism? And more importantly, what is the work of the Holy Spirit, and how do we follow Him in our evangelistic endeavors? It is my desire to answer these two questions in what follows, and at the same time, to emphasize the fact that the good news of the gospel is just that, Good News. The gospel is not a sales pitch.

2. THE EXAMPLE OF CHRIST

In answering the question concerning where prayer fits in our evangelism, let's first examine the example of Christ as He called individuals to follow Him. And as we do so, it would serve us well to observe that Christ dealt with people on both an individual level and a corporate level. At times, the individualism of modern evangelism is highly criticized. And well it might be, when it does not lead to corporate fellowship and service in the body of Christ. But, be this as it may, it must be observed that Christ did deal with individuals in a very pointed fashion as a part of His mission to a lost world.

For example, in Matthew 9:9 it says, "And as Jesus passed on from there, He saw a man, called Matthew, sitting in the tax office; and He said to him, 'Follow Me!' And he rose and followed Him." Here Jesus dealt with this individual, Levi, on an individual basis. But more importantly, for our purposes, a simple call was made, "Follow Me." Obviously there was the decision on the part of Levi to get up and follow Jesus. That is, Levi committed himself to this person, Jesus Christ. He determined to follow Him as a disciple.

But note two things very clearly. First, there was no "sales pitch" set forth by our Lord. Far from it! There was a simple call, "Follow Me." And Levi, confronted with the Christ and confronted with the proposition that he ought to follow Christ, was forced to determine his next course of action. "And he rose, and followed Him." But second, because there was no sales pitch, there was no traditional closing of the presentation. There was a simple exhortation. Then came a simple response. There was no verbal pressure applied. And there was no request for Levi to pray on the spot with Jesus. The narrative is quite clear. The sequence of events is very plain. Exhortation: "Follow Me!" Response: "And he rose, and followed Him."

Another individual with whom Jesus dealt was the woman at the well. The narrative found in John 4:1-42 is often used to explain how everyday situations and simple elements of creation can be used to point individuals to the Savior. And such is the case. But although Jesus uses the water and the well to illustrate His point, the main thing to consider is that Jesus simply presents Himself to this woman. "The woman said to Him, 'I know that Messiah is coming (He who is called the Christ); when that One comes, He will declare all things to us'" (John 4:25). Note the response of Jesus, "I who speak to you am He" (John 4:26).

Here we have a situation similar to the one outlined above. This woman, like Levi, was confronted with the Christ, and she knew it. Having been confronted with the Christ, this woman was forced to determine her next course of action. "So the woman left her waterpot, and went into the city, and said to the men, 'Come, see a man who told me· all things that I have done'" (John 4:28-29). Note again the absence of anything that smacks of a sales presentation. There is no verbal or emotional constraint placed upon this woman by Jesus. And there is no request for the woman to pray with Jesus there by the well. Quite to the contrary, the conversation is [and we might say, 'unfortunately'] interrupted by the arrival of the disciples and the woman went her way.

But what was the result of the evangelistic conversation with the woman at the well? John 4:39 tells us, "And from that city many of the Samaritans believed in Him because of the word of the woman who testified, 'He told me all the things that I have done.'" Needless to say, there are lessons here regarding the personal "testimony." But these will have to be saved for another time. Important for our purpose is the observation that the encounter Jesus had with this single woman by the well resulted in the conversion of many others in her city.

One final example of Christ dealing with an individual is Luke 19:1-10, which relates the story of Zaccheus. Jesus was in Jericho. Zaccheus was a chief tax-gatherer who was quite rich. He wanted to see

Jesus, and so he climbed a tree. "And when Jesus came to the place, He looked up and said to him, 'Zaccheus, hurry and come down, for today I must stay at your house'" (Luke 19: 5). Here again we see the same sort of circumstance as found in the previous two narratives discussed. Zaccheus is confronted with the Christ. He hears an exhortation from the lips of Jesus. He must now decide his next course of action. "And he hurried and came down, and received Him gladly" (Luke 19:6). Note again the lack of modern evangelistic procedure. There is no request for Zaccheus to pray with Jesus there at the foot of the tree or later at home. But we do know of Zaccheus' salvation. "Jesus said to him, 'Today salvation has come to this house'" (Luke 19:9).

There have been times when I have felt guilty about not properly taking advantage of a situation after a conversation about the Lord. I have asked myself, "Should I not have prayed with this person?" I have also heaped guilt upon myself when such a conversation was 'interrupted' by the appearance of another Christian. I am grateful for the examples of Jesus just cited. This is not to excuse an inadequate presentation of Christ. In the cases to which I have referred, Levi, the woman at the well, and Zaccheus were each squarely confronted with Christ. Our purpose ought to be the same. It ought to be in line with the apostle Paul who says, "I determined to know nothing among you accept Jesus Christ, and Him crucified" (1 Cor. 2:2). And what about prayer with an individual who desires to follow Christ? I'll speak to that later. For now, it is enough to see that Christ did not use such a procedure.

You may now be inclined to think that I am leading people away from an established procedure that has borne much fruit. I respond: Is our standard a long held tradition that is based upon a worldly procedure or is our standard for evangelistic work Holy Scripture? We must follow the examples of Scripture. Other procedures will lead people astray. In the last section of this chapter, I will attempt to outline some dangers inherent in the non-biblical procedure that I have experienced. As just stated, it is enough to see that Jesus did not use modern evangelistic techniques. But lest you feel that you might be losing out by not following such long established methodologies, allow me to give you a contemporary example.

Charles Colson tells the story of and elderly lady in Northern Ireland who visited Belfast's Maze Prison. One Christmas Eve, Miss Gladys Blackburne, a retired school teacher in her mid sixties, went to the prison and was directed to a young man by the name of Chips McCurry. Chips had been committed to terrorism since the age of twelve when the IRA killed his father. Note two things about this story. First, Miss Blackburne clearly presented Christ. Second, although there was no call for prayer at the moment, God had His way in the life of Chips McCurry.

> When Gladys entered his cell on Christmas Eve, Chips recognized her. He had often seen her in prison and knew, like most of the other inmates, that 'if you don't want to hear the gospel, then you'd better run when you see Miss Blackburne coming.' But there was nowhere to run. Miss Blackburne took the chair at the small desk directly opposite Chip's cot and asked if she could read some Scriptures. Chips prepared himself for a recitation of the Christmas story. Instead, Miss Blackburne opened her Bible to Luke 23, the account of the Crucifixion. She stopped when she came to the words of the thief on the cross: "Lord, remember me when you come into your kingdom."

> "Now who was this thief calling 'Lord?'" Miss Blackburne asked Chips, her pale blue eyes looking intently into his. "Here was a man who had a crown of thorns thrust into his head. Here was a man who was spat upon, stripped, beaten, whipped, and so disfigured He was unrecognizable. Does that look like a Lord to you? But this thief called Him 'Lord'—Because Jesus was still Lord on the cross." Chip's eyes fell. He didn't know quite why, but Gladys Blackburne's words made him aware of all the hatred and bitterness that had consumed him for years. For the first time he caught a glimpse of the con-

nection between Christ's death and himself. *Christ was perfect,* Chips thought. *And I am full of evil—the Sin He had to die for.*

He looked at the small woman. "How do I become a Christian?" he asked.

"You need to accept Christ as Lord, just like the thief on the cross," she said. "You need to turn away from your sins and believe that He died for them. And you need to confess Him as Lord to others."

Confess Christ as Lord? Chips hesitated. He had taunted enough Christians himself to know how hard it was in prison.

Miss Blackburne didn't push it. "Let me show you one more verse," she said. "Then I need to go visit some other friends." She flipped the pages of her worn New Testament and read him John 6:37: "He who comes to me I will in no wise cast out."

"If you come to Christ," she said, "He will never let you go."

After Miss Blackburne left, Chips McCurry sat in his cell thinking. Finally, late that night, he knelt by his cot and committed his life to Jesus Christ. He had seen the self-perpetuating emptiness of violence and the impotence of political philosophy. He realized he had finally met the Truth.[1]

This true story recounts a classic gospel presentation after the pattern of our Lord. It closely follows the requirements of Scripture outlined above in Part Two, Presenting the Gospel. There is no "sales pitch" for Christ. To present day evangelical standards, it is astounding that, after such a forceful presentation of Christ, no call to prayer is made. In actuality, the prayer came before the visit. More must be said on this later. Miss Blackburne presented Christ and left Chips. As in each of the Biblical examples given above, Chips was left to determine his next course of action.

---

1. Charles Colson, *Kingdoms in Conflict* (Grand Rapids: Zondervan, 1987), 351-352.

3. EXAMPLES FROM THE BOOK OF ACTS

Another excellent example of one-on-one evangelism is seen in the story of Philip and the Ethiopian. An Ethiopian court official had been in Jerusalem to worship. This man was educated and had obtained a copy of portions of the Old Testament Scriptures. He was riding in a chariot or carriage and was reading from Isaiah 53 when Philip encountered him. Philip was invited to explain the teaching of the Scriptures. "And Philip opened his mouth, and beginning from this Scripture he preached Jesus to him. And as they went along the road they came to some water; and the eunuch said, 'Look! Water! What prevents me from being baptized?'" (Acts 8:35-36). As the narrative continues, Philip baptizes the Ethiopian and is subsequently taken on to further work.

Again we see two characteristic elements in this story. First, there is a forceful presentation of Christ. There is little doubt that the Ethiopian is confronted with the Lord Jesus Christ and His work on the cross on behalf of sinners. Isaiah 53 is a classic prophecy fulfilled in detail by the sacrificial work of Christ. There is no sales pitch. On the contrary, the Scriptures are explained and expounded. As a result, the Ethiopian must determine his next course of action. Second, we see no insistence on the part of Philip that the Ethiopian pray with him there beside the road. In this instance, the response to the gospel is quite different. The Ethiopian wanted to be baptized. And so, in this case, it is baptism and not formula prayer that is the response to the gospel.

When we look at the ministry of the apostle Paul, we see the same thing. Acts 16:14-15 reads:

> And a certain woman named Lydia, from the city of Thyatira, a seller of purple fabrics, a worshiper of God, was listening; and the Lord opened her heart to respond to the things spoken by Paul. And when she and her household had been baptized, she urged us saying, 'If you have judged me faithful to the Lord, come into my house and stay.' And she prevailed upon us.

Now this businesswoman was the object of Paul's preaching along with other women who had gathered at a place of prayer by a riverside. These women had gathered to go through the Jewish ritual prayer service. When Paul spoke, Lydia listened. We see no indication of a sales pitch here. Paul's procedure in situations like this one was much like Philip's. He "reasoned ... from the Scriptures," (Acts 17:2), "testifying to the Jews that Jesus was the Christ" (Acts 18:5).

During this time, Christ, from His place in glory, opened Lydia's heart. In other words, He "caused her to be born again" by the power of the Spirit (1 Pet. 1:3). This was not Lydia's doing, "The wind blows where it wishes and you hear the sound of it, but do not know where it comes from or where it is going; so is every one who is borne of the Spirit" (John 3:8).

And why was Lydia's heart opened? Lydia's heart was opened for the specific purpose of properly responding to the preaching of Paul. This is why, in addition to there being no "sales pitch," there is no call for a prayer of decision on the part of the apostle Paul. The Lord Himself is working to elicit the proper response to the gospel by opening Lydia's heart. And so, having been forcefully confronted with the gospel of Christ, Lydia next determines her course of action. And what is her response? Again, the response is baptism. Paul does not insist that Lydia follow him in a particular prayer. No mention is made of such a procedure. Had the procedure been essential, we can be sure that the Holy Spirit would have so guided Paul. But what is given to us is the baptism of Lydia and the baptism of her household. This is what is recorded in Scripture.

We see a similar case in the incident involving the Philippian jailer. Paul and Silas were in jail. They were "praying and singing hymns of praise to God" (Acts 16:25). The Scriptures tell us that there was a great earthquake. "All the prison doors were opened, and everyone's chains were unfastened" (Acts 16:26). When the jailer realized what had taken place, he thought it best to kill himself.

> But Paul cried out with a loud voice, saying, "Do yourself no harm, for we are all here!" And he called for lights and rushed in and trembling with fear, he fell down before Paul and Silas; and after he brought them out, he said, "Sirs, what must I do to be saved?" And they said, "Believe in the Lord Jesus and you shall be saved, you and your household." And they spoke the word of the Lord to him together with all who were in his house. And he took them that very hour of the night and washed their wounds, and immediately he was baptized, he and all his household (Acts 16:28-33).

Paul presented Christ to the jailer and his household. And Paul presented the requirement to trust in Christ alone for salvation. Where is the sales pitch? As in the case of Lydia, it is conspicuously absent. And what was the response to this presentation of Christ? Baptism. Absent is any hint that Paul required the jailer to pray with him either in the jail or in his home.

Paul's methodology is in keeping with the Great Commission. "Go therefore and make disciples of all the nations, baptizing them in the name of the Father and the Son and the Holy Spirit, teaching them to observe all that I commanded you" (Matt. 28:19-20). We are to be in the business of making disciples and not just converts. Baptism brings converts into the visible body of believers, the church, where discipleship is to take place. And so baptism is a vital part of the process of making disciples.

The response of baptism is also in keeping with the pattern set down by Christ. Although in the examples given above, we do not see Christ baptizing those whom he called, we can be sure that baptism was a vital part of His ministry. John 4:1-2 relates, "When therefore the Lord knew that the Pharisees had heard that Jesus was making and baptizing more disciples than John (although Jesus Himself was not baptizing, but His disciples were) ... "

And so the procedure of likening the gospel to a sales presentation to be closed by requiring individuals who are the objects of our evangelism to pray a prescribed prayer with us does not bear up under the scrutiny of Scripture.

But let me hasten to emphasize that this observation is not set forth to disparage prayer with others. Interestingly enough, the Westminster Shorter Catechism states, "The preface of the Lord's Prayer, [which is, *Our Father which art in heaven*] teacheth us to draw near to God with all holy reverence and confidence, as children to a father, able and ready to help us; and that we should pray with and for others" (Answer 100). The controversy is not about praying with others. The controversy is over treating the gospel like a set of encyclopedias, treating its presentation as a sales pitch, and manipulating the objects of our evangelism with a prayer that is supposed to clinch the sale. The Biblical data simply does not support this procedure.

4. THE PLACE OF PRAYER

Given the material outlined above, what is the place of prayer in our evangelistic methodology? Jesus again points us in the right direction.

> And when you pray, you are not to be as the hypocrites; for they love to stand and pray in the synagogues and on the street corners, in order to be seen by men. Truly they have their reward in full. But you, when you pray, GO INTO YOUR INNER ROOM, AND WHEN YOU HAVE SHUT YOUR DOOR, pray to your Father who is in secret, and your Father who sees in secret will repay you (Matt. 6:5-6).

Here we find some basics with regard to prayer. First and foremost, when you pray, "go into your inner room." This inner room is a room within a room. We might liken it to a large walk-in closet in a modern bedroom. Your room is your bedroom. Your inner room is the walk-in closet. And you are to go into your inner room. That is, you are to be "in secret." No one knows where you are. No one knows what you are doing. You are not going to prayer to impress anyone. This is an earnest time in secret.

In this secret place you find your Father. Unlike other members of your family, unlike your neighbors and friends, God, your Father sees you in secret. He meets with you in secret. And so, there, in secret, you pray.

In relation to your evangelism, there are two important applications. First, you pray for those to whom you may have opportunity to present Christ. Here is the root of the matter. You must pray for these people specifically. You must pray that the Lord will open their hearts to respond to the things you present to them concerning Christ. I have in mind the work of the Lord in opening the heart of Lydia. We know that God does have His elect in the world around us. As Paul says specifically with regard to Jewish people, "In the same way then, there has also come to be at the present time a remnant according to God's gracious choice" (Rom. 11:5). And so if God has called you to do the work of an evangelist among Jewish people, you should pray in secret that your Father will open the hearts of those to whom you speak to respond to the message of the gospel. Is this praying in accordance with God's will? Indeed it is. As a result,

> This is the confidence we have before Him, that, if we ask anything according to His will, He hears us. And if we know that He hears us in what ever we ask, we know that we have the requests which we have asked from Him (1 John 5:14-15).

Having earnestly prayed for the Lord to open the hearts of His elect, you can present the gospel in confidence that He will indeed open the hearts of His people to respond properly to the gospel.

In like manner, God's election of grace is not reserved for Jewish people only; it is also extended to Gentiles. As Paul so eloquently puts it,

> What if God, although willing to demonstrate His wrath and to make His power known, endured with much patience vessels of wrath prepared for destruction? And He did so in order that He might make known the riches of His glory upon vessels

of mercy, which He prepared beforehand for glory, even us, whom He also called, not from among Jews only, but also from among Gentiles (Rom. 9:22-24).

Yes, there is an election of grace among Gentiles also. And so, you may pray that the Lord will open the hearts of His elect among all the nations of the earth. Some of those people are in your own neighborhood and community. As you pray for these people, you can pray with confidence that you are indeed praying in God's will. You can expect God to hear and answer. He will pave the way for you as you seek to present the gospel to those in need of Christ.

You must also pray for the convicting work of the Holy Spirit. As the Lord opens the hearts of lost men and women, the first great work of the Holy Spirit that these people should experience is conviction. Jesus again puts it plainly in His exposition of the work of the Spirit. "And He, when He comes, will convict the world concerning sin, and righteousness, and judgment" (John 16:8). The world is the spiritual realm opposed to God and to Christ. It is the domain of darkness and of those who reside in darkness. The very first work of the Spirit is to convict those in the world concerning their sin. Without the conviction of sin, there is no understanding of the need of Christ, the answer to the problem of sin.

The righteousness of which Christ speaks is at once both the righteous requirements of God's moral law and the righteous fulfillment of those requirements by the Lord Jesus Christ. Real conviction relates to both. On one side, there is an understanding of loss, an understanding that the individual is under condemnation because of failure to meet God's righteous demands. On the other side, there is a heartfelt conviction that Christ's righteousness is the individual's only gain in the sight of God.

At the same time, there is conviction concerning judgment. This is conviction concerning the judgment that all will face. This is conviction that individuals found in sin will stand before God's judgment seat and will be pronounced guilty. They will hear the sentence of eternal death. Since the first work of God's Spirit is the work of conviction, it is the will of God to bring such conviction upon those He intends to convert. When you pray for the Holy Spirit to carry out this work of conviction, you pray according to the will of God. Again, you may be confident that God will answer such prayer. The heart opened by the Lord will experience the application of this convicting work of the Holy Spirit. As a result, the Spirit will bless forthright presentations of responsibility before God, sin, and judgment. And Christ will be received as the only solution to the personal problem of sin.

And so, your prayer for individuals in private should be earnest. It should include prayer for the work of the Spirit to bring conviction. It should include prayer that the Lord will open the hearts of those to whom you may present the gospel. This is the first important application concerning secret prayer.

The second application involves the prayer of those to whom you may be privileged to present the gospel. The exhortation of Jesus is to private and secret prayer. Jesus is concerned about those who pray, "in order to be seen by men" (Matt. 6:5). The person who is on the receiving end of the gospel needs to settle accounts with God. This is not a matter with which to trifle. A prayer said at the close of a gospel presentation in order to please the person making the presentation will be of no avail. Jesus says very plainly, "Pray to your Father who is in secret, and your Father who sees in secret will repay you (Matt. 6:6). The individual concerned for the welfare of his or her soul must come to terms with the living God. If such an individual has been brought under conviction by the Holy Spirit and if such an individual's heart has been opened to respond to the gospel, there will be earnest heartfelt prayer to God in secret until the benefits of salvation are experienced and understood. And so, an application of our text would be to encourage individuals to whom we present the gospel to seek the Lord in private. Might sample prayers be given to such people? I see no reason to withhold such samples. But again, "meaningless repetition" (Matt. 6:7) of such prayers must be discouraged.

What I have said runs counter to current evangelical thought and practice. We might fear that we will lose converts if we do not press this matter of prayer with an individual after a gospel presentation. But are we presenting the gospel of Jesus Christ or are we using the wisdom of men in making a sales pitch that we feel we must close in order to guarantee the results? And in following the latter course, do we not betray our lack of confidence in the work of the Holy Spirit? Do we not also betray our lack of faith in Christ who Himself opens the hearts of men and women "to respond to the things spoken" in the gospel (compare Acts 16:14)? On the contrary, we should exhort men and women to "seek the Lord while He may be found" (Isa. 55:6). We should follow the apostle Paul who said, "My message and my preaching were not in persuasive words of man's wisdom, but in demonstration of the Spirit and of power, that your faith should not rest on the wisdom of men but on the power of God" (1 Cor. 2:4-5).

Yes, the power of God is found in the power of the Holy Spirit resident in the gospel and the Spirit's personal application of that gospel to the hearts of individuals. And so, Jesus gives us incentive to pray for the Spirit. He says, "If you then, being evil, know how to give good gifts to your children, how much more shall your heavenly Father give the Holy Spirit to those who ask Him?" (Luke 11:13). Your heavenly Father will give you the Holy Spirit *when you ask Him*! Therefore, you must ask Him to give you the Holy Spirit as you present Christ to those in need. This is a must so that your gospel presentation will rest in "demonstration of the Spirit and of power." You must also pray for the outpouring of the Spirit upon those to whom you speak the gospel. This is also absolutely essential in order that the faith of those to whom you present Christ may not rest upon the cunning of your salesmanship "but on the power of God."

This is the real place of prayer in the work of evangelism. It must precede and undergird that work. When we understand the proper place of prayer in the work of evangelism, we also see the real emphasis of that work. Evangelism is the work of presenting Christ and exhorting men and women to repent of sin and to trust in Christ as the only answer to their sin. If the real emphasis in evangelism is the presentation of Christ, we must work at presenting Christ and the need of men and women for Christ. A false emphasis is brought into our evangelistic work when the prayer of decision is made the keystone of the presentation. This likens the gospel to a case full of brushes peddled by a door-to-door salesman. However, as we have been emphasizing, the gospel is not a sales pitch. "It is the power of God unto salvation" (Rom. 1:16).

But now, allow me to comment on two important areas of probable concern. The two areas of concern are first, praying with people desirous of following Christ and second, the requirement of God to confess Christ before others. What about prayer with others who desire to follow Christ? First of all, prayer with others is always in order. And so, prayer with and for those to whom you present the gospel is also in order. But you ought to remember that a prepared prayer of decision recited with an individual is not a necessary ingredient to commitment to Christ. Circumstances may arise where such a prayer is appropriate. But care must be taken not to push people. Pushing people into a decision with such a prayer is never appropriate.

Again and again, in the examples given above, we have seen that the gospel was presented and then a commitment was made to follow Christ. Let that commitment be made and carried out! And as I will state in a moment, that commitment must also be verbalized. But it need not be formalized on the spot by a formula prayer. It is far more important that a commitment to Christ be formalized by a life full of zeal for the Lord and conduct that is becoming to the name Christian. This is the Biblical pattern. As I will also show, too often the decision formalized on the spot with a prayer for the benefit of men is a deception. Christ says as much in Matthew 6:5. Concerning those who are hypocritical and who pray in order to be seen by men Jesus says, "Truly I say to you, they have their reward in full." It must also be remembered that you will rarely be prepared to pray with others if you have not previously been in prayer for them in secret. Again, private secret prayer for others and yourself must take precedence.

And what about the public confession of Christ required by God? You say, "You would have us send men and women to their prayer closets when God requires them to make a public stand for Christ." But is the prayer closet incompatible with the public confession of Christ required of God? No, it is not. In the book of Acts, what was the public ceremony engaged in by every new convert? Men and women of old took their stand for Christ when they and their children were formally taken into the visible body of Christ by way of baptism. In each case, baptism is seen as the public response to the gospel that is made before men.

By way of baptism, individuals were separated from the world and made part of the fellowship of believers (Acts 2:41). In keeping with the Great Commission, baptism introduced converts into the fellowship in which they received the teaching and encouragement that propelled them on the road of discipleship (Acts 2:42). Today there is not so high a view of the visible church and the sacraments even though baptism is commanded as a vital part of the Great Commission. As a result, many new converts are not properly brought into the visible fellowship of believers in order to take their stand with the church against the world. In many cases, a public confession of Christ and a public stand with the visible church is replaced with going forward in an evangelistic service and formalizing that decision with a prayer in the counseling room. However, the former approach is Biblical while the latter has been developed on the basis of pragmatism. This brings me to the final section involving the inherent dangers in viewing the gospel as a sales pitch.

5. DANGERS THAT YOU CAN AVOID
It has been my privilege to lead many young men and women to Christ. I recall a young lady who was raped. She was pregnant when I met her and she was in great need. She was contemplating abortion.

It was my privilege to talk to her about Christ and the new way of life found in Him. By the grace of God, she grasped her need of Christ and embraced Him as Lord and Savior. In the succeeding months, with the help of a young Christian couple, we worked together to place her baby in an adoptive home when born. The mother never saw her baby but was grateful for his care. Where this woman is now, I have no idea. And I need not. I trust she is serving Christ wherever she may be. Others were led to the Savior in jail. They had been on drugs or had other problems. These men and women were always ready to talk. And many of them made commitments to Christ.

One particular case I recall, a bride-to-be and the prospective in-laws brought a young man to me. We talked about Christ and I encouraged the young man to pray with me to accept Christ. I was uneasy about the situation, as was he. But we went through the motions. And as it turned out, that's exactly what we did; we only went through the motions. The prospective in-laws were grateful for the encounter but the young man rode off on his motorcycle laughing. I doubt that any good work was begun in his life.

How often do such an encounters take place? I have no idea. However, this illustrates the point that, although good is done in many lives by such gospel presentations and pressing for prayers of commitment, there are dangers involved. The greatest danger is to perpetuate the notion that the gospel is about as valuable as a vacuum cleaner, when we treat it as such in our presentations. The results can be devastating.

Let me illustrate by recounting another situation. A mother called me frantically one day because her young daughter had been dragged through the motions at the vacation Bible school of a neighborhood church. The youngster had indicated her willingness to follow Jesus after a gospel presentation. Whether this was by raising her hand or the use of some other device I do not recall. The girl was then summarily baptized and sent home. When she reported what had taken place to her mother, I received a call. The problem was simple. After discussion with her daughter, this mother knew that her daughter had little or no understanding as to what she had done. Yet she was told that she had become a Christian. Here was the grand deception. The youngster had no conception of what real commitment to Christ means. But because this youngster believed she was a Christian, further efforts to explain the truth of the gospel were made difficult. And the results have been sad. This young lady got in trouble with an unbelieving fellow and became pregnant. Now, the two of them, along with their children, are outside of Christ.

Such incidents are too often repeated in this day of easy believing and calling for decisions. People are deceived into thinking they are Christians because they have repeated a prayer at the request of a sincere Christian. Yet there is no new life to back up the profession that has been made. These people are stillborn rather than new born. The first child of my wife and me was stillborn. The child was born dead. Those who make a bare decision for Christ that is not founded upon the grace of God operative in their lives are also stillborn. There is a lack of conviction regarding sin. The Lord has not opened their hearts to respond to the things spoken in the gospel. They have gone through the motions and have been encouraged to believe that their decision makes them a Christian. And subsequently, more Biblical presentations of the gospel fall on deaf ears. The great danger here is that men and women are led away from the kingdom of God rather than brought into it. This can and does happen when the gospel is treated as a sales pitch.

Allow me to give you another illustration that sticks in my mind. Several years ago shortly after a move, our family learned that the church we were attending was involved in community evangelistic meetings. The churches of the small Kansas community had come together to bring in an evangelist to preach the gospel. As many people as possible were encouraged to attend the meetings that were held in the school gymnasium. Counselors had been trained and music was arranged. The meetings were well attended and each evening there were several who responded to the call of the evangelist to come forward. Counselors then met with each individual to discuss the gospel and to confirm their decision with a prayer of commitment. Then teams were also established to do follow-up work. Needless to say, the effort was well organized.

What were the results? Almost a year later, one of the ladies in the congregation we attended requested prayer. She had been involved in the follow-up effort after the evangelistic campaign. And she was greatly distressed. Of the over ninety people who had made commitments during the evangelistic meetings, none of them had taken the step of aligning themselves with the people of God in any of the churches of that community. In other words, the communitywide evangelistic campaign had little lasting effect on the life of the community or the churches of the community. May I again make the plea? The gospel is not a sales pitch.

This sad story was repeated in a large congregation in the city from which we recently moved. This large church had a week of evangelistic meetings in which many decisions were recorded. The subsequent observation of the pastor was telling. Those making decisions during the evangelistic meetings were conspicuous by their absence in the ongoing life of the church. It must be confessed that this congregation is well known for what we might call the hard sell. But again, the gospel is not a sales pitch. Treating it as such has its dangers.

How can these dangers be avoided? These dangers can be avoided by following Christ and the apostles and by placing emphasis, where it belongs, on the gospel. Emphasis must be upon Christ and the need of every unbeliever for Him. We must start where Paul starts. We must start with responsibility toward God, define sin carefully, and warn people of the judgment to come. At the same time we must pray for the work of the Holy Spirit to bring conviction of sin, and of righteousness, and of judgment. Then we must present Christ as the only alternative to facing judgment for sin. And we must call men and women everywhere to repent of sin and trust in Christ for their salvation. In addition, we must exhort people everywhere to bow before Christ and confess Him as Lord. At the same time we must pray that God will be pleased to open the hearts of men and women to respond to the exhortations to repent and to turn to Christ.

Here is where we must labor. We must labor to present Christ in all of His glory. We must labor to present the requirements of the gospel, defining repentance and faith as those requirements. With proper emphasis placed upon the message itself and the Biblical response to the message, we can trust the God of the message to make it effective and draw men to Christ. This was the experience of the great preachers of old like George Whitefield and Charles Spurgeon. Like them, we need not resort to modern sales techniques to twist the hearts of listeners into a decision. It is when inadequate emphasis is placed upon the presentation of Christ and the Biblical requirements for true conversion that misplaced emphasis can easily be placed upon the gospel as a sales pitch and the closing of the sale with a prayer of decision.

Parts One and Two, set forth above, outline the Biblical approach to unbelievers and the gospel of Christ along with its requirements. There is no need to review that ground here. Emphasize the gospel and its requirements. Simply give men and women Christ's invitation as set forth in POINT C of the gospel presentation. Tell men and women, "The Lord Jesus Christ freely offers Himself to you saying: 'Come to Me, all who are weary and heavy-laden, and I will give you rest'" (Matt.11:28). At the same time, trust the Lord to carry out the work He alone is able to do. Then we will see men and women come to Christ and serve Him. And this will be the case all the more if we reject the notion that the gospel is a sales pitch.

SECTION TWO:
GOING ABOUT THE TOWN

1

GOING ABOUT THE TOWN

Jesus was going through all the cities and villages.
~MATT. 9:35

1. INTRODUCTION

Have you ever thought about doing house-to-house calling? Well, if you are like many pastors and lay people, your reaction to this task is, "Argh, I hate it and it's not productive." Yes, house-to-house visitation has traditionally been one of the least productive types of evangelism. All you need to do is review the statistics. Why have results so often been so poor? I'll give you one good reason. Door-to-door calling for the church has too often been viewed as an end in itself. The pastor or layperson has spent an hour delivering brochures or gospel tracts to a hundred homes and he expects immediate and automatic results. When neighborhood people do not flock to Sunday worship, the response is, "See, I knew such visitation was nonproductive."

However, house-to-house visitation is not an end in itself. I say it again, door-to-door calling in not an end in itself. In addition, knocking on doors is certainly not, by itself, evangelism. However, going from house to house can be used as a method of contacting men and women in order to evangelize them. The difference must be understood. *Ultimately, I want us to see the difference between making contact and evangelizing.* At this point, to begin to understand the difference, we need to look at the ministry of our Lord and Savior Jesus Christ. Matthew 9:35-38 sets before us a good picture of His ministry.

> And Jesus was going about all the cities and the villages, teaching in their synagogues, and proclaiming the gospel of the kingdom, and healing every kind of disease and every kind of sickness. Seeing the multitudes, He felt compassion for them, because they were distressed and down cast like sheep without a shepherd. Then He said to His disciples, "The harvest is plentiful, but the workers are few. Beseech the Lord of the harvest to send out workers into His harvest."

These are familiar words. Our first lesson centers on the clause, "And Jesus was going about all the cities and villages." My objective is to show, whether you are a pastor or a layperson, it is not sufficient for you to sit in your church building or in your home and wait for the people to come to you. Rather, you must be out, around the town, meeting others and going into their homes.

2. THE EXAMPLE OF JESUS

To accomplish my objective, I ask you to follow me as we first take a look at the specific meaning of the words, "And Jesus was going about all the cities and villages." Yes, Jesus was going. He was going about. He was going around. This was a continuous activity. Jesus was going about and passing through all the cities and villages.

Now there are two sides to the travels of Jesus that Matthew describes. On one side we see a very similar statement being made in Matthew 4:23, "And Jesus was going about in all Galilee." You notice that "in all Galilee" is substituted for "all the cities and villages." Galilee was a county sized district in northern Israel. It was probably about twenty-five miles wide and forty miles long. Jesus traveled the length and breadth of Galilee. He went from city to city and from village to village. This is the first way to understand Matthew 9:35.

There is a second way to take Matthew 9:35. Jesus not only went from city to city. Jesus passed through and went about in each of the cities to which he came. Jesus did not just sit in one place in each city and village expecting the people to flock to Him. No. He made the rounds in each and every city or village. This fact must be emphasized. Jesus continuously went from place to place in a particular city or village.

Notice too that Jesus went about all "the cities and the villages." The cities spoken of were the population centers, the main cities, perhaps seats of government. These cities were characterized by the fact that they were fortified. They were towns enclosed by walls having gates.

In contrast, the villages were small towns, the tiny country communities, and the little hamlets. They were without fortifications or walls. By our standards, these places were insignificant. But Jesus was out, going around, in even those tiny villages. And Jesus did not just go to the town square to sit with the elders of the city or village. He went out into the shops and homes.

One of the cities Jesus frequented was Capernaum. Here was a city nestled on the northwest shore of the Sea of Galilee. And Matthew 4:12-13 says: "Now when He heard that John had been taken into custody, He withdrew into Galilee; and leaving Nazareth, He came and settled in Capernaum, which is by the sea, in the region of Zubulun and Naphtali." It appears that Jesus made His home in Galilee. This city became the headquarters for His Galilean ministry. Capernaum is therefore one of the cities that Jesus "went about." How did He do this? Let's look at some examples of how Jesus "went about" Capernaum.

We start with Matthew 4:18-19, "And walking by the sea of Galilee, He saw two brothers, Simon who was called Peter, and Andrew his brother, casting a net into the sea; for they were fishermen. And He said to them, 'Follow Me, and I will make you fishers of men.'" Jesus went down to the beach to call Peter and Andrew. Jesus did not wait in one place for them to come to Him. He was busy going out around the city.

After Jesus' Sermon on the Mount, we again see Him on the move. Matthew 8:5-7, "And when He had entered Capernaum, a centurion came to Him, entreating Him, and saying, 'Sir, my servant is lying paralyzed at home, suffering great pain.' And He said to him, 'I will come and heal him.'" Jesus readily goes into the home of a Roman centurion. Were the Romans well thought of by the Jews? No, they were not. In fact, the Romans were despised. Nevertheless, Jesus said, "I will come and heal him." Jesus was not waiting for folks to come to Him. He went to them.

Again we see Jesus went into the homes of people in the city. Matthew 8:14-15, "And when Jesus had come to Peter's home, He saw his mother-in-law lying sick in bed with a fever. He touched her hand, and the fever left her; and she arose, and began to wait on Him." Here is a most interesting scene. Our first thought is that Jesus went to Peter's home for the specific purpose of seeing Peter's mother-in-law. The text suggests something quite different, as do the parallel passages (Mark 1:29-30; Luke 4:38-39). Jesus did not go to this home in order to visit Peter's mother-in-law. He found Peter's mother-in-law ill when He went to visit Peter's home. This speaks volumes concerning the character of Jesus' ministry.

We move ahead to Matthew 9, "And getting into a boat, He crossed over, and came to His own city" (v. 1). Jesus left Capernaum and crossed the Sea of Galilee; now He was returning home. "And as Jesus passed on from there, He saw a man, called Matthew, sitting in the tax office; and He said to him, 'Follow Me!' And he rose, and followed Him" (v. 9). Notice the emphasis. Jesus was passing from place to place within the city. Now He is in the tax office, of all places.

Verse 10 goes on to say: "And it happened that as He was reclining at the table in the house, behold many tax-gatherers and sinners came and joined Jesus and His disciples at the table." Now Jesus is in another home. It is likely that this is the house of Matthew (see Luke 5:29). I emphasize this. Jesus is in another home eating and teaching. Jesus was indeed "going about" the city of Capernaum.

We follow Jesus a little further in Matthew 9.

> While He was saying these things to them, behold, there came a synagogue official, and bowed down before Him, saying, "My daughter has just died; but come and lay Your hand on her, and she will live." And Jesus rose and began to follow him, and so did His disciples (vv. 18-19).

Jesus goes out with the synagogue official. The narrative continues:

> And behold, a woman who had been suffering from a hemorrhage for twelve years, came up behind Him and touched the fringe of His cloak; for she was saying to herself, "If I only touch His garment, I shall get well." But Jesus turning and seeing her said, "Daughter, take courage; your faith has made you well." And at once the woman was made well (vv. 20-22).

On the way to the synagogue official's house, not while sitting in one place, Jesus meets this woman in need. Would this encounter have taken place if Jesus had not been busy going about the town? The answer is, "No."

> And when Jesus came into the official's house, and saw the flute players, and the crowd in noisy disorder, He began to say, "Depart; for the girl is not dead, but is asleep." And they were laughing at Him. But when the crowd had been put out, He entered and took her by the hand; and the girl arose. And this news went out into all the land (vv. 23-26).

After healing the woman with the hemorrhage, Jesus went into the house of the synagogue official. The crowd and the jeering did not deter our Lord. His pattern for ministry took Him where the people lived, their places of business and their homes.

"And as Jesus passed on from there, two blind men followed Him, crying out, and saying, 'Have mercy on us, Son of David'" (v. 27). Jesus did not remain in the home of the synagogue official. He "passed on from there." We find here, in verse 27, the very same words used in verse 9. Jesus is again going about the town. At this point, He meets two blind men.

> And after He had come into the house, the blind men came up to Him, and Jesus said to them, "Do you believe that I am able to do this?" They said to Him, "Yes, Lord." Then He touched their eyes, saying, "Be it done to you according to your faith" (vv. 28-29).

Was it the house of the blind men that Jesus now entered? There is every likelihood this is the case. So we find Jesus in another home healing the blind.

How can we avoid seeing Jesus going about the town of Capernaum? He was down at the seashore on the beach. There is warrant for beach ministry here. He was in the business districts. He even went to the tax office. Would we dare to go to the local office of the Internal Revenue Service to call disciples to Christ? Jesus also purposefully went to people's homes. How we must emphasized this fact. All of what we have discussed is given in Scripture to flesh out the words, "And Jesus was going about all the cities and villages."

3. THE EXAMPLE OF THE DISCIPLES

Another crucial question faces us. Since it was Jesus' practice to go about each city and village, what did He expect from His disciples? We need only look into Matthew 10 to find our answer. "And having summoned His twelve disciples, He gave them authority over unclean spirits, to cast them out, and to heal every kind of disease and every kind of sickness ... And these twelve Jesus sent out after instructing them ... " (vv. 1 and 5). Jesus sent the disciples. He sent them out into the cities and villages. He told the disciples:

> Into whatever city or village you enter, inquire who is worthy in it; and abide there until you go away. And as you enter the house, give it your greeting. And if the house is worthy, let your greeting of peace come upon it; but if it is not worthy, let your greeting of peace return to you. And whoever does not receive you, nor heed your words, as you go out of that house or that city, shake off the dust of your feet (vv. 11-14).

The disciples were not to sit in one place with their knowledge of Christ and His kingdom. Apparently these disciples were to follow the pattern set by Jesus. They were to go about all the cities and villages where Jesus sent them. Again, Matthew 10:12 says, "And as you enter the house give it your greeting." The disciples were to go into various homes in individual cities. The parallel verse in Luke 10:7 gives the further instruction of Jesus, "And stay in that house, eating and drinking what they give you; for the laborer is worthy of his wages. Do not keep moving from house to house." The procedure seems to have been this: "Having established themselves in the homes of those who are worthy, the apostles must now go from home to home, bringing the gospel."[1]

Jesus instructed the disciples to set up a headquarters in each city or village. They were to approach worthy individuals, those known to be supporters of the ministry of Jesus, concerning room and board. When such people were agreeable, the apostles were to use their home for a base of operations. That the disciples did not remain fixed in this headquarters house in each city seems evident from verse 14, "And whoever does not receive you, nor heed your words, as you go out of that house or that city, shake off the dust of your feet." It was not a single house in each individual city that the apostles were to visit. Notice what Jesus says, "As you go out of that house or that city." You see, when the disciples left a particular house, they did not necessarily leave the city. They very likely went to house after house until they had gone completely through that city. Then they moved on. That this was the procedure will be confirmed when we look at the ministry of the apostles in Jerusalem.

Another point that is quite important must be added. What the early disciples did might be characterized as first time or "cold turkey" visitation. Luke 10:1 proves the point. "Now after this the Lord appointed seventy others, and sent them two and two ahead of Him

---

1. William Hendriksen, *Exposition of the Gospel According to Matthew* (Grand Rapids: Baker, 1973), 459.

to every city and place where He Himself was going to come." What did Jesus do? Jesus sent the disciples "ahead of Him ... where He Himself was going to come." Jesus did not prepare the way, He sent disciples out to prepare the way, to break the ground.

You see, at some time and at some place, cold-turkey ground breaking activity must take place. *Jesus sent His disciples out to do this.*

Yes, it was Jesus' practice to go about each town He entered. A part of Jesus' ministry involved going into people's homes. Jesus expected His disciples to do the very same thing. Are you now getting a better grasp of what it means to be "going about all the cities and villages"?

4. THE EXAMPLE OF THE APOSTLES

How well did the disciples learn from the example and teaching of Jesus? Acts 5:42 gives a direct answer as it describes the ministry of the apostles in Jerusalem after Pentecost. "And every day, in the temple and from house to house, they kept right on teaching and preaching Jesus as the Christ." The apostles had two main methods of ministry in Jerusalem. First, they taught in public, in the temple. The public proclamation of the Word of God was a vital part of the ministry.

The apostles also went from house to house in the city. They took the gospel into individual homes going from house to house. After the example and following the instructions of Christ, the apostles went about the city of Jerusalem. From house to house they went about teaching and preaching Christ.

Notice how often this was taking place. This house-to-house calling and teaching from door to door was taking place "every day." The disciples did not reserve one evening a month for house visitation. No. They went out "every day." No wonder the church in Jerusalem grew as it did.

If the twelve apostles seemed to learn from Jesus, the apostle Paul was not far behind. Paul describes his ministry in Ephesus for us in Acts 20:18-21.

You yourselves know, from the first day that I set foot in Asia, how I was with you the whole time, serving the Lord with all humility and with tears and with trials which came upon me through the plots of the Jews; how I did not shrink from declaring to you anything that was profitable, and teaching you publicly and from house to house, solemnly testifying to both Jews and Greeks of repentance toward God and faith in our Lord Jesus Christ.

Paul's ministry followed the pattern set by Christ and exemplified by the other apostles. He taught the Word of God publicly. But by his testimony, Paul also went from house to house in the city "For a period of three years" (Acts 20:31). Paul busied himself going about the city of Ephesus visiting house after house. As J. A. Alexander indicates, "The church has yet invented nothing to supply the place or rival the effect of church and household preaching."[2] Such examples from the work of the apostles confirm what we have said it means to be "going about all the cities and villages."

5. YOUR PERSONAL WORK
Which brings us to the crucial question. Are you willing to follow the instruction of Jesus, the apostles, and the Bible? Is it sufficient for you to sit in your home or in your church building week after week waiting for people to come to you to learn about Christ? Jesus did not think it was adequate. He got up and got out and went about the town. As we have seen, as an example, He went out and walked all over the city of Capernaum. He also sent out His disciples two at a time to do the very same thing. There was to be no sitting and waiting. You too must go out into the city and go all over the city, your city. It is not sufficient for you to sit and wait for others to come to you. Such a posture is contrary to the teaching of the Bible.

What procedure should be used as you go about the town? Jesus

---

2. J. A. Alexander, *Acts of the Apostles* (Carlisle: Banner of Truth, 1980), 2:243

went to people's places of business and to their homes. Jesus also instructed His disciples to go to people's homes. The apostles, following Jesus' example, went from house to house in Jerusalem every day. Paul did the same thing in Ephesus for three years. The result was the church grew rapidly. You too must go out through your city going door-to-door, carrying the gospel from house to house. Are you willing to follow the example and teaching of Jesus in this?

Some will say door-to-door calling is the job of the pastor and the elders, after all, wasn't the Great Commission given to the apostles of Christ. Surely evangelism of the type you are describing, and judging from the examples you use, is to be conducted by the ordained officers of the church and not by the laypeople.

This objection may be answered quite readily. Acts 8:1 says, "And on that day a great persecution arose against the church in Jerusalem; and they were all scattered throughout the regions of Judea and Samaria, except the apostles." When persecution arose against the church in Jerusalem, men and women, members of that church, were scattered abroad. What did they do? "Those who had been scattered went about preaching the word" (Acts 8:4). Literally, these people were evangelizing. Acts 11:19 tells us of some of their activity, "So then those who were scattered because of the persecution that arose in connection with Stephen made their way to Phoenicia and Cyprus and Antioch, speaking the word to no one except to Jews alone." Notice there is no mention of these people being ordained to an office in the church. Had there been a firm requirement that those going about "speaking the word" had to be ordained, surely the Holy Spirit, speaking through Dr. Luke, would have made that requirement abundantly clear. Yet He does not. Rather the Scriptures go on to say,

> But there were some of them, men of Cyprus and Cyrene, who came to Antioch and began speaking to the Greeks also, preaching the Lord Jesus. And the hand of the Lord was with them, and a large number who believed turned to the Lord (Acts 11:20-21).

Chapter 1: Going About the Town

Here we see the planting of the church in Antioch. Men from the island of Cyprus and from North Africa accomplished it. It is very possible that some of those who evangelized the Gentiles in Antioch were recent converts to Christ from Cyprus and Cyrene. Again, the Scriptures make no special point of the need of those who evangelize the lost to be ordained. In fact, we are left with a startling truth. The church at Antioch was begun by laypeople who were committed to Christ and took the Gospel into that city. The question may be asked, "Shouldn't evangelistic work be left to the pastor and the elders?" The answer remains an emphatic, "No!"

Some of you will no doubt have other reservations and objections. "I can't go from house to house and talk about Jesus." But the apostle Paul said, "I can do all things through Him who strengthens me" (Phil. 4: 13). Surely Christ will strengthen you to follow His will outlined in the Bible. "But," you say, "if I go out into this town and go from house to house, I'll be accused of proselytizing." The apostles stirred up such a fuss in Jerusalem that they were thrown into jail. They went right back out on the streets to talk about Jesus. You see, the real question is this: Are you willing to go from house to house in your town or city?

2
TALKING WITH UNBELIEVERS

For they exchanged the truth of God for a lie, and worshiped and served the creature rather than the Creator, who is blessed forever. Amen. ~ROM. 1:25

1. INTRODUCTION

In the last chapter, I began looking at one method of making initial contact with people. The ultimate goal is to evangelize them. The method under discussion is door-to-door visitation.

We saw Jesus purposely went into people's homes. He also instructed the disciples to do the same. As a result, the Bible says of the early disciples, "Every day, in the temple and from house to house, they kept right on teaching and preaching Jesus as the Christ" (Acts 5:42). In this way, Jesus and the disciples took the gospel to the multitudes. We must do the same.

Now the question arises as to what you should actually say when you approach an individual in his or her home. What point of contact do you have with unbelievers? How do you use this point of contact in talking with someone who is outside of Christ? And more importantly, what does the Bible say about these things? What follows reviews, confirms, and fleshes out the argumentation in Section One, "You Cannot Escape from God," with further discussion and examples.

2. A FIRST STEP: RECOGNIZE ROOT SIN

The Bible gives us some hints about the direction we should take. We look at the basic and ultimate sin of human beings. The apostle Paul describes the root sin of humankind in Romans 1:22-25. Paul says of fallen men and women:

> Professing to be wise, they became fools, and exchanged the glory of the incorruptible God for an image in the form of corruptible man and of birds and four-footed animals and crawling creatures. Therefore God gave them over in the lusts of their hearts to impurity, that their bodies might be dishonored among them. For they exchanged the truth of God for a lie, and worshipped and served the creature rather than the Creator, who is blessed forever. Amen.

Human beings have wantonly exchanged the glory of the incorruptible God for the meanness of corruptible inferior creatures. As a result, fallen sinful human beings have "worshipped and served the creature rather than the Creator." Here is the basic sin of every human being. It is rejection of the Creator and worship of the creature.

During the first missionary Journey, Paul and Barnabas met a blatant form of this sin in the city of Lystra. By the grace of God, Paul dramatically healed "a certain man, without strength in his feet, lame from his mother's womb, who had never walked" (Acts 14:8). Upon seeing this great miracle, the people of the city could not contain themselves. "They began calling Barnabas, Zeus, and Paul, Hermes, because he was the chief speaker. And the priest of Zeus, whose temple was just outside the city, brought oxen and garlands to the gates, and wanted to offer sacrifice with the crowds" (Acts 14:12-13). Imagine, seeing the miracle of healing, these people prepared to offer sacrifices to Paul and Barnabas. They very literally "worshipped and served the creature rather than the Creator" (Rom. 1:25). Their worship of Paul and Barnabas was not unlike the kind of worship the Roman emperor expected and demanded from his subjects.

Notice how Paul and Barnabas responded.

> When the apostles, Barnabas and Paul, heard of it, they tore their robes and rushed out into the crowd, crying out and saying, "Men, why are you doing these things? We also are men of the same nature as you, and preach the gospel to you in order that you should turn from these vain things to a living God, who made the heaven and the earth and the sea, and all that is in them" (Acts 14:14-15).

Immediately, Paul and Barnabas directed the attention of their would be worshippers to the Creator, the Maker of heaven and earth. Paul and Barnabas could not accept the worship of other men and women. They urged the people to turn from such empty and useless things to the living God, the Creator. Paul wanted to reverse the basic sinful tendency of these people, to turn them around, to bring them to true worship. And so, Paul began pointing them to the Creator.

The fact that Paul made the Creator of the universe his starting point in this encounter is of more than passing interest. Paul had a profound reason for speaking to the people of Lystra as he did.

What was it? Paul tells us in Romans 1:18-21.

> For the wrath of God is revealed from heaven against all ungodliness and unrighteousness of men, who suppress the truth in unrighteousness, because that which is known about God is evident within them, for God made it evident to them. For since the creation of the world His invisible attributes, His eternal power and divine nature, have been clearly seen, being understood through what has been made, so that they are without excuse. For even though they knew God, they did not honor Him as God ...

Paul knew certain things about every unbelieving heart. Paul knew unbelievers, all unbelievers, "suppress" or "hold down" the truth about God within them. That is, Paul knew that human beings have indisputable knowledge of God that "is evident within them." This knowledge of God includes an understanding of "His eternal power and divine nature." Every unbeliever has a knowledge that

God exists and is very powerful. This is truth that all unbelievers possess; and unbelievers, Paul says, always "suppress the truth."

How do men and women come into possession of this truth? Again, Paul answers. This truth is "understood through what has been made." Creation and the providential governing of creation by God in history reveal His eternal power and divine nature.

> But just what does Paul mean when he claims that human beings "see" and "understand" from creation and history that a powerful God exists? Some think that Paul is asserting only that people have around them the evidence of God's existence and basic qualities; whether people actually perceive it or become personally conscious of it is not clear.[1]

The *Evangelical Dictionary of Theology* takes this position. "Read in context, Rom. 1 and 2 teach that the pagan's natural knowledge of God is distorted and turned only to his judgment, in no way to the reasonable deductions of theological truths."[2]

> Paul's wording suggests more than this. He asserts people actually come to "understand" something about God's existence and nature. How universal is this perception? The flow of Paul's argument makes any limitation impossible. Those who perceive the attributes of God in creation must be the same as those who suppress the truth in unrighteousness and are therefore liable to the wrath of God.[3]

Professor John Murray concurs. He says, "[W]hat is sensuously imperceptible is nevertheless clearly apprehended in mental conception ... [I]t is the seeing of understanding, of intelligent conception."[4] Murray goes on to say,

> We must not tone down the teaching of the apostle in this passage. It is a clear declaration to the effect that the visible creation

---

1. Douglas J. Moo, *The Epistle to the Romans* (Grand Rapids: Eerdmans, 1996), 105.
2. Walter A. Elwell, *Evangelical Dictionary of Theology* (Grand Rapids: Baker, 1984), 753.
3. Moo, *The Epistle to the Romans*, 105.
4. John Murray, *The Epistle to the Romans* (Grand Rapids: Eerdmans, 1965), 38-39.

as God's handiwork make manifest the invisible perfections of God as its Creator, that from these things which are perceptible to the senses cognition of these invisible perfections is derived, and thus a clear apprehension of God's perfections may be gained from his observable handiwork. [5]

Human beings are also a part of the creation of God. God created human minds, hearts, and consciences. Just as God reveals Himself in the outside world of His creation, he also reveals Himself within created hearts and minds and consciences. There is internal revelation as well as external revelation. It therefore follows that God's eternal power and divine nature are revealed within the minds and hearts and consciences of every human being. This is why Paul says, "That which is known about God is evident within them."

The sum of what we are saying is that human beings cannot avoid knowing God as their Creator. The logical deduction is for unbelievers to immediately see themselves as creatures of God. Men and women may indeed "suppress the truth" that is "evident," but their refusal to honor the God they know as God renders them "without excuse." Therefore, in Lystra, when faced with the prospect of being worshipped by pagan idolaters, the apostle Paul does not hesitate to talk about "a living God, who made the heaven and earth and sea, and all that is in them" (Acts 14:15).

3. A SECOND STEP: TOUCH GOD'S SELF-REVELATION

Paul sheds further light on God's internal revelation of himself, in Romans 2:14-15.

> For when Gentiles who do not have the Law do instinctively the things of the Law, these, not having the Law, are a law to themselves, in that they show the work of the Law written in their hearts, their conscience bearing witness, and their thoughts alternately accusing or else defending themselves.

---

5. Ibid., 40.

The law that Paul is talking about here is the summary of the moral law of God found in the Ten Commandments. Ancient Israel received this law in written form at Mount Sinai. The Gentile nations did not receive this Law from God in written form. This was the special privilege of Israel.

Yet the apostle Paul says the same people "who do not have the Law" before them in written form "do instinctively the things of the Law." They do "by nature" the things of the law. What is done by nature or instinctively is done by spontaneous impulse. "'By nature' is contrasted with what is derived from external sources and refers to that which is engraved on the natural constitution."[6] Paul contrasts the internal revelation of the Law with the external revelation of God in creation.

> What is done "by nature" is done by native instinct or propension, by spontaneous impulse as distinguished from what is induced by forces extraneous to ourselves. The things done by nature are said to be "the things of the law." It is to be observed that the apostle does not say that they do or fulfill the law and he must have intentionally refrained from that expression. "The things of the law" must mean certain things which the law prescribes and refer to those things practiced by pagans which are stipulated in the law ... [7]

For example, who teaches the robin how to build his nest? No one. The robin knows instinctively how to build a nest. In the same way, those who have not been taught the moral law of God instinctively follow the precepts of the law. Again, Paul does not say such people fulfill the law. Quite to the contrary! Only those who have hearts renewed by the Holy Spirit are capable of living lives that even begin to conform to the standard of the Ten Commandments. And Paul tells us in Romans 8:7, "The mind set on the flesh is hostile toward God; for it does not subject itself to the Law of God, for it is not even able

---

6. Murray, *The Epistle to the Romans*, 73.
7. Ibid

to do so." Paul's point is that all human beings are moral creatures. Even people who have never seen the Ten Commandments follow some of the things required in the Ten Commandments.

Paul goes on to say that when people "do instinctively the things of the Law," they "are a law to themselves." This means pagan unbelievers, "by reason of what is implanted in their nature, confront themselves with the law of God. They themselves reveal the law of God to themselves—their persons [are] the medium of revelation.[8]

Why are these people a law to themselves? They "are a law to themselves, in that they show the work of the Law written in their hearts" (Rom. 2:15). As already mentioned, the work of the law amounts to the things required by the law. What God requires in the way of upright and moral living has been inscribed in every human heart. These are things "such as their pursuit of lawful vocations, the procreation of offspring, filial and natural affection, the care of the poor and sick, and numerous other natural virtues required by the law."[9] "Paul's point is that Gentiles outside of Christ regularly obey their parents, refrain from murder and robbery and so on."[10] In the end, no human being can escape the requirements of God's moral law. Unbelievers, by instinctive action, "attest knowledge of divine moral standards."[11]

Let me emphasize a point emphatically. Paul does not say the law itself is written on the hearts of unbelievers. The Promise of the New Covenant is that the law will be written on the human heart (Jer. 31:31-33). Paul is careful to speak of "the work of the law" rather than the law itself because he is not talking about born again believers in Christ. "As Luther puts it, 'The knowledge of the work is written, that is, the law that is written in letters concerning the works that have to be done, but not the grace to fulfill the law.'"[12]

---

8. Ibid.
9. Ibid.
10. Moo, *The Epistle to the Romans*, 150.
11. Ibid., 151.
12. Ibid., 152.

Yes, Paul teaches us every unbeliever knows God as his or her Creator. Paul also teaches us unbelievers confront themselves daily with the moral demands of God summarized in the Ten Commandments. Unbelievers must therefore know God as the Author of the moral requirements pressing in upon them. Not only so, if "that which is known about God" (Rom. 1:19) includes a knowledge of God as both Creator and Lawgiver, then unbelievers must also know God as their Judge. This follows inevitably from the prior knowledge of God as the giver of the law. If the Creator of the universe demands a certain standard for living that is summarized in specific commandments, then this same Creator is bound to judge all those who do not live up to the standard He prescribes. Such knowledge is imbedded in the very fiber of every unbeliever's being. It is inescapable. This is why the apostle Paul points to the creator when he attempts to overturn the idolatry of those in Lystra.

4. A THIRD STEP: BE CONSCIOUS OF CONSCIENCE

Do we make too much of a leap here? I do not think so. Romans 2:14-15 points to the mind and conscience. Look at it again.

> For when Gentiles who do not have the Law do instinctively the things of the Law, these, not having the Law, are a law to themselves, in that they show the work of the Law written in their hearts, their conscience bearing witness, and their thoughts alternately accusing or else defending them.

"The conscience could be the source of moral norms (as in our popular use of the term), but it is usually viewed as a reflective mechanism by which people can measure their conformity to a norm."[13] In the case before us, the norm is the moral law of God. Con-science is knowledge, science, which stands alongside or with the norm or standard. Conscience "bears witness" to the actions of unbelievers. It testifies regarding their conformity to the moral law of God. When

---

13. Ibid.

conscience bears witness against them, they feel guilty. This moral mechanism is ever present.

Paul adds "that their thoughts alternately accusing or else defending them." "Accusation or excusation,[14] whether of ourselves or others, are activities which evidence moral consciousness and therefore point to our indestructible moral nature, the only rationale of which is the work of the law of God in the heart."[15]

All of this proves we are moral beings and that there is an absolute moral standard, God's law, by which we constantly judge ourselves, consciously or unconsciously, and by which we will be judged.

> The clause, "their thoughts among themselves both accusing or else defending them" might add a second independent idea to the witness of the conscience, but it probably expands it; the witness of conscience consists in the mixed verdict of one's thoughts.
>
> This debate among the thoughts goes on constantly, but its ultimate significance will be revealed in the last judgment ... The excusing and accusing testimony of the thoughts within each person's conscience portends the verdict of the one who will bring every thought to light.[16]

All of this not only proves we are moral beings and that there is an absolute moral standard, but it also leads unbelievers inevitably to God, the Judge of all, whether they see fit to admit it or not. "It is appointed for men to die once and after this comes judgment" (Heb. 9:27). Unbelievers do not see fit to embrace this truth. They "suppress the truth in unrighteousness (Rom. 1:18). However, denials of the truth do not alter the truth.

I had an amusing but serious debate with an avowed atheist, Jeff, by e-mail. He read a devotional of mine on the Internet. I accused atheism of being unscientific. Jeff was very angry and indignant. In

---

14. To give an excuse or apology
15. Murray, *The Epistle to the Romans*, 76-77.
16. Moo, *The Epistle to the Romans*, 153.

his opinion, I was quite wrong. What right did this atheist have of being "angry" and telling me I was "wrong"? What was his basis or norm? "Why are you angry?" I asked. "You are wrong," Jeff responded. "Do you believe in ultimate right and wrong?" I asked. "No, I do not," he answered. "Then what right do you have of making a moral judgment regarding my statement?" Jeff responded, "Well, I'll say your statement is incorrect. Let's leave morality out of the discussion." Could we leave morality out of the discussion? I think not. Jeff was *angry* because it was *wrong* for me to make, what he viewed, as an incorrect statement. I might hurt people and lead them astray. It is not right to *hurt* people and lead them astray. To say I'm not *right* and to be *angry* because of my error is to admit there is a norm or standard of right and wrong. Our little debate confirmed Paul's analysis in Romans 2:14-15. We cannot escape the moral dilemma.[17]

Notice again, Paul's appeal. It is wrong for you people of Lystra to worship the likes of us. We are men as yourselves and not gods. We come to preach to you about the living and true God, the Creator. It is wrong for you to worship men. Turn from this evil. Turn to God. "He did not leave Himself without witness, in that He did good and gave you rains from heaven and fruitful season, satisfying your hearts with food and gladness" (Acts 14:17). In the end, this is an appeal to conscience.

5. CONCLUSION

Taking what we learn from Romans 1 and 2, what do we have? Every unbeliever knows God exists as the Creator. Every unbelieving human being is a moral being and instinctively holds to right and wrong. The basis is the Creator's moral requirements. All unbelievers have consciences and debate the propriety of their actions. They often sense guilt for their failures. By implication they know they face judgment for failing to properly honor God. Beyond doubt, unbelieving

---

17. Along this line, see my discussion, "God Must Exist to Play Basketball" in Section Two, Chapter 7.

men, women and children suppress this truth about their relationship with God. This does not alter the truth.

The apostle Paul therefore unabashedly presents the truth. He points men and women to their Creator. He refers immediately to the moral requirements of God. He speaks of their guilt before God, guilt they experience as their consciences bear witness and their thoughts alternately excuse and accuse them.

In like manner, we must challenge unbelievers to acknowledge and accept the truth about themselves. Following Paul, we may do so on three levels, the knowledge of God from creation, the innate knowledge of God's law, and the activity of conscience under God and His law. Only when unbelievers stop covering up the truth will they see their need of Christ. Only then will Christ's salvation make sense to them.

In the end, Paul's presentation and ours, ought to be directed to conscience, conscience under God, and conscience under the law of God. Here is a sample conversation you might have with someone you encounter going door-to-door. We jump into this conversation called "Talking with a Stranger" after certain preliminaries have been covered.[18]

> AL: I see that. But I'm wondering how you intend to continue this conversation.
>
> JOHN: Can we go back to the cockroaches?
>
> AL: How can that possibly help your case?
>
> JOHN: I suppose you'd say that the overrunning of your house was a bad thing, right?
>
> AL: Well, it sure was bad for me. But, as I said, from the standpoint of the universe as a whole, it doesn't much matter.
>
> JOHN: What about the flight attendant's taking your briefcase?

---

18. For the complete conversation, see: John M. Frame, *Apologetics to the Glory of God* (Phillipsburg, NJ: P & R, 1994), 204-217.

AL: That was wicked! Seriously, they should have notified me when I picked this seat that I would be deprived of my briefcase for a time. To me, that is a more serious matter than whether I get a window or aisle seat, or even whether I sit in the smoking or nonsmoking area.

JOHN: Would you say, then, that the airline was wrong?

AL: Sure—not that I would make a federal case out of it, though.

JOHN: Now, tell me how an atheist or agnostic decides what is right and what is wrong.

AL: Conscience, I suppose.

JOHN: Conscience is a moral sense; it senses right and wrong as the eye senses light and color. But the eye doesn't create light and color. Would you say that your conscience creates right and wrong?

AL: Well, some people would. But I'm uncomfortable with that idea; I mean, if right and wrong are my own inventions, why should anyone else care about them?

JOHN: Exactly. And you think that others ought to care; that, too, is a moral judgment. But it's something more than just a feeling of yours. It's something objective that obligates you and them.

AL: Yes, I can see the importance of objective moral values.

JOHN: Then these values bind us; they impose obligations.

AL: Yes.

JOHN: But why? Why are we obligated to accept those values?

AL: I guess it's just part of the way the universe is. In the physical universe, what goes up must come down. So, in the moral universe, he who hurts others incurs guilt.

JOHN: But physical laws don't obligate me to do anything. I can't imagine anything merely material that could impose an obligation. Can you?

AL: Well, I do sense that the obligation is there. Where else could it come from?

JOHN: Look at the alternatives: either the universe is ultimately impersonal (i.e., everything reduces to matter, motion, space, time, and chance) or it is personal (an ultimate being creates and uses matter, motion, etc., for his own purposes). Which is the more likely origin of moral obligation?

AL: I don't see that either is likely. Even if a person tells me what to do—say, a policeman—I am not thereby obligated to do what he says.

JOHN: Sure. A policeman can be wrong. He can exceed his authority. And even when he is right, he doesn't create moral obligations any more than you or I do.

AL: I'm confused. I thought you were leading me in the direction of a personalistic account of morals.

JOHN: I am, but of course moral values cannot be entirely explained by finite personalities.

AL: Oh, of course! This is your proof for God!

JOHN: Well, think it through! Moral values are rather like loyalty, aren't they? In fact, loyalty is a moral value, and it obligates us to behave in certain ways. Now how do we get into positions where we find ourselves loyal to someone or something?

3

RECOGNIZING THE HARVEST

Seeing the people, He felt compassion for them,
because they were distressed and dispirited like sheep
without a shepherd. ~MATT. 9:36

WE HAVE NOW LAID A FOUNDATION upon which we can build. We have seen that "Jesus was going about all the cities and villages" (Matt. 9:35). In part, this "going about" involved house-to-house calling or visitation. Jesus also directed the disciples to go to the homes of people. And so they did. They took the gospel to house after house in Jerusalem. We too must take the gospel into the homes of our communities.

We have also learned that we have a vital point of contact with all unbelievers. This point of contact is certain knowledge about God within every human heart. We have seen that all unbelievers know God as their creator, lawgiver, and judge. And although they suppress this truth about God as it wells up from within them, this knowledge of God provides a vital point of contact with the unbelieving heart.

And so now, as you go from house to house with the confidence that you can, with the help of the Holy Spirit, really challenge unbelievers with the truth, another question arises. How did Jesus, how did His disciples, and how can you recognize real opportunities to present the gospel. Even though you have a point of contact with everyone, not every person will be receptive to the truth. How is God's harvest, the harvest of God's elect, to be recognized? We see an answer to this crucial question in Matthew 9:36, "And seeing the multitudes, He felt compassion for them, because they were distressed and downcast like sheep without a shepherd."

The text speaks of Jesus "seeing the multitudes." Yes, Jesus had been "going about all the cities and villages" in Galilee. And now, in His mind's eye, Jesus sees the multitudes in city after city and in village after village. At this point Jesus has more than just the crowd of people before Him in mind. He is seeing all of the people in all of the cities and villages he has visited. And Jesus characterizes these multitudes as the harvest. "And seeing the multitudes, He felt compassion for them." Then He said to His disciples, "The harvest is plentiful, but the workers are few" (Matt. 9:36-37).

The multitudes that Jesus sees in all the cities and villages amount to the harvest of God's people. Jesus is not talking about the harvest at the end of the age. In that harvest the angels will be the reapers, the wheat and the tares will remain mixed until the harvest, and the tares will be thrown into the fire (Matt. 13:36-43).

The harvest Jesus is talking about is the present harvest of the Lord. Jesus says, "The harvest *is* (present tense) plentiful." Labor is presently needed because "the workers are few." Men and women are the reapers in this harvest and men and women are needed. "Therefore beseech the Lord of the harvest to send out workers into His harvest," cries Jesus (Matt. 9:38). It seems that much seed has already been sown. "Multitudes, multitudes [are] in the valley of decision" (Joel 3:14). Truly the harvest is plentiful.

Now Jesus characterizes this harvest of people for God's kingdom in three ways. First, Jesus sees people who are "distressed." Here were a troubled and weary people. "They fainted" (KJV). They were "harassed" (RVS). Here were individuals who were exposed to the elements and beaten down by the cares of life. On the other side, it may be said that these are people without the peace that passes understanding. They include the husband and father who just lost his job. Among them is the wife who has just learned that her husband is having an affair with another woman. Here we find the teenager who goes to school filled with anxiety because her parents have just had another fight over her father's drinking. These are people who are "distressed."

Second, Jesus sees people who are "downcast." These are people who are dejected about life. As a result, their countenances, the expressions on their faces, are fallen. They are downcast. The same word is used in other places in the New Testament to describe demons casting down those whom they possess. Here is the youngster who is in the habit of cheating at school. Here we find the executive who is losing his grasp on the details of his business because he drinks too much. Here Jesus also sees the woman who is living with a man who is not her husband. These people are dejected because their sin is catching up with them. They are cast down with burdens of guilt.

The King James Version of the Bible translates the term we are discussing, "scattered." In other words, the lives of these people have crumbled around them. Their lives have been shattered by the trauma of a divorce or the loss of a loved one. Now they act like wandering scattered people. They do not have any direction. They do not have an anchor for their souls. The result is that they are "downcast."

Then third, Jesus describes the people he sees, the harvest, as those who are "like sheep without a shepherd." No domestic animal is more helpless than a sheep when left by itself. And these people, fatigued and forlorn, are like lost sheep. They are sheep that are untended, unsought, unprotected and harassed by the world, the flesh and the devil. Beyond any doubt, here is a picture of lost sinners left alone in a hostile world. They are like sheep without a shepherd. They are people who are in desperate need of guidance, who are in need of being led. This is how Jesus describes the harvest. It is composed of people who are downcast, like sheep without a shepherd.

The further point is that these descriptions amount to outward visible characteristics. In other words, Jesus gives us a guide, a guide by which we too may recognize the harvest. Now this does not mean that we are given an infallible prescription. Jesus did have the edge on each of us. He could look into people's hearts. Jesus could judge the heart. But we can only judge by the outward appearance. And so we may make mistakes. God knows this. Nevertheless, Jesus gave us three outward characteristics by which we are to recognize the harvest. Those who are a part of the plentiful harvest before us are people who are (1) distressed, {2) downcast, and (3) like sheep without a shepherd.

Now if these are the three recognition factors we are to use, when will they most likely come into play? When will we utilize them most fully and thus actually see the harvest? The answer should be plain. When we are out in the midst of the harvest. It was when Jesus was out in the middle of the harvest, when he "was going about all the cities and the villages" that he said, "The harvest is plentiful." And it was when Jesus and the disciples were working in the harvest that Jesus pointed out the three recognition factors.

What was Jesus doing? Again Matthew 9:35 tells us. Our Lord was "teaching in their synagogues, and proclaiming the gospel of the kingdom, and healing every kind of disease and every kind of sickness." Yes, Jesus was going about the towns and little hamlets ministering. He was serving the people by bringing them the gospel of the kingdom and by bringing them healing. You see, it is when you are in the midst of ministry, when you are involved in bringing the gospel to others and when you are immersed in diaconal service to the needy, that you see the harvest for what it is.

To put it bluntly, you do not see and recognize the harvest unless you are out working in it. If you are in the harvest, bringing the gospel of the kingdom, then you see it. This is why you must go out from house to house. To engage in such visitation is to get out into the harvest. And if you take the instruction given by Jesus with you out there, you too can begin to recognize the harvest.

Now to help build some confidence, we carry our lesson one step further. What should you expect when you present a gospel tract or when you outline the gospel itself to someone who is like a sheep without a shepherd? John 10:24-28 gives us some interesting instruction on this question.

> The Jews therefore gathered around Him, and were saying to Him, "How long will you keep us in suspense? If you are the Christ, tell us plainly." Jesus answered them, "I told you, and you do not believe; the works that I do in My Father's name, these bear witness of Me. But you do not believe, because you are not My sheep. My sheep hear My voice, and I know them, and they follow Me; and I give eternal life to them, and they shall never perish; and no one shall snatch them out of My hand."

Jesus says to the Jews confronting Him, "You do not believe." These were the same scribes and Pharisees, and people like them, upon whom we have already seen Jesus pronounce woe. They did not believe and follow Jesus. Why? Jesus answers by saying, "Because you are not My sheep." These Jews were not like sheep without a shepherd. Of these same Jews Jesus said, "You are of your father the devil, and you want to do the desires of your father (John 8:44). The point is once again that these particular Jews were not Jesus' sheep; they might have been lost but they were not lost sheep, they were goats (Matt. 25:31-33). Not only so, because they were not lost sheep, these particular Jews were not like sheep without a shepherd. Quite to the contrary their shepherd was the devil. And these people knew exactly what they were about. They wanted to destroy Jesus. In other words, they wanted to do the desires of their father. The lesson is that when you approach people like this, who are not like sheep without a shepherd, you should not expect the gospel to be well received. And you should not be shocked when it is not well received.

On the other hand, how will Jesus' lost sheep respond to His call? Again our Lord answers for us, "My sheep hear My voice, and I know them, and they follow Me" (John 10:27). Beyond doubt they will recognize Jesus' voice and they will follow their shepherd. When Jesus freely offers Himself saying, "Come to Me, all who are weary and heavy-laden, and I will give you rest" (Matt. 11:28), those who are Jesus' lost sheep, who are genuinely like sheep without a shepherd, will respond positively to that invitation. And knowing this should give you no small amount of confidence.

And so, be prepared to follow the guidelines set forth by Christ. Understand that the characteristics of Jesus' lost sheep are primarily three. They are described as distressed and downcast and like sheep without a shepherd. It is to people like this that you should be prepared to freely offer the gospel. They will not always accept Christ as their Lord and Savior. You will make some mistakes in identifying those who are like sheep without a shepherd. But you know that Christ's lost sheep will come to Him when they hear His voice.

Finally, in a much more specific way, let's relate what we have been saying to you going about the town. Here is the scene. You are out in the harvest. You are going from house to house as the early disciples did. You know that Christ described the harvest in three ways. And your first objective as you go from one house to another is to locate people, men and women and children, who are like sheep without a shepherd. As you go, you can expect to meet two different circumstances

First you will encounter people who are not like sheep without a shepherd. These may be confirmed unbelievers like the Pharisees. You go to the door. When the door is answered, you introduce yourself and you invite the family to attend worship. The man or woman at the door is not interested. You leave your literature. Always leave a gospel tract. Perhaps God will use the tract to speak to this family. Then you go to the next house. You are looking for those who are like sheep without a shepherd.

Next you may come to the home of a fervent member of another church. When the resident responds to your knock at the door, you introduce yourself and you invite the family to worship. At this point, you learn that the family is very active in their own church. You express appreciation and leave your literature. You should also leave a gospel tract at this home. You want these people to know that you and your church take a stand for the gospel too. The people living in this home are not like sheep without a shepherd and so you go on.

The other category of people you will meet include those who fit the description given in Matthew 9:36. These people may be unbelievers, but they will act like sheep without a shepherd. When the door is answered, you introduce yourself and once again invite the family to come to worship. Then this resident just stands quietly at the door. And there is silence. Perhaps you become a little embarrassed by the silence. I have seen this take place many times while standing at a door. And the result has been an invitation into the person's living room. Very often the silence is an invitation to say more. In fact, it is very likely that you are now faced with a person who expects you to say more and wants you to say more. And before you know it, you are in the house talking to a person who is lonely, or dejected, or sad because of a loss. You have come to the home of a person who is like a sheep without a shepherd.

Behind the next door there may be a person who is already a believer and who has a church home but is wandering. You introduce yourself and you again invite the family to attend worship. This resident is pleased and seeks more information. In conversation you learn that the family has not been in church for some time and has been burdened with guilt as a result. You have come to another family whose members are like sheep without a shepherd. In each of these cases you have the opportunity to pray with people, present the gospel, and/or return for Bible study. You were out in the harvest looking for those like sheep without a shepherd and you have found them.

Presenting Your Faith:
Relating Your Hope

And do not fear their intimidation, and do not be troubled, but sanctify Christ as Lord in your hearts, always being ready to make a defense to everyone who asks you to give an account for the hope that is in you, yet with gentleness and reverence. ~ 1 Pet. 3:14-15

PART ONE:
THE ANSWER TO FEAR

THE FOLLOWING STUDY INTRODUCES one way to prepare yourself to relate your personal hope to men and women and young people who may be "distressed and downcast like sheep without a shepherd" (Matt. 9:36). Part One of the study addresses the fears you and I encounter. Part Two outlines what it means to relate your hope to others. Part Three will guide you in the preparation of a short, Biblically based, testimony in which you can briefly relate your Christian hope to others. This three part study unfold the truths of 1 Peter 3:14-16 and builds on what we have already learned about talking with unbelievers.

1. THE POSSIBILITY OF SUFFERING
Let's get the context of the text before us. The paragraph we are examining begins with 1 Peter 3:13. Peter renews his discussions of suffering.

> Who is there to harm you if you prove zealous for what is good? But even if you should suffer for the sake of righteousness, you are blessed. And do not fear their intimidation, and do not be troubled, but sanctify Christ as Lord in your hearts, always being ready to make a defense to everyone who asks you to give an account for the hope that is in you, yet with gentleness and reverence; and keep a good conscience so that in the thing in which you are slandered, those who revile your good behavior in Christ will be put to shame (1 Pet. 3:13-16).

In general, no one is going to harm you for taking a stand for the righteousness of God summarized in the Ten Commandments. In general, I say. Specific circumstances may arise when you are persecuted for your stand for Christ. Such persecution is actually a blessing in disguise. Those who persecute you see your stability in Christ. Because of the work of Christ in you, you are a very hopeful person. Those persecuting you despise your confidence and hope. They attempt to counter your zeal for good by intimidating you with the prospect of real suffering, economic, physical, emotional and spiritual. Peter is aware of all of this. In contemporary jargon he would say, "Been there; done that."

In the text before us, Peter counters the fear we have of doing good in the face of hostility, intimidation and suffering. In the last part of 1 Peter 3:14 the apostle exhorts, "And do not fear their intimidation, and do not be troubled." What is the answer to fear? Peter tells us in verse 15, "But sanctify Christ as Lord in your hearts." In the last part of verse 14 Peter recognizes three things. First, unbelievers will attempt to intimidate you if you prove zealous for good. Second, as a result, you may really become fearful of doing good. Third, as a final result, you may become confused and troubled. Because Peter recognizes these three things, he exhorts, "Do not fear their intimidation." Thankfully Peter does not stop with the negative. He also gives the positive answer to the fear of doing good. "But sanctify Christ as Lord in your hearts." Notice this is *the* positive solution to fear we may apply in all manner of situations.

In this lesson we look at Peter's exhortation not to fear and the positive solution. I'm particularly interested in what Peter has to say from an evangelistic perspective. Fear or intimidation seems to be the single largest factor deterring people from active evangelism. I think this text offers the answer to this critical problem. I've been called upon to offer this solution to the fear of doing evangelism on several occasions in several congregations. May God be pleased to work His solution to fear into your heart so that you might always be "ready to make a defense to everyone who asks you to give an account for the hope that is in you" (1 Pet. 3: 15).

2. FEAR NOT

First of all, from Peter's exhortation we see Peter recognizes that several things can happen when you are truly zealous for good. Unbelievers may attempt to intimidate you or they may threaten you. Literally the text says, "And do not fear their fear." The King James Version reads, "And be not afraid of their terror." The text simply means, "Do not fear them."

Peter has in mind those who might harm you by causing you to suffer. Peter asks, "Who is there to harm you if you prove zealous for what is good" (1 Pet. 3:13)? The possibility of bodily injury or emotional harm exists. Peter adds, "But even if you should suffer for the sake of righteousness, you are blessed" (1 Pet. 3:14). Remember, Jesus said the same thing.

> Blessed are those who have been persecuted for the sake of righteousness, for theirs is the kingdom of heaven. Blessed are you when people insult you and persecute you, and falsely say all kinds of evil against you because of Me. Rejoice and be glad, for your reward in heaven is great; for in the same way they persecuted the prophets who were before you (Matt. 5:10-12).

What is Peter's reaction to the real possibility of persecution? Do not fear. Easier said than done. Those who oppose your stand for good may intimidate you and threaten you. Their objective is to keep you from doing good and from following Christ. You may be threatened with loss of property, the loss of reputation, the loss of friends or even the loss of life itself. Fear arises. Fear of loss keeps you from doing good. Peter knows what he is talking about from bitter experience. He remembers his own fear and the fear of the disciples when Christ was crucified. "Now Peter was sitting outside in the courtyard, and a servant-girl came to him and said, 'You too were with Jesus the Galilean'" (Matt. 26:69-70). Peter was afraid of being identified as a follower of Christ. Peter thought he too might be put to death. What was Peter's first instinct in this situation? "But he denied it before them all, saying, 'I do not know what you are talking about.'" Peter was afraid. He was afraid of being hauled before the Sanhedrin as Jesus was. He was intimidated by the words of a little servant girl. Peter did not stand up for truth and good. He denied any knowledge of Christ.

To put it bluntly, Peter lied. He broke the Ninth Commandment. God says, "You shall not bear false witness." Following this commandment requires us to take a stand for truth and righteousness. Yet rather than taking such a stand for Christ, rather than taking a stand for truth, he lied. Peter was not zealous for good. Peter confirms his lack of zeal with a second denial. "When he had gone out to the gateway, another servant-girl saw him and said to those who were there, 'This man was with Jesus of Nazareth.' And again he denied it with an oath, 'I do not know the man'" (Matt. 26:71-72).

Peter lied a second time with an oath. In other words, Peter publicly perjured himself. Look at the Westminster Shorter Catechism, "What is required the ninth commandment? The ninth commandment requireth the maintaining and promoting of truth between man and man and of our own and our neighbor's good name, especially in witness bearing" (Q&A 77). Peter does not promote the truth. He denies his knowledge of Christ by swearing an oath that his lie is actually the truth. As Peter stands before God, this is perjury on the witness stand of life.

Matthew 26:73-74 relates a third and similar incident, "A little later the bystanders came up and said to Peter, 'Surely you too are one of them; for even the way you talk gives you away.' Then he began to curse and swear, 'I do not know the man!' And immediately a rooster crowed." Peter lied a third time. This time Peter added cursing and swearing. Peter's language is no better than that found in many bars and on many ball fields in our day.

What is the problem? Fear turns Peter away from standing up for the truth and the good. How often this is true with you and me. How often children lie to parents out of fear of loosing special privileges. How often Christian professionals, intimidated by the bosses' desire to balance the office budget, pad billing records. How often Christian students in high schools and colleges, fearful of low grades, cheat on exams and plagiarize on papers. Hence the exhortation, "Do not fear."

I am familiar with the chief executive officer of an educational institution. He often used and no doubt continues to use intimidation as a key element of his leadership style. When subordinates do not line up with him he threatens them with their jobs. I have seen him try to turn staff members against each other in order to ward off criticism. Such tactics breed fear. The best solution is to always stand for truth. Always be truthful. Never compromise. This is not easy. It is the way of Christ.

3. DO NOT BE TROUBLED

The final outcome of all this is what Peter calls, being troubled. "And do not fear their intimidation, and do not be troubled" (v. 14). The word refers to being confused, stirred up and disconcerted. Peter speaks of a troubled and confused state of mind and heart. Jesus says in John 14:1, "Let not your heart be troubled." In John 14:27, He assures, "Peace I leave with you; my peace I give to you; not as the world gives, do I give to you. Let not your heart be troubled, nor let it be fearful." There you have it. Being troubled and fearful is the exact opposite of peace of heart.

What usually happens to bring on this troubled state of mind? Here is the common sequence of events. When you fear what someone may think, you do not take a stand for good as you should. You compromise. You lie. You cheat on your expense sheet. Your heart naturally becomes troubled because of your sin. There is internal dissonance and discord. Your heart is a confusion of feelings. You lament, "Why did I do that?" You lack peace. You are troubled.

Peter knows exactly how you feel. Look at his action and reactions.

> A little later the bystanders came up and said to Peter, "Surely you too are one of them; for even the way you talk gives you away." Then he began to curse and swear, "I do not know the man!" And immediately a rooster crowed. And Peter remembered the word which Jesus had said, "Before a rooster crows, you will deny Me three times." And he went out and wept bitterly (Matt. 26:73-75).

Peter told that terrible lie a third time. Immediately the cock crowed. Peter was crushed. "He went out and wept bitterly." All of this is in the background of Peter's exhortation to you and me. Do not be intimidated and fearful and wind up with a troubled heart.

There are some beautiful Biblical examples of what Peter is talking about. The parents of Moses are a good example. Hebrews 11:23 tells us, "By faith Moses, when he was born, was hidden for three months by his parents, because they saw he was a beautiful child; and they were not afraid of the king's edict." Notice, Moses' parents did what was right despite the decree of the king. They did not fear.

Then there is Moses himself. "By faith he left Egypt, not fearing the wrath of the king; for he endured, as seeing Him who is unseen" (Heb. 11:27). Moses did not fear the king of Egypt. He did what was right in the sight of God.

Do you remember the three young men, Shadrach, Meshach, and Abednego?

> Then Nebuchadnezzar in rage and anger gave orders to bring Shadrach, Meshach and Abednego; then these men were brought before the king. Nebuchadnezzar responded and said to them, "Is it true, Shadrach, Meshach and Abednego, that you do not serve my gods or worship the golden image that I have set up? Now if you are ready, at the moment you hear the sound of the horn, flute, lyre, trigon, psaltery and bagpipe and all kinds of music, to fall down and worship the image that I have made, very well. But if you do not worship, you will immediately be cast into the midst of a furnace of blazing fire; and what god is there who can deliver you out of my hands?" Shadrach, Meshach and Abednego replied to the king, "O Nebuchadnezzar, we do not need to give you an answer concerning this matter. If it be so, our God whom we serve is able to deliver us from the furnace of blazing fire; and He will deliver us out of your hand, O king. But even if He does not, let it be known to you, O king, that we are not going to serve your gods or worship the golden image that you have set up" (Dan. 3:13-18).

Shadrach, Meshach and Abednego did not fear Nebuchadnezzar's threat. They put trust in God who could deliver them from the fire. They stood their ground. They shunned idolatry. They refused to worship a golden image.

Who can forget Daniel and his stand for truth and good?

> It seemed good to Darius to appoint 120 satraps over the kingdom, that they would be in charge of the whole kingdom and over them three commissioners (of whom Daniel was one), that these satraps might be accountable to them, and that the king might not suffer loss. Then this Daniel began distinguishing himself among the commissioners and satraps because he possessed an extraordinary spirit, and the king planned to appoint him over the entire kingdom. Then the commissioners and satraps began trying to find a ground of accusation against

> Daniel in regard to government affairs; but they could find no ground of accusation or evidence of corruption, inasmuch as he was faithful, and no negligence or corruption was to be found in him. Then these men said, "We will not find any ground of accusation against this Daniel unless we find it against him with regard to the law of his God" (Dan. 6:1-5).

Rather than discontinue appointed times of prayer to the living and true God, Daniel was willing to be thrown to the lions. He did not fear the king.

Did Peter learn his lesson? Scripture indicates he did. Peter and the other apostles boldly proclaimed the resurrection of Christ in obedience to the Savior. The Jewish high council threw them in prison for their preaching. An angel subsequently released them and their preaching continued. The authorities again took them into custody. Acts 5:28-29 records the challenge of the high priest and Peter's response. "We gave you strict orders not to continue teaching in this name, and yet, you have filled Jerusalem with your teaching and intend to bring this man's blood upon us." But Peter and the apostles answered, "We must obey God rather than men."

We too must put away our fears. We too must obey God rather than men. It is time to resist the intimidating tactics of those who oppose Christ. It is time to stop fearing them and be zealots for good like Moses and his parents, and like Shadrach, Meshach and Abednego. We must dare to be Daniels. We must follow in the bold footsteps of Peter.

4. SANCTIFY CHRIST AS LORD IN YOUR HEART

Putting away fears is the negative side. There is also a positive side. Peter presents this positive solution to fear in verse 15. "And do not fear their intimidation, and do not be troubled, but sanctify Christ as Lord in your hearts" (1 Pet. 3:14-15). We oppose fear by taking specific action. We must sanctify Christ as Lord in our hearts. To "sanctify" means to set aside, set apart, or to separate for a special purpose. The word is usually used of God taking action on us by sanctifying us.

Here, Peter uses the word with reference to the action of Christians. Christians must sanctify Christ. Christians must set apart Christ as special. The King James Version says, "But sanctify the Lord God in your heart." The more ancient manuscripts speak particularly of Christ. The reading in the New America Standard Version is probably better.

Now Christians cannot really sanctify Christ or set Christ apart as special. Christ is what He is and He is special. He already is Lord. He is Lord of all. He sits right now in all splendor and glory on the throne of God. The basic confession of the church is simple: Jesus Christ is Lord. The basic gospel message is the gospel of the kingdom. It is the good news Jesus Christ, the crucified risen savior, is Lord of all.

When we sanctify Christ as Lord we simply acknowledge Him as Lord. We set Christ apart. He is higher than any other allegiance. We recognize Christ for who He is, the Lord. Personally and individually this means we treat Christ as He should be treated. If He is King and Lord, we reverence Him and we reverence His Word found in the Bible. To sanctify Christ as Lord is to rely on His power. To sanctify Christ as Lord is to trust in His faithfulness. To sanctify Christ as Lord is to submit to His wisdom. To sanctify Christ as Lord we reverence Him as Lord.

Look again at our text. "And do not fear their intimidation, and do not be troubled, but sanctify Christ as Lord *in your hearts*" (1 Pet. 3:14-15, italics added). Peter says this sanctification of Christ is a matter of heart. Christians should beware of a superficial and external sanctifying of Christ. Remember how Jesus rebuked the Pharisees? "This people honors me with their lips but their heart is far away from me" (Matt. 15:8). Lip service is insufficient. Simply calling Christ Lord will never do.

> Many will say to Me on that day, "Lord, Lord, did we not prophesy in Your name, and in Your name cast out demons, and in Your name perform many miracles?" And then I will declare to them, "I never knew you; depart from Me, you who practice lawlessness" (Matt. 7:22-23).

Paul also ties together our hearts and our lips. "If you confess with your mouth Jesus as Lord, and believe in your heart that God raised Him from the dead, you will be saved" (Rom. 10:9). Our confession of Christ stems from heartfelt conviction. In your heart you love, esteem, fear, and trust Christ. In your heart you recognize His total Lordship over you. In your heart you bow before Christ and worship and serve Him.

Peter gets this basic idea from the prophet Isaiah.

> You are not to say, "It is a conspiracy!" In regard to all that this people call a conspiracy, and you are not to fear what they fear or be in dread of it. It is the Lord of hosts whom you should regard as holy. And He shall be your fear, and He shall be your dread. Then He shall become your sanctuary (Isa. 8:12-13).

To sanctify the Lord is to regard Him as Holy. Isaiah 8:12-14 relates two ways to do this. First, to sanctify Christ as Lord in your hearts, you must make Him your fear and your dread. In other words, more than anything else, you fear offending Christ. More than anything else you dread not pleasing Christ. This simply means that you love Christ so much that you are sold out to Him and are prepared in every way to serve Him as Lord. The King James Version says, "Sanctify the Lord of hosts Himself; and let Him be your fear and let Him be your dread."

Second, to sanctify Christ as Lord in your hearts, He must become your sanctuary. This means He is your place of refuge. You flee to Christ for strength, help, and comfort. This means you love Christ as a Father. If Christ is truly your sanctuary, you cast all of your cares on Him knowing that He cares for you. To sanctify Christ as Lord in your hearts you make Him your fear and your dread. You make Him a sanctuary.

5. CONCLUSION

Now let's put the two parts of our text together as Peter does. On one hand Peter says, "Do not fear their intimidation." On the other hand,

Peter exhorts, "But sanctify Christ as Lord in your hearts." Do you see the connection? The solution to fear is this process sanctifying Christ as Lord in your hearts. And as we have seen, part of sanctifying Christ as Lord in your hearts is making Him your fear and making Him your dread. The opposite of this is fearing the intimidation of those who oppose Christ.

When we talk about doing good and being zealots for what is good, it all boils down to this: Whom do you fear? Do you fear the displeasure of other men and women and so compromise with Christ? Or do you fear displeasing Christ and so put His will first in your life? The problem with most of us is that we fear the displeasure of other human beings.

The solution to this problem is very basic. "Sanctify Christ as Lord in your hearts." When we fear standing up for what is right and good and just, there is only one cure. Flee to Christ; go to Christ; serve Christ. To fear what others think and compromise what is right is sin. Christ is always the cure for sin. The cure for the fear that leads to compromise is also Christ, fleeing to Christ, cleaving to Christ, following Christ. This is why Peter exhorts you and me, "Sanctify Christ as Lord in your hearts." When I was an army chaplain in Vietnam, other chaplains carried side arms. One chaplain in our brigade had a machine gun mounted on his jeep. All the soldiers knew chaplains, by international law, are considered non-combatants. Many fellow officers encouraged me to carry a pistol. After all, the Viet Cong were not known for their adherence to international legal standards. What was I to do? I was afraid. A fellow could get killed driving around alone in the jungle.

First Peter 3:14-15 was my solution. Do not fear. Sanctify Christ as Lord in your heart. I went before God with many prayers for safety. I sought to serve Christ as a man who was in the care of the Sovereign Lord. Riflemen in our unit noticed my stand. I came home whole in body and spirit. In this instance, I stood for what is right and good. Christ overcame my fears.

When I first did any door-to-door evangelism, I was frightened. This is a common reaction. The best way to overcome this fear is to get out and regularly do this evangelistic work. In preparation, you must understand the gospel yourself. You must practice making gospel presentations. You must seek the face of God for those to whom you will have opportunity to talk. You must pray for personal boldness. All of this amounts to sanctifying Christ as Lord in your heart. This process is the answer to personal fear. It is the answer to the intimidation tactics you are bound to meet in our fallen world.

Are you fearful of standing up for what is good? Peter responds to your fears. Take His advice. It is the advice of the Holy Spirit speaking through him. "Do not fear their intimidation, and do not be troubled, but sanctify Christ as Lord in your hearts" (1 Pet. 3:14-15).

5

PRESENTING YOUR FAITH: RELATING YOUR HOPE

And do not fear their intimidation, and do not be troubled, but sanctify Christ as Lord in your hearts, always being ready to make a defense to everyone who asks you to give an account for the hope that is in you, yet with gentleness and reverence. ~ 1 Pet. 3:14-15

PART TWO:
THE HOPE OF THE RESURRECTION

1. GET READY

Are you prepared; are you ready; are you on alert? Are you equipped to defend the hope within you? "Awe, not me," you say. "Leave that to the professionals. Leave that to the preacher. After all, I don't know that much; and after all, we pay the preacher to do that. I've got a job and a family and children to worry about you know. I just don't have the time for Bible study and reading other books like the preacher does."

Although this is how you may feel, look at 1 Peter 3:15. "Sanctify Christ as Lord in your hearts, always being ready to make a defense to everyone who asks you to give an account for the hope that is in you, yet with gentleness and reverence." Peter is not just talking to preachers. He speaks forthrightly to all Christians.

As you recall, Peter is laboring at the point that the prospect of unjust suffering may be just around the corner. Peter is very cognizant that fear of harm may keep you from doing what is good. He has been there. He has done that. Now Peter gives the positive solution to the very fear to which he once succumbed. "Sanctify Christ as Lord in your hearts."

The second part of verse 15 gives us one of the ways we may sanctify Christ. We can divide what Peter has to say here into four parts. First, Peter urges all Christians to be "ready to make a defense." Second, *what* must Christians to defend? "The hope that is in you," answers Peter. Third, when are Christians to make their defense? *Whenever* someone asks you about the hope that is within you. Fourth, *how* must Christians make their defense? Peter commands us to defend our hope with gentleness and fear. We examine these four points as we examine the first way you ought to sanctify Christ as Lord in your heart: "Always being ready to make a defense to everyone who asks you to give an account for the hope that is in you, yet with gentleness and reverence" (1 Pet. 3:15).

The apostle Peter speaks of "always being ready to make a defense." The word translated "defense" has its background in the old Greek city-states. "In Athens, every citizen was expected to be able to join in the discussion of state affairs."[1] "[E]very citizen had to defend himself *personally* if he were brought to trail."[2] The word refers to giving an answer, or self-justification. This might be in a formal situation as when Paul spoke before King Agrippa. This defense or answer might be very informal, over coffee. Simply taken, the defense Peter is talking about is the answer or reply you give when asked to speak a word about your faith.

Now, if you are *ready*, as Peter says, to make a defense, you must know exactly what you are defending. That is, you must know the

1. A. T. Robertson, *Word Pictures of the New Testament* (Nashville: Broadman, 1964), 6:114.
2. Jay E. Adams, *Trust and Obey* (Phillipsburg: Presbyterian and Reformed, 1978), 110.

exact content of the faith you are defending. We will look at this more closely under our second point. For now, it must be said, if you are to know, really know, the faith you may be called on to defend, you must read and study. You must read and study the Bible. You must have an understanding of the Bible and the content of the Bible. You must be able to find your way around the Bible. You must regularly read the Bible. You must read the Bible daily. If you do not have a private time each day when you read the Bible, you should. You should also have family times when you read the Bible. In our family, we have scheduled family devotions after meals. This is a good time to read the Bible and pray together.

You should also study the Bible regularly. Devotional reading and study are quite different. You must look more deeply into the Bible. You must search out its truth. This means using other books and helps and guides. This means spending time in reading for study. It takes time and you must make time to do these things. How much time do you spend in the Bible reading and studying in contrast to the time spent given to the TV screen, for instance?

Peter speaks of *always being ready to make a defense*. To be ready means to be prepared and that means making preparation. If you are to be prepared to give an answer concerning your faith, you must prepare your answer in advance. In other words, you should have a well thought out answer. You might even write out a testimony to God's grace as part of your preparation. I'll have something to say about preparing a testimony in a following chapter.

This well thought out answer should always be ready. You should frequently review your prepared response. You should regularly improve your reasoned response. You should always be prepared to actually speak, to give your answer to others.

Always being ready to defend your faith also involves prayer. You must be spiritually prepared as well as intellectually prepared. You ought to pray for the fullness of the Holy Spirit in your life. You ought to have times of private prayer, daily, seeking God's face. You ought to have times of family prayer. Failure in these areas will mean a lack of readiness to defend your faith.

2. YOUR HOPE

Now, more specifically, *what* are Christians to defend? Look at 1 Peter 3: 15 once again. "But sanctify Christ as Lord in your hearts, always being ready to make a defense to everyone who asks you to give an account for *the hope that is in you*, yet with gentleness and reverence" (italics added). Peter says you are to be prepared to defend the hope that is in you. This hope is the essence of your faith. Peter speaks of this hope in chapter 1 and verses 3-5,

> Blessed be the God and Father of our Lord Jesus Christ, who according to His great mercy has caused us to be born again to a living hope through the resurrection of Jesus Christ from the dead, to obtain an inheritance which is imperishable and undefiled and will not fade away, reserved in heaven for you, who are protected by the power of God through faith for a salvation ready to be revealed in the last time.

You have a living hope because Christ was raised from the dead. This is the hope of an inheritance reserved for you in heaven. It is hope of final salvation, the hope you too will participate in the resurrection of the dead. First Peter 1:13 says something similar. "Therefore, prepare your minds for action, keep sober in spirit, fix your hope completely on the grace to be brought to you at the revelation of Jesus Christ."

When Christ comes a second time in glory, the dead will be raised incorruptible. The great hope of the Christian is this resurrection. Once Christians are raised from the grave, they will live forever in heaven with Christ. The hope Peter is talking about is the resurrection. It includes the resurrection of those who believe in Christ. It is the hope of eternal life.

This hope is the center of the gospel. When the apostle Paul reviews the gospel, he sets down three important facts.

> Now I make known to you, brethren, the gospel which I preached to you, which also you received, in which also you stand, by which also you are saved, if you hold fast the word which I preached to you, unless you believed in vain. For I delivered to you as of first importance what I also received, that Christ died for our sins according to the Scriptures, and that He was buried, and that He was raised on the third day according to the Scriptures (1 Cor. 15:1-4).

When we think of the gospel, three points should come to mind immediately. These three points are of primary importance. One: Christ died for our sins according to the Scriptures. Two: He was buried. Three: He was raised on the third day according to the Scriptures. The resurrection is central to the good news of Christ.

The Lord Jesus Christ plainly states, "For God so loved the world, that He gave His only begotten Son, that whoever believes in Him shall not perish, but have eternal life" (John 3:16). When you trust in the risen Christ, you gain eternal life. You have the hope of partaking of the resurrection of the dead when Christ comes again. This is your life. This is your hope.

The apostle Paul provides a good example of one who was always ready to defend the hope within him. Acts 24:10-15 is part of one defense.

> When the governor had nodded for him to speak, Paul responded: "Knowing that for many years you have been a judge to this nation, I cheerfully make my defense. Since you can take note of the fact that no more than twelve days ago I went up to Jerusalem to worship. Neither in the temple, nor in the synagogues, nor in the city itself did they find me carrying on a discussion with anyone or causing a riot. Nor can they prove to you the charges of which they now accuse me. But this I admit to you, that according to the Way which they call a sect I do serve the God of our fathers, believing everything that is in accordance with the Law and that is written in the Prophets;

having a hope in God, which these men cherish themselves, that there shall certainly be a resurrection of both the righteous and the wicked."

Paul is defending himself before Governor Felix. As Paul begins, he uses the same word, *defense*, as Peter uses in 1 Peter 3:15 (Acts 24:10). Paul also speaks of his hope in God. What is this hope? Based upon the promises of the Old Testament, Paul declares, "there shall certainly be a resurrection of both the righteous and the wicked" (Acts 24:15). The hope Paul is called upon to defend is *the hope of the resurrection*.

Acts 26:1-8 gives us another example from the life of the apostle Paul.

> Agrippa said to Paul, "You are permitted to speak for yourself." Then Paul stretched out his hand and proceeded to make his defense: "In regard to all the things of which I am accused by the Jews, I consider myself fortunate, King Agrippa, that I am about to make my defense before you today; especially because you are an expert in all customs and questions among the Jews; therefore I beg you to listen to me patiently. So then, all Jews know my manner of life from my youth up, which from the beginning was spent among my own nation and at Jerusalem. Since they have known about me for a long time, if they are willing to testify, that I lived as a Pharisee according to the strictest sect of our religion. And now I am standing trial for the hope of the promise made by God to our fathers; the promise to which our twelve tribes hope to attain, as they earnestly serve God night and day. And for this hope, O King, I am being accused by Jews. Why is it considered incredible among you people if God does raise the dead?"

Again, Paul is making a defense. This time it is before King Agrippa. We again find the basic root word translated defense in verse 1. This is also a defense of Paul's hope (Acts 26:6-7). This hope is the hope of the Jewish nation. It is rooted in the promises of the Old Testament. What is this hope? Paul tells us by way of a question in verse 8. "Why is it considered incredible among you people if God does raise the dead?" Peter declares we must be ready to defend this hope.

As we go back to 1 Peter 3: 15, we must realize the hope of the resurrection is not just academic. The hope of the resurrection is a hope that grips the soul. This is why Peter speaks of the hope that is in you. Those who have resurrection life in them possess this hope. Those who are born again have *living* hope in them. "Blessed be the God and Father of our Lord Jesus Christ, who according to His great mercy has caused us to be born again to a living hope through the resurrection of Jesus Christ from the dead" (1 Pet. 1:3). The Spirit of Christ, the very life of Christ, surges in their souls.

This is what the apostle Paul calls, "Christ in you, the hope of glory" (Col. 1:27). This is the hope to which Paul refers in his prayer in Ephesians 1: 18-21. We must realize our lives as Christians are transformed and upheld by resurrection power.

> *I pray that* the eyes of your heart may be enlightened, so that you will know what is the hope of His calling, what are the riches of the glory of His inheritance in the saints, and what is the surpassing greatness of His power toward us who believe. *These are* in accordance with the working of the strength of His might which He brought about in Christ, when He raised Him from the dead and seated Him at His right hand in the heavenly *places*, far above all rule and authority and power and dominion, and every name that is named, not only in this age but also in the one to come.

Note the source of converting power. It is the resurrection. It is resurrection power brought to bear on your sin filled and spiritually dead soul. The consequence is new life. Your inner soul throbs with the pulse beat of resurrection life.

Is this really the case in you? Paul lays down a challenge in 2 Corinthians 13:5, "Test yourselves to see if you are in the faith; examine yourselves! Or do you not recognize this about yourselves, that Jesus

Christ is in you unless indeed you fail the I test?" The hope you must prepare to defend is no academic thing. It is a hope that is living in you, animating you.

3. ALWAYS BE READY

When are Christians to make a defense of the hope that is in them? Our text is very clear at this point. You make your defense when asked. It is to those who ask you that you are to be prepared to speak, to give a reason for the hope that is within you.

You may expect three types of inquiries into your faith. First, the civil authorities might request you to answer for your faith. The situation in Peter's day required Christians to expect this. We do not see a lot of this type of thing in our country today. However, challenges from government authorities are increasing. Such inquiries are common in the Middle East. Second, those who want to ridicule Christianity will require you to defend the hope that is in you. Academics often ridicule Christianity. Third there will be sincere inquiries about your eternal hope from those seeking truth.

Inquiries, questions, from these sources will come to all Christians. Pastors, ministers and seminary teachers are not the only people who are requested to make a defense of the hope that is in them. It is not only ruling elders or deacons who will be posed such questions. Every Christian may receive inquiries about his or her hope. Every Christian ought to be ready to make a defense to every one who asks them concerning the hope of the resurrection. This means each of you should be ready to make a defense to everyone who asks you. Most importantly, you should be prepared to handle those sincere inquiries about Christ.

This brings us to another aspect of our text. We should live our lives before a watching world so as to actually appear to others as people of hope. Our world is full of despair. Depression is a rising phenomenon in our culture. Why is this the case? When we cut ourselves off from the living God, we cut ourselves off from the source and fountain of hope. Stress, anxiety and various forms of mental disease are bound to increase. Look at how Paul describes people outside the faith. He says to the Christians at Ephesus, recalling their life in paganism, "Remember that you were at that time separate from Christ, excluded from the commonwealth of Israel, and strangers to the covenants of promise, *having no hope and without God in the world*" (Eph. 2:12, italics added). They were once without hope. Now it is different.

Unbelievers should see you and me as people of hope. When we exude that hope, our countenances are affected. Questions arise. At least this should be the case.

If Christians are only an anxious downcast lot, how can we expect unbelievers to be attracted to Christianity. People will ask the question of Genesis 4:6, "Why has your countenance fallen?" When believers are hopeful creatures of God, unbelievers are constrained to ask another question. Why are you so hopeful? This question opens the door to speak of the hope of the resurrection.

4. GENTLENESS AND FEAR

Finally, *how* are you to make your defense? Peter answers: "Make a defense to everyone who asks you to give an account for the hope that is in you, *yet with gentleness and reverence*" (italics added). Peter cautions you and me. Make your defense. But do it with gentleness and fear. You ought not to be boastful or proud. You have the hope of the resurrection. This means God has given you hope. You did not work up this hope yourself. God's grace is responsible. All boasting is excluded. "For by grace you have been saved through faith; and that not of yourselves, it is the gift of God; not as a result of works, so that no one may boast" (Eph. 2:8-9).

So Peter says, make your defense with gentleness and fear. Gentleness is a fruit of the Spirit (Gal. 5:23). The Authorized Version calls this quality "meekness." Peter has already urged Christian wives to adorn themselves "with the imperishable quality of a gentle and quiet spirit, which is precious in the sight of God" (1 Pet. 3:4). The exhortation applies to men too. It applies to children. "A gentle answer turns away wrath, but a harsh word stirs up anger (Prov. 15:1). When you make a defense of or give a reason for the hope within you, you should not be defensive or hostile. To the contrary, be gentle yet firm. The fear Peter mentions is the fear of God. It is reverence for God. To be in fear means you are struck with a sense of awe before God. You know God's resurrection power is your hope. You know you are privileged to speak on behalf of God. God is holy. He will not share His glory. "I am the Lord, that is My name; I will not give My glory to another" (Isa. 42:8). You may neither misrepresent God nor puff up yourself.

You know it is the resurrection power of God that changes men and women from despair to hope. You stand in awe of this power and you fear offending the God of this power more than you fear offending any human being. You follow the injunction of Isaiah 8:13. "It is the Lord of hosts whom you should regard as holy. And He shall be your fear, and He shall be your dread."

Not only so, you fear the judgmental power of God. You know it is real. You see the agony of Christ in the garden. You see the suffering of Christ on the cross. You know this same judgment is yours except for the grace of God. Your reverence for God's power to punish turns to fear for others outside of Christ.

What is the result? When you give a defense regarding your hope, you have awe in your heart for God's power to heal the broken hearted. When you give others a reason for the hope within you, you fear the judgment of God poised over the life of the unbeliever to whom you talk. You speak with gentleness and fear.

5. CONCLUSION

These points are, very briefly, the four points of our text. First, Peter is urging all Christians to always be ready to defend their Christianity. Second, *what* specifically do Christians defend? Christians defend the resurrection hope within them. Third, *when* do Christians make their defense? Answer: Whenever someone asks them about their hopefulness. Finally, *how* do Christians defend their hope in Christ? They do so with gentleness and fear.

Taking action on what Peter says will have important results in your life. It will result in greater practical knowledge of Christ as Lord. Being ready to defend the hope that is in you is one way you can sanctify Christ as Lord in your heart. This is one of the points of the outline we are following. Look again at our text. "Sanctify Christ as Lord in your hearts, always being ready to make a defense to everyone who asks you to give an account for the hope that is in you, yet with gentleness and reverence."

Another result is that the fear of God will prevail over fear of man. This result is true because the positive solution to fear is sanctifying Christ as Lord in your heart. This point is another result in the outline we are following. Here is what the outline of 1 Peter 3:14-15 looks like.

A. *The Problem of Fear*: And do not fear their intimidation, and do not be troubled.

B. *The Answer to Fear*: but sanctify Christ as Lord in your hearts,

> *How you Sanctify Christ*: always being ready to make a defense to everyone who asks you to give an account for the hope that is in you, yet with gentleness and reverence.

Where do you stand? Do you experience fear? What is the answer? Sanctify Christ as Lord in your heart. What steps can you take to really set apart Christ as Lord in your heart? The very first step you can take is to prepare yourself to talk to those who ask you to give an account of the hope that is in you. Are you prepared? "Sanctify Christ as Lord in your hearts, always being ready to make a defense to everyone who asks you to give an account for the hope that is in you, yet with gentleness and reverence" (1 Pet. 3:15).

6

Presenting Your Faith:
Relating Your Hope

And do not fear their intimidation, and do not be troubled, but sanctify Christ as Lord in your hearts, always being ready to make a defense to everyone who asks you to give an account for the hope that is in you, yet with gentleness and reverence. ~ 1 Pet. 3:14-15

PART THREE:
YOUR TESTIMONY

We are dealing with 1 Peter 3:15 and responding to people who ask us to give a reason for the hope within us. You must not fear the intimidation tactics of those who oppose Christ. Rather, "Sanctify Christ as Lord in your hearts, always being ready to make a defense to everyone who asks you to give an account for the hope that is in you, yet with gentleness and reverence."

As we have already said, if you are going to be ready to speak to others about your hope in Christ, you must get ready to do so. Readiness means putting together a short presentation you can relate to others over coffee. My purpose is to examine this process and set an example before you from the apostle Paul. First of all, let's do a little review.

1. OUR PERSPECTIVE

You have hope in this life because of what God has done for you in Christ. God raised Jesus Christ from the grave (Acts 3:15). This resurrection defeated death (1 Cor. 15:55). You therefore also have the hope of being raised from the dead (Acts 24:15). The Holy Spirit gives you assurance regarding this future resurrection through His Word (Eph. 1:14).

A common error in giving witness to the grace of God is to place the accent on ourselves and to point men and women to ourselves. The more dramatic the story told, the more we highlight ourselves. We tend to be quite self-centered, quite man-centered, even when we talk about the grace of God. Several years ago I watched and heard Norma Zimmer sing a popular hymn, "To *God* be the Glory," on television. At the close of the hymn, there was a deep bow, the audience applauded wildly, and Norma Zimmer said, "Thank you very much." I could not help but think this scene presented a typical contradiction. To God be the glory. Bow and accept applause from the audience. It is subtle for many of us, perhaps too subtle. In giving witness to the magnificent grace of God, we too often accept the applause *ourselves* and say, "Thank you."

However, our witness must be God-centered not man-centered. I am talking about a point of view, a way of thinking. Paul exhorts in Romans 12:1-2:

> Therefore I urge you, brethren, by the mercies of God, to present your bodies a living and holy sacrifice, acceptable to God, which is your spiritual service of worship. And do not be conformed to this world, but be transformed by the renewing of your mind, so that you may prove what the will of God is, that which is good and acceptable and perfect.

Our whole culture is geared toward self-enjoyment. This is the very opposite of the Biblical picture. Listen to the Westminster Shorter Catechism. Question: What is the chief end of man? Answer: Man's chief end is to glorify God and to enjoy Him forever (Q&A 1). God does not call us to the primary goal of enjoying ourselves. We are called to enjoy Him first and foremost. We find our joy in Him. This will be the case eternally. Again, the Westminster Shorter Catechism asks: What benefits do believers receive from Christ at the resurrection? Answer: At the resurrection, believers being raised up in glory, shall be openly acknowledged and acquitted in the day of judgment, and made perfectly blessed *to the full enjoying of God to all eternity* (Q&A 38, italics added).

We therefore defend our hope with this viewpoint. We do not tell people about Christ so they will enjoy themselves more in this life. We point people to Christ so they will learn to enjoy God. This does not mean a lack of joy for God's people. It is a different perspective on joy, an eternal rather than temporal standpoint. Eternal bliss does not mean enjoying yourself. Eternal bliss refers to the full enjoyment of God. We find our greatest joy when we enjoy the one we love most. This is true with God and with Christ.

This is why the primary call to men and women by Scripture is the call to repentance. Here are several texts. "Now in those days John the Baptist came, preaching in the wilderness of Judea, saying, 'Repent, for the kingdom of heaven is at hand'" (Matt. 3:1-2). "From that time Jesus began to preach and say, 'Repent, for the kingdom of heaven is at hand'" (Matt. 4:17). "Now after John had been taken into custody, Jesus came into Galilee, preaching the gospel of God, and saying, 'The time is fulfilled, and the kingdom of God is at hand; repent and believe in the gospel'" (Mark 1:14-15).

> Now when they heard this they were pierced to the heart, and said to Peter and the rest of the apostles, "Brethren, what shall we do?" Peter said to them, "Repent, and each of you be baptized in the name of Jesus Christ for the forgiveness of your sins; and you will receive the gift of the Holy Spirit" (Acts 2:37-38).

"Therefore repent and return, so that your sins may be wiped away, in order that times of refreshing may come from the presence of the Lord" (Acts 3:19). "I did not shrink from declaring to you anything that was profitable, and teaching you publicly and from house to house, solemnly testifying to both Jews and Greeks of repentance toward God and faith in our Lord Jesus Christ" (Acts 20:20-21). "I did not prove disobedient to the heavenly vision, but kept declaring both to those of Damascus first, and also at Jerusalem and then throughout all the region of Judea, and even to the Gentiles, that they should repent and turn to God, performing deeds appropriate to repentance" (Acts 26:19-20). Here is the main point. The message of repentance is the message of turning away from self to God. For this reason, your testimony, the defense of your hope, must center upon what God has done. This is central. Everything hinges on this central message.

2. THE EXAMPLE OF THE APOSTLE PAUL

With this brief word regarding our perspective, we look at how the apostle Paul made his defense, how he related the hope that was within him. We'll use Acts 26:1-18 as our guide and take the text point by point. "Agrippa said to Paul, 'You are permitted to speak for yourself.' Then Paul stretched out his hand and proceeded to make his defense" (Acts 26:1). Note that 1 Peter 3: 15 speaks of making an apology for our hope, giving a reason, making our defense. This is exactly what Paul is doing before king Agrippa.

Before we deal with the defense proper, I acknowledge what we have is a summary of Paul's defense. This point seems important. We need to learn to summarize our position before Christ to others. Several years ago I went through this lesson with a group of people in a Reformed Presbyterian Church. I emphasized the fact that what we have here is a summary. I asked the people to put together a similar summary. One individual came with several typewritten pages. The reading took perhaps forty-five minutes. What is before us is quite different. It is a two-minute presentation of something like four hundred words. This example is taken from Scripture. It is one we can use. Once we get the basic outline under our belts, we can expand the message. But watch the outline and the content of the message under each point of the outline.

Chapter : Presenting Your Faith: Relating your Hope, Part 3

Introduction

Paul's introduction comes first.

> In regard to all the things of which I am accused by the Jews, I consider myself fortunate, King Agrippa, that I am about to make my defense before you today; especially because you are an expert in all customs and questions among the Jews; therefore I beg you to listen to me patiently (Acts 26:2-3).

Paul makes a very polite introduction. He gives thanks for King Agrippa. He acknowledges that Agrippa's understanding of Jewish customs make him a worthy judge in the matter at hand. Paul asks Agrippa to listen and to listen patiently. Really hearing what Paul has to say is important.

We too can make a polite introduction when someone challenges us regarding our hope in Christ. We might even appeal to the individual's status and position in business or education as putting us in a privileged position in speaking with them. We should not hesitate to make an appeal for patience in listening and also understanding. The introduction is short. In the New American Standard Version, it is only fifty-five words.

Point One: My Former Manner of Life Without Christ

Paul's first major point begins with Acts 26:4-5. Here, the apostle speaks of his former manner of life.

> So then, all Jews know my manner of life from my youth up, which from the beginning was spent among my own nation and at Jerusalem; since they have known about me for a long time, if they are willing to testify, that I lived as a Pharisee according to the strictest sect of our religion.

Paul is forthright about his past but also circumspect. In sum, he says he was very religious. This is a claim many people have. People are very religious without Christ. In our culture you can be fanatical about sports, money and cars. You can be a respectable church person who has high moral standards. You can even be a harlot or you can be gay as long as you act out of love in your relationships and act out of religious convictions.

Paul continues this point regarding his former manner of life in verses 9-11.

> So then, I thought to myself that I had to do many things hostile to the name of Jesus of Nazareth. And this is just what I did in Jerusalem; not only did I lock up many of the saints in prisons, having received authority from the chief priests, but also when they were being put to death I cast my vote against them. And as I punished them often in all the synagogues, I tried to force them to blaspheme; and being furiously enraged at them, I kept pursuing them even to foreign cities.

Paul acknowledges he used religion to justify all sorts of evil. He admits he even stooped to murder. His religion justified his evil actions. Mormon missionaries are often observed to be very cleancut, upright and moral individuals. This is the appearance. I have received some of the most vulgar, profane, and blasphemous letters from those who classify themselves Mormon elders. They are very religious people. Yet they are often very profane.

Perhaps this was the case in your life. You used religion as a cloak for evil. I once belonged to a Boy Scout Troop sponsored by a church. I received the God and Country award. I was not a Christian. I was a very vulgar and profane schoolboy. Some men work very hard to support their families. They are religious about their work. They use their work addiction to justify ignoring their wives and children. At the same time, they use their hard work to justify heavy drinking or extramarital affairs. They are very honorable in their own eyes. But they are deeply deceived. We can all use good to shroud evil in our lives.

This point is obviously for those converted later in life. These are people who have a former life to which they may point. If you grew up in a Christian home, this point may or may not apply to you. You may have been a very rebellious child rejecting the gospel until your college days. This is not unusual. If this is the case in your life, this first point applies. You have a religious background about which you can testify. How did you use religion as a cover for evil in your life?

On the other hand, you may not know a day without Christ. This is a great blessing. You do not have a former manner of life in the sense about which Paul speaks. Remember, this does not lessen what Christ has done. In fact, it heightens the work of Christ. Grace abounded. You are privileged beyond measure. You should not feel bad that you do not have a seamy former life to talk about. You should feel good about that. This first point in Paul's presentation does not specifically apply to you. Wonderful. Gladly leave it out.

Point Two: What Christ Did
The first point is not the major portion of the defense or testimony. In the New American Standard Version it is only one hundred and fifty-two words. The major point in this presentation follows. What Christ did, Acts 26:12-18. In the New American Standard Version this section is two hundred and four words. I know, perhaps I'm placing too much weight on the number of words. I will talk about this more. For now, get a sense of proportion here. Understand this is the longest section in Paul's presentation.

In Acts 26:12 Paul exclaims, "While so engaged as I was journeying to Damascus with the authority and commission of the chief priests." While Paul was in the midst of his sinful activity, Jesus Christ arrested him on the Damascus road. Compare Romans 5:8. "But God demonstrates His own love toward us, in that while we were yet sinners, Christ died for us." It is while we are sinners that Christ comes to us. He dies on the cross for helpless sinners. "For while we were still helpless, at the right time Christ died for the ungodly" (Rom. 5:6). This is the case for each of us. Christ comes to us *in our sin*.

Acts 26:13-15 continues,

> At midday, O King, I saw on the way a light from heaven,

brighter than the sun, shining all around me and those who were journeying with me. And when we had all fallen to the ground, I heard a voice saying to me in the Hebrew dialect, "Saul, Saul, why are you persecuting Me? It is hard for you to kick against the goads." And I said, "Who are You, Lord?" And the Lord said, "I am Jesus whom you are persecuting."

Christ revealed Himself to Paul. If you are a Christian, Christ revealed Himself to you too. How did He reveal himself to you? You did not receive a revelation from heaven while walking down the street. You did, however, receive a revelation from heaven in the form of God's Word in the Bible. Christ came to you in His Word and through this Word. It is always through the instrumentality of the Word that Christ reveals Himself in a saving way. "You have been born again not of seed which is perishable but imperishable, that is, through the living and enduring word of God" (1 Pet. 1:23). The point to catch here, however, is that Christ took the initiative. He revealed Himself to Paul. He also revealed Himself to you.

In Acts 26:16-18, Christ continues to speak to Paul. He gives Paul specific directions.

> But get up and stand on your feet; for this purpose I have appeared to you, to appoint you a minister and a witness not only to the things which you have seen, but also to the things in which I will appear to you; rescuing you from the Jewish people and from the Gentiles, to whom I am sending you, to open their eyes so that they may turn from darkness to light and from the dominion of Satan to God, that they may receive forgiveness of sins and an inheritance among those who have been sanctified by faith in Me.

Christ gave Paul a specific purpose for his life. This is how we come to understand our purpose for living. Christ comes to us. Christ reveals Himself to us. Christ directs us. Was this not the case in your life? Sure, it was not so dramatic. But in the end, was it not the same?

Again, note that the bulk of the testimony involves a statement concerning the work of Christ, what Christ has done. There are two main sub-points here. First, we speak of what Christ did in revealing Himself to us. How did this occur in your life? I'll relate how this took place in my life momentarily. Second, we speak of what Christ did in speaking to us and directing us through His Word. We do not look for special revelations from heaven today. We have Scripture. It is a sufficient revelation. How did Christ speak to you from Scripture? I will relate how Christ spoke to me from Scripture in a moment to give you an example. For now, let these two points concerning the work of Christ sink in.

Point Three: The Hope of the Resurrection
In Acts 26:6-8, Paul completes his defense by pointing to the hope he has in Christ.

> And now I am standing trial for the hope of the promise made by God to our fathers, the promise to which our twelve tribes hope to attain, as they earnestly serve God night and day. And for this hope, O King, I am being accused by Jews. Why is it considered incredible among you people if God does raise the dead?

This brings us full circle. We must be prepared to defend the hope within us whenever asked to do so by those who may challenge us. Peter simply says, "Sanctify Christ as Lord in your hearts, always being ready to make a defense to everyone who asks you to give an account for the hope that is in you, yet with gentleness and reverence." We are reviewing one example of such a defense given by the apostle Paul. The apostle calls attention to his hope. "I am standing trial for the hope of the promise made by God to our fathers" (Acts 26:6).

What is this hope? Paul tells us by way of a question. "Why is it considered incredible among you people if God does raise the dead?" (Acts 26:8). The hope of the resurrection is the hope you too are called upon to defend to a listening world. Why should it be considered incredible if the Creator of the universe should raise the dead? This is the hope presented in the Bible. This is the hope revealed to you by the resurrected, living Christ. This is the hope to which you testify because you have experienced renewal with resurrection power when you were born again. The gift of the Spirit is given to you as a down payment. When you receive the Spirit, you know you have the promise of future resurrection with Christ. You can now testify to this hope because you have experienced it.

The Three Points
These three points are a concise defense of the faith. Here is the breakdown. Introduction: 55 words, 11% of the presentation; Point One: 152 words, 32%; Point Two: 204 words, 43% of the presentation; Point Three: 62 words, 13.5%. I don't want to be legalistic about following Paul here. However, because the Spirit gave to us what we have through Paul, I think we should pay attention to this defense and use it as a pattern. When we do so, we have a two-minute speech. We have a presentation we can make over coffee on the spur of the moment.

3. A PERSONAL EXAMPLE
The following applies the outlined derived from Paul in Acts 26. It attempts to put into practice what we learn from the apostle. This example is 363 words in length. Write out your testimony using the same outline. Make it simple and brief.

Introduction (36 words)

> Thanks for this opportunity to briefly talk to you about my faith in Christ. I hope you will take what I have to say seriously and not disregard my words as coming from some fundamentalist fanatic.

My former life without Christ (107 words)

> When I was a youngster and in high school and college, I was

like a lot of kids. I attended church pretty regularly with my friends. I was active in the Boy Scouts and even won the God and Country Award. I also played varsity football in high school and was later captain of the West Point rugby team. In college I attended chapel services regularly and often attempted to read the Bible. Something was missing. I couldn't really pray and I didn't understand the Bible. Most of all, my religious convictions were shallow. They did not keep me from drinking heavily and carousing with the crowd.

What Christ did in revealing Himself to me (163 words)

When I graduated from West Point, my first military assignment was in Korea. We called it the armpit of the world. Here God began to deal with me. I made a commitment not to live a totally immoral life with prostitutes. Later, I came to realize this was the beginning of repentance. This was God at work in my life. You see the Bible tells us real repentance is a gift from God.

Then one day I felt compelled to visit with the chaplain. He challenged me right away by asking, "Have you ever accepted Jesus Christ as your Lord and Savior?" I hadn't. The chaplain opened the Bible. For the first time I understood this book. God showed me, through the Bible, I was a sinner. God showed me He sent Christ into the world to die on the cross to pay for my sins. Finally, God showed me, from the Bible, Christ is alive, that He was raised from the grave.

My hope as a result of what Christ has done (57 words)

Through the Bible, God also showed me the way to hope and eternal life is through faith in Jesus Christ. The chaplain led me in prayer and I did trust Christ. Because of what Christ did for me in dying and rising again, I have real hope. I have the hope of heaven to come. Do you?

4. A SECOND PERSONAL EXAMPLE (315 words)

This example omits point two, my past life. I spend more time on what Christ has done. This is the main point for you and me.

> I am being asked to give an account of the hope that is within me. I am constrained to declare my great and personal hope is the hope of eternal life and the hope of being raised again from the dead. What is the reason for this hope? My hope and confidence rest in Jesus Christ and what He has done.
>
> When I was 24 years old, I first understood the really good news about Jesus Christ. I learned that Jesus died on a cross to pay the penalty due to me for my sins. There was little doubt I was a sinner and deserved God's wrath. I also learned Jesus was raised again from the grave. This proved He was and is God. Because this Jesus is now alive and is God, He could give me the ability to lead a new life. A chaplain in the Army talked to me about all this and this chaplain showed me Romans 10:9, "If you confess with your mouth Jesus as Lord, and believe in your heart that God raised Him from the dead, you shall be saved." I committed my life to Christ. My life was changed. I experienced forgiveness for my sins. I experienced new life; it was the resurrection life of Christ. I found God had given me a new heart. I realized I was born again. There was a new joy in my life because of what Christ had done for me.
>
> Yes, I have great hope, hope that does not disappoint because the love of God has been poured out within my heart by the Holy Spirit who was given to me. You see, "I know Whom I have believed and am convinced that He is able to guard what I have entrusted to Him until that day"(2 Tim. 1:12). Is this the kind of hope and confidence you have?

God Must Exist to Play Basketball

*In Him we live and move and exist, as even some of your
own poets have said, "For we also are His children."*
~ Acts. 17:28

BLUE 35 IS IN THE LANE, her feet firmly planted. Red twenty-four is driving for the basket. There are only seconds on the clock and the score is tied. The conference championship is on the line. Red twenty-four crashes into her opponent. The whistle sounds and to the amazement of the crowd the hand single of the official indicates a block. Red twenty-four has two shots with only three seconds on the clock. The game is determined by a call that even the winning coach admits should have gone the other way. Some fans are outraged. Others are in disbelief. The home crowd is exuberant with its championship.

But why was there any debate over that final call anyway? In fact, why were there officials and why are there rules by which to play? Why are the officials charged with making judgments in accord with the pre-established rules? Well, silly, you can't play a basketball game without rules and without officials. True. But the nagging question remains. Why? The answer is startlingly simple. It goes back to God. God must exist to play basketball or any other sport. God must exist to play by the rules or to live in the world by the rules. Let me explain.

The very fact that basketball fans of any background, either gender, any race, or any religious conviction, either applaud or castigate basketball officials testifies to the existence of right and wrong. The fact that coaches will argue vehemently with an official about a call saying it's wrong, with the fans backing up the coach, testifies to the existence of right and wrong. The existence of officials on the floor enforcing preexistent rules argues for the existence of truth and error. For an official to make a good call, following the rules and for the fans to show appreciation argues for the existence of truth. But for the same official to make a bad call and for the same fans to display utter disapproval attests to the existence of error.

Further, the applause after a call or the proverbial, "get in the game ref," affirms our desire for justice. We instinctively cry for justice. We want to see it on the basketball floor and we want to see it in the courtroom. A game that is decided on the basis of poor officiating smacks of injustice. It is not fair, it is not just, when a team looses, not on the merits of its play, but on the demerits of the officiating. We can hardly tolerate such injustice.

The existence of officials in basketball games, the existence of rules, and the officiating itself, not only point to the existence of right and wrong, truth and error, justice and injustice, they firmly testify to the existence of absolutes. We have no problem saying that an official who calls a blocking foul against a defensive player whose feet are firmly planted on the floor is wrong. The call should have been charging. We do not, we cannot, say that the truth is relative here. The call is either right or wrong. There may be debate over whether the offensive player drove her shoulder into the defensive player. There may also be debate over whether the defensive player was shuffling her feet on the floor. But if instant replay shows a shoulder down and feet firmly planted in the lane, a blocking foul is not only wrong it is absolutely wrong. Because our sense of fairness is injured we argue against the call. Because we seek justice, we argue with the call. The call is wrong. It is absolutely wrong.

And so we are immediately plunged into the arena of moral absolutes. On one hand we may claim such absolutes do not exist. On the other hand we live our lives on the basis they do exist. And every time we say something is right or wrong, true or in error, we are appealing to a standard of right and of truth. In addition, we recognize that standard cannot be arbitrary. It must be fixed. To be sure, the rules of a basketball game can be changed. But capricious application of the rules is unacceptable. Breaking the rules in basketball is wrong. For the officials to refuse to enforce the rules of the game on the court is wrong. It is absolutely wrong. Such officials should be replaced. And so we are back to moral absolutes. We cannot escape them; we cannot live without them.

But if basketball or any other game cannot be played without the existence of moral absolutes, surely life cannot be lived without them. If simple games require absolute truth, absolute definitions of right and wrong, and absolute justice, to be understood and played, surely these games, which we teach to be microcosms of life, truly display that life cannot be lived without an appeal to absolutes.

Interestingly enough, if moral absolutes are as integral to life as they are to basketball, they must come from somewhere. If absolute truth does exist, as basketball suggests, there must be an absolute standard of truth. And if the longing of the human heart for justice on the basketball court is to be fulfilled, there must be absolute and final justice in the universe.

What or whom does absolute and final justice require? Think about it. The officiating at a basketball game leads us to the concept of absolute truth and justice. But absolute justice requires an Official who knows all. The reason absolute justice is not found on the basketball court is that no official can see everything and know everything that takes place on the court. Absolute justice requires omniscience, someone who knows all. For perfect justice to exist, the judge must not only be omniscient, this judge must also be perfectly righteous and good. This judge must be incapable of error. In addition, the judge must have the power to execute just judgment. The judge must be omnipotent, all-powerful. His power must be pervasive and inescapable. *Only the God of the Bible fits these qualifications.*

Here is the sum of it. To play basketball, or to live in this world, requires the existence of moral absolutes. No judgment regarding truth and error can be made without them. But as soon as we begin talking about making judgments, the concept of justice looms large. As justice is sought on the basketball court, our hearts long for absolute justice based upon absolute standards. From this we are driven back to God. And we realize that God must exist to play basketball.

SEEK THE LORD!

Seek the Lord while He may be found;
Call upon Him while He is near.
Let the wicked forsake his way,
And the unrighteous man his thoughts.
~ Isa. 55:6

A PRIORITY IN EVANGELISM should be to invite people to attend church with God's people, to listen to the sermons, to read the Bible, and to "Seek the Lord while He may be found" (Isa. 55:6). In doing door-to-door calling, you invite people to attend church. You want them to be connected with the church. You want them to be exposed to the Scriptures and to the gracious working of the Spirit in the midst of God's people as they worship together. You want them to hear the gospel. You want them to be born again. You want them to repent of sin and turn to Christ as the only source of salvation from sin and death and hell. You want them to seek the Lord as exhorted in Isaiah 55:6.

This procedure is a vital part of Biblical and Reformed evangelism. Although not well known, this methodology is called *seeking evangelism*. It was the evangelism of Jonathan Edwards and the Great Awakening. In it we implore sinners to place themselves under the hearing of the Word of God. We encourage them to read the Bible. In the mean time, we urge men and women to turn away from sinful ways. We warn them of the dangers of hell. And we tell them that their only hope is in Jesus Christ.

A sharp criticism is immediately raised. The apostle Paul quotes Psalm 14 to the effect, "There is none who seeks for God" (Rom. 3:11). In other words, on their own, unbelievers do not seek God, cannot seek God, and will never properly seek God. And so seeking evangelism falls before it gets started. The issue is that seeking evangelism seems to urge totally depraved sinners to do what they are incapable of doing. However, is the answer to move directly to the step of calling sinners to repentance and faith? Is this not to require of them that which they cannot and will not do? The response is that we depend on the Holy Spirit to regenerate the sinner and provide the gifts of repentance and faith. Exactly! We must honor the Holy Spirit in our evangelism. And it is my contention that seeking evangelism is the method that most thoroughly does this.

Before going further however, let me show you that seeking evangelism is Biblical. In the Old Testament we read,

> And Asa did good and right in the sight of the Lord his God, for he removed the foreign altars and high places, tore down the sacred pillars, cut down the Asherim, and commanded Judah to seek Lord God of their fathers and to observe the law and the commandment (2 Chron. 14:2-4).

Here is the testimony of God. It is good to encourage men and women caught in the web of idolatry and heathenism to seek the Lord. This is a very important point. To encourage men and women to seek the Lord is a good thing in the eyes of God.

Why is this the case? Paul answers us in his sermon on Mars Hill.

> The God who made the world and all things in it, since He is Lord of heaven and earth, does not dwell in temples made with hands; neither is He served by human hands, as though He needed anything, since He Himself gives to all life and breath and all things; and *He made from one, every nation of mankind to live on all the face of the earth*, having determined their appointed times, and the boundaries of their habitation, *that they should seek God*, if perhaps they might grope for Him and find Him,

though He is not far from each one of us; for in Him we live and move and exist, as even some of your own poets have said, 'For we also are His offspring' (Acts 17:24-28, italics added).

Note that Paul tells us very clearly that human beings were placed on this earth for the purpose of seeking God. Sin does not set aside this purpose of God. Human inability does not abrogate responsibility. Therefore, understanding this purpose of God, it must be a very good thing to encourage people to seek the Lord as set forth in 2 Chronicles 14:2-4. Much more could be said but, let's do that in conjunction with a discussion of seeking evangelism and the five points of Calvinism.

First, seeking evangelism begins with the utter sinfulness of fallen humanity. It recognizes that sinners will not seek the Lord on their own. It recognizes that God acts through many providential circumstances to literally cause men and women to seek Him. Psalm 83:13-16 confirms this truth.

> O my God, make them like the whirling dust;
> Like chaff before the wind.
> Like fire that bums the forest,
> And like a flame that sets the mountains on fire,
> So pursue them with Thy tempest,
> And terrify them with Thy storm.
> Fill their faces with dishonor,
> That they may seek Thy name, O Lord.

God will often bring terror into people's lives so they will seek Him. So-called natural disasters such as earthquakes and tornados are meant to break human pride and induce seeking. A young man encountered by a deacon in the Sterling congregation was terrified because of dreams he was having. This fear brought about opportunity to urge this young man to seek the Lord. But how often we pat people on the back in circumstances like this and tell them everything will be all right. Everything will not be all right! Such people need to seek the Lord. The point here is that fallen sinners can read the Bible. They can place themselves under the preaching of the Word. They can be invited to and many will attend evangelistic Bible studies. We need to urge unbelievers to do such things. We need to urge them to seek the Lord.

Second, seeking evangelism emphasizes the doctrine of unconditional election. Seeking evangelism lets people know that God elects sinners. It emphasizes that knowledge of our position with relation to the electing work of God is of ultimate importance. Seeking evangelism also recognizes that the seeker may ask, "Will God save me?" The proper answer is, "I don't know. God is sovereign. God may save those who seek Him. He may not." Jesus was clear on this, "Strive to enter by the narrow door; for many, I tell you, will seek to enter and will not be able" (Luke 13:24).

Note two things from these words of Jesus. First, we are all to strive to enter. The word here is "agonize to enter." This means seeking the Lord is work. It requires time and effort. It requires study of the Word. It requires time with believers discussing, praying over, and debating the Word. And unbelievers must place top priority on this task. But second, and according to Jesus, there are no guarantees. Many seek to enter and are not able. This is tough. But it is true. That God is sovereign is all the more reason to seek the Lord. The question of the individual's election must be answered.

But, you may respond, this doctrine will deter people from seeking the Lord. Perhaps. But if people reject the sovereign electing God of the Bible, they reject the only author of salvation.

And they should be told that they are rejecting the only possible salvation there is. And so they must seek this sovereign God.

Third, seeking evangelism accentuates the doctrine of limited atonement. Seeking evangelism does not say, "God loves you and has a wonderful plan for your life." This popular statement compromises both unconditional election and limited atonement. Seeking evangelism therefore cannot tell people that they must simply accept the

Christ who died for all men. Seeking evangelism explains the doctrine of limited atonement. Then the exhortation is, "Seek the Lord while He may be found; call upon Him while He is near" (Isa. 55:6). Why? The objective is for sinners to find the answer to the question of their eternal state before God. Only God can answer this question. Thus the only proper way to get the answer is to seek the Lord. The hope is for the individual to legitimately be able to say with Paul, "I live by faith in the Son of God, *who loved me, and delivered Himself up for me*" (Gal. 2:20, italics added).

Fourth, seeking evangelism is rooted in the doctrine of sovereign regeneration. For the most part, present day evangelism assumes that unregenerate people have the ability to place faith in Christ. But when people embrace this false claim regarding their own ability and on this basis make a commitment to Christ, spurious faith results. It is "faith" generated by the power of the flesh. And to this extent "the demons also believe" (Jas. 2:19).

As already said, seeking evangelism urges men and women to place themselves under the hearing of the word. It is here that the Spirit of God is most likely to act. In such circumstances, He may regenerate the seeker. You see, seeking evangelism does stress the need to be born again. It explains that sinners cannot lovingly embrace Christ except they be born again. And it tells the seeker that the new birth is a sovereign act of God. It explains that this is why people must place themselves under the teaching of the word. "For you were born again not of seed which is perishable but imperishable, that is, through the living and abiding word of God ... And this is the word which was preached to you" (1 Pet. 1:23-25).

Seeking evangelism also emphasizes the need for sinners to repent of sin and trust in Christ. But it makes very plain that repentance and faith are gifts of the Spirit. It is the Spirit who works repentance and faith in us. And so, because seeking evangelism takes depravity and the need for regeneration seriously, seeking evangelism also takes the gospel call seriously. Jesus said, "Come to Me, all who are weary and heavy-laden, and I will give you rest" (Matt. 11:28). Seeking evangelism sees this gospel call coming to those who are weary and heavy-laden because of sin. Others may hear the call. But they do not take the call seriously because they do not take their sin seriously. God has convicted those who take their sin seriously. This is the work of the Spirit (John 16:8). The prospect of hell frightens them. They are therefore impelled to seek God. And in the midst of this seeking, that is, while sitting under the preaching or teaching of Scripture, God may grant the gifts of repentance and faith.

This is a place to note that seeking evangelism puts assurance in the proper context. Seekers who are regenerated by God realize that the faith in Christ they express and the change of life they experience comes from God. Their assurance is therefore rooted in the sovereign and gracious work of God. This is a wonderful outcome.

Fifth, seeking evangelism upholds the doctrine of the perseverance of the saints. You see, seeking the Lord does not end upon conversion. Seeking the Lord continues throughout the Christian life. Why is this so important? To desist in such seeking is a sign of a lack of conversion. Yes, the truly converted person no longer needs regeneration. But the truly converted person does need growth and sanctification. And so such a person will seek the Lord. This is the kind of seeking to which Jesus refers when He says, "Ask, and it shall be given to you; seek, and you shall find; knock, and it shall be opened to you" (Matt. 7:7).

It was in this way that I came to faith in Christ. The lifestyle of many in the army disturbed me. I began to go to chapel services. And then under the ministry of an army chaplain, I came to faith in Christ. In retrospect, although I did not know it, my conversion came about in the midst of my seeking the Lord. As I look at my children, I think the same thing can be said. From the time they were very young, my wife and I taught them the Word of God. We also prayed for the sovereign work of the Spirit. And in the midst of this "seeking" God was gracious. A young man in a congregation I served confesses that it was through this process of seeking that he came to Christ, although he did not know it at the time. Examples could be multiplied.

Putting this methodology to work requires us to be bolder in our instructing people in the doctrines of sovereign grace. It requires us to be bolder in telling people of their need to study the Bible and attend a church where the Bible is faithfully taught. And at the same time it requires that we persistently call men and women, young people and children, to, "Seek the Lord while He may be found" (Isa. 55:6).

For example, I was recently asked to lead a small Bible study one evening at Kansas State University. A young lady in attendance had many questions. She seemed to be searching. One of her questions concerned the meaning of the new birth. After some explanation, this young lady needed to be encouraged to attend church, listen to the preaching, read the Bible, and to "Seek the Lord while He may be found (Isa. 55:6).

9

SCRIPTURE'S EXAMPLE: PAUL'S CONVERSION

Now Saul, still breathing threats and murder against the disciples of the Lord, went to the high priest, and asked for letters from him to the synagogues at Damascus, so that if he found any belonging to the Way, both men and women, he might bring them bound to Jerusalem. As he was traveling, it happened that he was approaching Damascus, and suddenly a light from heaven flashed around him; and he fell to the ground and heard a voice saying to him, "Saul, Saul, why are you persecuting Me?" And he said, "Who are You, Lord?" And He said, "I am Jesus whom you are persecuting, but get up and enter the city, and it will be told you what you must do." The men who traveled with him stood speechless, hearing the voice but seeing no one. Saul got up from the ground, and though his eyes were open, he could see nothing; and leading him by the hand, they brought him into Damascus. And he was three days without sight, and neither ate nor drank.

Now there was a disciple at Damascus named Ananias; and the Lord said to him in a vision, "Ananias." And he said, "Here I am, Lord." And the Lord said to him, "Get up and go to the street called Straight, and inquire at the house of Judas for a man from Tarsus named Saul, for he is praying, and he has seen in a vision a man named

Ananias come in and lay his hands on him, so that he might regain his sight." But Ananias answered, "Lord, I have heard from many about this man, how much harm he did to Your saints at Jerusalem; and here he has authority from the chief priests to bind all who call on Your name." But the Lord said to him, "Go, for he is a chosen instrument of Mine, to bear My name before the Gentiles and kings and the sons of Israel; for I will show him how much he must suffer for My name's sake." So Ananias departed and entered the house, and after laying his hands on him said, "Brother Saul, the Lord Jesus, who appeared to you on the road by which you were coming, has sent me so that you may regain your sight and be filled with the Holy Spirit." And immediately there fell from his eyes something like scales, and he regained his sight, and he got up and was baptized; and he took food and was strengthened. ~ACTS 9: 1-19

1. INTRODUCTION

Scripture devotes more space to the conversion of the apostle Paul than any other subject outside of the passion of Christ. For this reason alone, Paul's conversion to faith in Christ merits study.

The space in Scripture given to the conversion of Paul suggests this conversion is a pattern to which we should look in both understanding the conversion experience in general and in assessing our own conversion and the conversions of others.

In this brief review, I suggest a specific time line that has implications for other portions of Scripture. In general, when we speak of Paul's conversion, we look at the Damascus road experience. He was converted on that road, we say without hesitation. I suggest actual conversion took place three days later. This conversion came about through the instrumentality of a disciple, Ananias by name, who spoke the truth in love to Paul. As we see below, two important phases of God's work in Christ took place prior to Paul's conversion itself.

2. PHASE ONE: BLINDED

> Now Saul, still breathing threats and murder against the disciples of the Lord, went to the high priest, and asked for letters from him to the synagogues at Damascus, so that if he found any belonging to the Way, both men and women, he might bring them bound to Jerusalem (Acts 9:1-2).

At this point Paul is an unbelieving murderer. As a Pharisee, he knows the Bible quite well. He says of his own life and training, "I am a Jew, born in Tarsus of Cilicia, but brought up in this city, educated under Gamaliel, strictly according to the law of our fathers, being zealous for God just as you all are today" (Acts 22:3). Paul is full of zeal for his own Jewish faith and reputation. Paul also knows many of the facts about Christ including the story of the resurrection. He rejects it all and desires to eradicate the Christian sect. He travels to Damascus under the auspices of the high priest. Again, Paul describes his own state of mind and position.

> I thought to myself that I had to do many things hostile to the name of Jesus of Nazareth. And this is just what I did in Jerusalem; not only did I lock up many of the saints in prisons, having received authority from the chief priests, but also when they were being put to death I cast my vote against them. And as I punished them often in all the synagogues, I tried to force them to blaspheme; and being furiously enraged at them, I kept pursuing them even to foreign cities (Acts 26:9-11).

At this point in his life, Paul says, "I was once alive apart from the Law" (Rom. 7:9). Paul was jealous for his religion and was alive to Judaism as few other Pharisees were. He was convinced he was doing God a favor by killing Christians. He saw no conflict between the Sixth Commandment, "You shall not murder," and his persecution of Christians. Paul was free, free to furiously torment and torture those opposed to him. Acts 9:3-8 then says,

> And it came about that as he journeyed, he was approaching

Damascus, and suddenly a light from heaven flashed around him; and he fell to the ground, and heard a voice saying to him, "Saul, Saul, why are you persecuting Me?" And he said, "Who art Thou, Lord?" And He said, "I am Jesus whom you are persecuting, but rise, and enter the city, and it shall be told you what you must do." And the men who traveled with him stood speechless, hearing the voice, but seeing no one. And Saul got up from the ground, and though his eyes were open, he could see nothing; and leading him by the hand, they brought him into Damascus.

The drama of this scene cannot be overstated. Christ reveals Himself to Paul. There is no doubt Paul hears an articulate voice, the voice of Christ. It is likely the others heard only a sound. Acts 22:9 says, "And those who were with me saw the light, to be sure, but did not understand the voice of the One who was speaking to me." Paul and his company fell to the ground. The Authorized Version adds that Paul was "trembling and astonished" (Acts 9:6). What does the voice say to Paul? "Saul, Saul, why are you persecuting Me?" (Acts 9:4).

On the ground, Paul cries out for an explanation. "Who are You, Lord?" (Acts 9:5). The answer is startling in its clarity. "I am Jesus whom you are persecuting" (Acts 9:5). It is Jesus. It is the One whom the Christians say is alive though crucified. Paul had spurned the doctrines, hated the perpetrators of them, and despised the Christ they represent. Now Paul hears the very voice of this Jesus. Is He actually alive as his followers proclaim? This question must suddenly pierce Paul's heart and soul.

The victorious Christ is riding forth. His sword is bound to His thigh. He fires gospel arrows into the hearts of the enemies of the King. Surely Paul is an enemy of King Jesus. Surely he feels the pierce of the arrow coming from the bow of Christ. Psalm 45:3-5 paints the picture for us. We see Christ. We see Paul.

> Gird Your sword on Your thigh, O Mighty One,
> *In Your* splendor and Your majesty!

And in Your majesty ride on victoriously,
For the cause of truth and meekness and righteousness;
Let Your right hand teach You awesome things.
Your arrows are sharp; the peoples fall under You;
Your arrows are in the heart of the King's enemies.

3. PHASE TWO: DARKNESS

The light of Christ now blinds Paul. He cannot see. This light, like a hundred suns, suddenly plunges Paul into utter terrible darkness. All Paul understood as truth is now brought into question and doubt. The man who was convinced he was on the path to heaven based on his own righteousness is now blind. Was he always wrong although convinced he was right? This is a frightening prospect. Paul's whole life and work is suddenly and mercilessly ripped out from under him like an oriental rug. Nothing, absolutely nothing, is left. Shaken and blind, Paul is led off to Damascus. He began the journey as a self-confident, proud, Pharisee on a mission for God. He completes his journey as a devastated humiliated blind man.

Again, Paul comments on his condition in Romans 7:9. "I was once alive apart from the Law; but when the commandment came, sin became alive and I died." Plunged into darkness, Paul must realize the light he thought he had is actually darkness. This is the very teaching of Jesus. "If then the light that is in you is darkness, how great is the darkness" (Matt. 6:23). Acts 9:9-11 accentuates the point.

> And he was three days without sight, and neither ate nor drank. Now there was a disciple at Damascus named Ananias; and the Lord said to him in a vision, "Ananias." And he said, "Here I am, Lord." And the Lord said to him, "Get up and go to the street called Straight, and inquire at the house of Judas for a man from Tarsus named Saul, for he is praying, and he has seen in a vision a man named Ananias come in and lay his hands on him, so that he might regain his sight."

What did Paul do during those three days? "And he was three

days without sight, and neither ate nor drink ... [H]e is praying." You can well imagine Paul fasting and praying. He was not celebrating his victory over the sect of the Christians and their leader. To the contrary, meeting the person he believed dead, Paul agonized. I cannot help but think he experienced the greatest of turmoil and anguish of soul. Paul thought he had it all put together. He thought he was certainly on the path to heaven. Now he realizes he is wrong. He realizes he is not on the path to heaven but that he is doomed. The road he is on leads to hell. How could he be so blind? How could he be so mistaken? For three days Paul prayed.

He must have also agonized over the Scriptures. Did he think of Psalm 45, which speaks of the coming of the Messiah and of that Messiah slaying His enemies? Did he contemplate Psalm 110:1-3, which also speaks of the Messiah?

> The Lord says to my Lord:
> "Sit at My right hand
> Until I make Your enemies a footstool for Your feet."
> The Lord will stretch forth Your strong scepter from Zion,
> *saying,*
> "Rule in the midst of Your enemies."
> Your people will volunteer freely in the day of Your power;
> In holy array, from the womb of the dawn.
> Your youth are to You as the dew.

Was Jesus the Messiah of God? Was He exercising His rule from heaven? Was this Jesus now directing Paul with the strong scepter from the heavenly Zion? For three days Paul was on his face before God in prayer wrestling with Scripture.

For three days Paul sought the face of God concerning all his past life and this encounter with the living Christ. For three days Paul agonized over his sins. Christ lived. Paul was a murderer, a violator of God's commandments. Paul thought, beyond doubt, he was righteous. The truth came crashing home. He was not righteous. He was a sinner. He was a dead man. "I was once alive apart from the Law; but when the commandment carne, sin became alive and I died" (Rom. 7:9). Sin arose from Paul's heart like a dead and evil corps arising from the grave. With the gravestone of Paul's heart removed, Paul saw within the darkness of hell itself.

The commandment that really came home to Paul was the Tenth Commandment. "I would not have come to know sin except through the Law; for I would not have known about coveting if the Law had not said, 'You shall not covet'" (Rom. 7:7). The word translated "covet" is the word "lust." You shall not lust! Paul was full of lust for his own program. He coveted nothing less than the eradication of Christianity. He would do everything in his power to achieve that goal. Now he sees his sin. "When the commandment came" in the power of the Holy Spirit, convicting Paul of sin and righteousness and judgment, Paul was devastated. He cries, "I was once alive apart from the Law; but when the commandment came, sin became alive and I died" (Rom. 7:9).

And so, the three days of blindness were three days of spiritual darkness. These were three days in which Paul had to reevaluate his life in total. If Jesus was alive, He was the Christ of God and Paul was the chief of sinners.

4. PHASE THREE: CONVERSION
Enter Ananias.

> Now there was a disciple at Damascus named Ananias; and the Lord said to him in a vision, "Ananias." And he said, "Here I am, Lord." And the Lord said to him, "Get up and go to the street called Straight, and inquire at the house of Judas for a man from Tarsus named Saul, for he is praying, and he has seen in a vision a man named Ananias come in and lay his hands on him, so that he might regain his sight." But Ananias answered, "Lord, I have heard from many about this man, how much harm he did to Your saints at Jerusalem; and here he has authority from the chief priests to bind all who call on Your

name." But the Lord said to him, "Go, for he is a chosen instrument of Mine, to bear My name before the Gentiles and kings and the sons of Israel; for I will show him how much he must suffer for My name's sake." So Ananias departed and entered the house, and after laying his hands on him said, "Brother Saul, the Lord Jesus, who appeared to you on the road by which you were corning, has sent me so that you may regain your sight and be filled with the Holy Spirit." And immediately there fell from his eyes something like scales, and he regained his sight, and he got up and was baptized; and he took food and was strengthened (Acts 9:10-19).

Initially, Ananias did not want to visit Paul. "Lord, I have heard from many about this man, how much harm he did to Your saints at Jerusalem; and here he has authority from the chief priests to bind all who call on Your name" (Acts 9:13-14). Go, Ananias. Why? The answer is crystal clear, "He is a chosen instrument of Mine" (Acts 9:15). "Here God stops [Ananias'] mouth immediately, by asserting His sovereignty, and preaching to him the doctrine of election."[1] Although Ananias was one of the disciples Paul sought to kill, and Ananias knew this was the case, he went to Paul at God's direction.

Ananias reiterated the commission Christ had for Paul. "And he said, 'The God of our fathers has appointed you to know His will and to see the Righteous One and to hear an utterance from His mouth. For you will be a witness for Him to all men of what you have seen and heard'" (Acts 22:14-15).

Then he made this astounding statement, "And now why do you delay? Arise, and be baptized, and wash away your sins, calling on His name" (Acts 22:16). Here was the need of the moment. The very Christ whom Paul had despised was the One upon whom he had to call to receive forgiveness and imputed righteousness. "Why do you delay, Paul?" We hear the echo of those wonderful words later

---

1. George Whitefield, "Saul's Conversion," *George Whitefield's Sermons* (New Ipswitch, NH: Pietan Publications, 1991), 1:179.

CHAPTER 9: SCRIPTURE'S EXAMPLE: PAUL'S CONVERSION 193

penned by the apostle in Romans 10:13, "Whoever will call upon the Name of the Lord will be saved." Paul knew those words spoken by the prophet Joel so well. Now he knew Jesus Christ was that Lord. He realized "that if you confess with your mouth Jesus as Lord and believe in your heart God raised Him from the dead, you shall be saved" (Rom. 10:9).

Paul called on the Lord Jesus. Paul was also baptized. He became a vital part of the body of Christ, the very body he determined to eradicate. This was his conversion. It came after Christ smote him, after three days of turmoil and darkness, after hearing wonderful words from Ananias, "Brother Saul, receive your sight" (Acts 22:13). At that moment everything made sense. Why do you delay, Paul? He waited no longer. He called upon Christ.

5. PHASE TWO: REVISITED

In the three days of darkness preceding his conversion, Paul was under deep conviction by the Spirit. George Whitefield gives this description of Paul's trial.

> [W]ho can tell what horrors of conscience, what convulsions of soul, what deep and pungent convictions of sin he underwent during these three long days? It was this that took away his appetite, (for who can eat or drink when under a sense of the wrath of God for sin?) and, being to be greatly employed hereafter, he must be greatly humbled now; therefore the Lord leaves him three days groaning under the spirit of bondage, and buffeted, no doubt, with fiery darts of the devil, that, being tempted like unto his brethren, he might be able hereafter, to succor those that were tempted. Had Saul applied to any of the blind guides of the Jewish church under these circumstances; they would have said he was mad, or going beside himself; as many carnal teachers and blind Pharisees now deal with, and so more and more, distress poor souls laboring under awakening convictions of their damnable state ... [By comparison] it

seems, that before these three days, Saul never prayed in his life: and why? Because before these three days, he never felt himself a condemned creature; he was alive in his own opinion, because without a knowledge of the spiritual meaning of the law; he felt not a want of, and therefore, before now, cried not after Jesus, and consequently, though he might have said, or made a prayer, as many Pharisees do in these days, he never uttered a prayer; but now behold! He prayed indeed; and this was urged as one reason he was converted.[2]

Paul appears to delineate his personal struggle, his bondage, and his final cry for deliverance in Romans 7:14-25. This is how George Whitefield sees it.[3] Read these verses with his interpretation in view. Then take a look at the diagram in Appendix B. Romans 7:14-25 completes a vital part of the picture of Paul's conversion. It fills in the gap of Paul's dark days. It explains the dark days of many people under conviction in this day. It leads us properly to the hope given to us by God in Jesus Christ. "Therefore there is now no condemnation for those who are in Christ Jesus. For the law of the Spirit of life in Christ Jesus has set you free from the law of sin and of death" (Rom. 8:1-2). To really appreciate these verses, consider the condemnation Paul undergoes in Romans 7:14-25.

> For we know that the Law is spiritual, but I am of flesh, sold into bondage to sin. For what I am doing, I do not understand; for I am not practicing what I would like to do, but I am doing the very thing I hate. But if I do the very thing I do not want to do I agree with the Law, confessing that the Law is good. So

---

2. Ibid., 176-178.
3. Today, Whitefield's view on Romans 7 is the minority report. Douglas Moo, *The Epistle to the Romans*, has a helpful review of the various positions on Romans 7:14-25 (443-451). As he indicates, "Most of the early church fathers thought that these verses describe an unregenerate person" (443). Moo also takes this position. "But when all the data have been weighed, I think that the balance tilts toward the interpretation of the egō in these verses as unregenerate" (449). Whitefield's position, and the one to which I subscribe in this chapter, is what Moo accurately indicates "is only 'halfway' to true Christian experience—under conviction but not yet 'reborn'" (444). After setting forth the data as he see it, John Murray, *The Epistle to the Romans*, says, "For these reasons we are compelled to conclude that 7:14-25 is the delineation of Paul's experience in the state of grace" (1:259).

now, no longer am I the one doing it, but sin which dwells in me. For I know that nothing good dwells in me, that is, in my flesh; for the willing is present in me, but the doing of the good is not. For the good that I want, I do not do, but I practice the very evil that I do not want. But if I am doing the very thing I do not want, I am no longer the one doing it, but sin which dwells in me. I find then the principle that evil is present in me, the one who wants to do good. For I joyfully concur with the law of God in the inner man, but I see a different law in the members of my body, waging war against the law of my mind and making me a prisoner of the law of sin which is in my members. Wretched man that I am! Who will set me free from the body of this death? Thanks be to God through Jesus Christ our Lord! So then, on the one hand I myself with my mind am serving the law of God, but on the other, with my flesh the law of sin.

Condemned by sin and recognizing his bondage, Paul cries out to God for mercy. This was his conversion. John Newton puts it similarly in his famous hymn, "'Twas grace that taught my heart to fear, And grace my fears relieved."

10

THE CONVICTION OF SIN AND
THE WORD OF GOD

*Now when they heard this, they were pierced to the heart,
and said to Peter and the rest of the apostles, "Brethren,
what shall we do?"* ~ACTS 2:37

THE FIRST STEP OF GOD in drawing men and women to Himself is the work of convicting them of their sin and showing them their need of Christ. Jesus tells us this is the first work of the Holy Spirit. "And He, when He comes, will convict the world concerning sin and righteousness and judgment" (John 16:8). *The Theological Dictionary of the New Testament* gives this definition of the Greek work translated "convict."

> It means "to show someone his sin and summon him to repentance." This may be a private matter as between two people, as in Mt. 18: 15; Eph. 5:11. But it may also be a congregational affair under the leader, as in the Pastorals: 1 Tm. 5:20; 2 Tm. 4:2; 1 Tt. 1:9, 13; 2:15. It is also the work of the Holy Spirit in the world (Jn. 16:8), the exalted Christ in the community (Rev. 3: 19), and of the Lord in the judgment at the *parousia* (Jd. 15).[1]

Conviction is a legal term. To convict means to expose, prove guilty, and reprove. Jesus uses the same word in Matthew 18:15. "And if your brother sins, go and reprove him in private; if he listens to you, you have won your brother." As in a courtroom, the proof is

---

[1]. Gerhard Kittel, ed., *Theological Dictionary of the New Testament*, trans. and ed., Geoffrey W. Bromiley (Grand Rapids: Eerdmans, 1966), 2:474.

not always accepted. The jury of reason and conscience may reject the exposure of sin.

> For when Gentiles who do not have the Law do instinctively the things of the Law, these, not having the Law, are a law to themselves, in that they show the work of the Law written in their hearts, their conscience bearing witness and their thoughts alternately accusing or else defending them (Rom. 2:14-15).

When reason and conscience reject the proof and reproof of conviction, further hostility is inevitable.

The Holy Spirit uses two primary means to produce conviction. They are God's spoken Word and God's providential dealings with men and women. It is the duty of Christians to expose the error and sin of unbelievers.

> Therefore do not be partakers with them; for you were formerly darkness, but now you are light in the Lord; walk as children of light (for the fruit of the light consists in all goodness and righteousness and truth), trying to learn what is pleasing to the Lord. And do not participate in the unfruitful deeds of darkness, but *instead even expose them*; for it is disgraceful even to speak of the things which are done by them in secret. But all things become visible when they are exposed by the light, for everything that becomes visible is light (Eph. 5:7-13, italics added).

To expose the deeds of darkness committed by men and women, young people and children, means to reprove and convict them regarding these sins. Believers ought to speak up concerning the sin of those around them to expose that sin for what it is.

What is sin? Sin is any want of conformity unto or transgression of the Law of God (WSC, Q&A 14). To expose sin and convict of sin, we must preach the moral law of God summarized in the Ten Commandments. "Now we know that whatever the Law says, it speaks to those who are under the Law, that every mouth may be closed, and all the world may become accountable to God; because by the works of the Law no flesh will be justified in His sight; for through the Law comes the knowledge of sin" (Rom. 3:19-20). When individuals have a true and accurate knowledge of their sin in their heads, the Holy Spirit may convict them in their hearts and consciences of these violations of God's law. They may then truly feel their guilt before God.

There are many outstanding examples of such conviction of sin. Peter described to the Jewish people how they falsely condemned and crucified the Son of God. "When they heard this they were pierced to the heart, and said to Peter and the rest of the apostles, 'Brethren, what shall we do?'" (Acts 2:37). Matthew Henry describes the situation this way.

> We are now to see another blessed fruit of the pouring out of the Spirit in its influence upon the hearers of the gospel. From the first delivery of that divine message, it appeared that there was a divine power going along with it, and it was mighty, through God, to do wonders: thousands were immediately brought by it to the obedience of faith; it was the rod of God's strength sent out of Zion, Ps. 110:2, 3. We have here the firstfruits of that vast harvest of souls which by it were gathered in to Jesus Christ. Come and see, in these verses, the exalted Redeemer riding forth, in these chariots of salvation, conquering and to conquer, Rev. 6:2.
>
> In these verses we find the word of God the means of beginning and carrying on a good work of grace in the hearts of many, the Spirit of the Lord working by it. Let us see the method of it.
>
> I. They were startled, and convinced, and put upon a serious enquiry, v. 37. When they heard, or having heard, having patiently heard Peter out, and not given him the interruption they had been used to give to Christ in his discourses (this was one good point gained, that they were become attentive to the word), they were pricked to the heart, or in the heart, and, un-

der a deep concern and perplexity, applied themselves to the preachers with this question, What shall we do? It was very strange that such impressions should be made upon such hard hearts all of a sudden. They were Jews, bred up in the opinion of the sufficiency of their religion to save them, had lately seen this Jesus crucified in weakness and disgrace, and were told by their rulers that he was a deceiver. Peter had charged them with having a hand, a wicked hand, in his death, which was likely to have exasperated them against him; yet, when they heard this plain scriptural sermon, they were much affected with it.

1. It put them in pain: They were pricked in their hearts. We read of those that were cut to the heart with indignation at the preacher (ch. 7:54), but these were pricked to the heart with indignation at themselves for having been accessory to the death of Christ. Peter, charging it upon them, awakened their consciences, touched them to the quick, and the reflection they now made upon it was as a sword in their bones, it pierced them as they had pierced Christ. Note, Sinners, when their eyes are opened, cannot but be pricked to the heart for sin, cannot but experience an inward uneasiness; this is having the heart rent (Joel 2:13), a broken and contrite heart, Ps. 51:17. Those that are truly sorry for their sins, and ashamed of them, and afraid of the consequences of them, are pricked to the heart. A prick in the heart is mortal, and under those commotions (says Paul) I died, Rom. 7:9. "All my good opinion of myself and confidence in myself failed me."[2]

As Matthew Henry says, Paul describes his personal experience with conviction in Romans 7:9. "I was once alive apart from the Law; but when the commandment came, sin became alive and I died." Paul

---

2. Matthew Henry, *Matthew Henry's Commentary on the Whole Bible*, (Westwood, NJ: Revell, n.d.), 6:25-26.

was self-satisfied and self-righteous as a Pharisee. He saw himself as headed for eternal life and heaven because of his own righteousness. "He is speaking of the unperturbed, self-complacent, self-righteous life which he once lived before the turbulent motions and convictions of sin ... overtook him."[3] Paul then made this bold confession:

> If anyone else has a mind to put confidence in the flesh, I far more: circumcised the eighth day, of the nation of Israel, of the tribe of Benjamin, a Hebrew of Hebrews; as to the Law, a Pharisee; as to zeal, a persecutor of the church; as to the righteousness which is in the Law, found blameless (Phil. 4:3-6).

When the commandments of God came home to him with the power of the Holy Spirit convicting him of sin, Paul saw he was a dead man. He saw the law condemned him. Both of these cases, the Jews on the Day of Pentecost and Paul apprehended by Christ on the Damascus road, had a positive issue. They ended in conversion. Acts 24:24-25 presents the opposite case, conviction of sin without conversion.

> But some days later Felix arrived with Drusilla, his wife who was a Jewess, and sent for Paul and heard him speak about faith in Christ Jesus. But as he was discussing righteousness, self-control and the judgment to come, Felix became frightened and said, "Go away for the present, and when I find time I will summon you."

Felix was a notorious philanderer. Bold, with the empowering of the Holy Spirit, Paul speaks to governor Felix about his sin, a serious lack of self-control. Paul knows the priority of the Spirit to "convict the world concerning sin and righteousness and judgment" (John 16:8). Paul speaks of the righteousness of God and of Christ and of the judgment we face for our failure to meet the standard of God's righteousness. Felix becomes frightened. Fear is a manifestation of the presence of conviction. Hearers become frightened because they see they are

---

3. Murray, *The Epistle to the Romans*, 1:251.

lost and stand condemned before God. In this case, Felix sends Paul away. Again, Matthew Henry aptly describes the circumstances.

We have here the result of Paul's trial before Felix, and what was the consequence of it ...

III. He had frequent conversation with him afterwards in private, once particularly, not long after his public trial, v. 24, 25. Observe,

1. With what design *Felix sent for Paul*. He had a mind to have some talk with him *concerning the faith in Christ* ... and this only to satisfy his curiosity, or rather the curiosity of *his wife Drusilla, who was a Jewess*, daughter of Herod Agrippa, that was eaten of worms ... [S]he was another man's wife when Felix took her to be his wife, and she lived with him in whoredom and was noted for an impudent woman ...

2. What the account was which Paul gave him of the Christian religion; by the idea he had of it, he expected to be amused with a mystical divinity, but, as Paul represents it to him, he is alarmed with a practical divinity. Paul, being asked *concerning the faith in Christ, reasoned* (for Paul was always a rational preacher) *concerning righteousness, temperance, and judgment to come*. It is probable that he mentioned the peculiar doctrines of Christianity concerning the death and resurrection of the Lord Jesus, and his being the *Mediator between God and man*; but he hastened to his application, in which he designed to come home to the consciences of his hearers.

(1.) He discoursed with clearness and warmth of righteousness, temperance, and judgment to come; and here he showed, [1.] That the faith in Christ is designed to enforce upon the children of men the great laws of justice and temperance. The grace of God teacheth us to live soberly and righteously, Tit. 2:12. Justice and temperance were celebrated virtues among the heathen moralists; if the doctrine Paul preaches, which Felix has heard of as proclaiming liberty, will but free him from an obligation to these, he will readily embrace it: "No," says Paul, "it is so far from doing so that it strengthens the obligations of those sacred laws; it binds all under the highest penalties to be honest in all their dealings, and to render to all their due; to deny themselves, and to keep under the body, and bring it into subjection." The world and the flesh being in our baptism renounced, all our pursuits of the world and all our gratifications of the desires of the body are to be under the regulations of religion. Paul reasoned of righteousness and temperance, to convince Felix of his unrighteousness and intemperance, of which he had been notoriously guilty, that, seeing the odiousness of them, and his obnoxiousness to the wrath of God for them (Eph. 5:6), he might enquire concerning the faith of Christ, with a resolution to embrace it. [2.] That by the doctrine of Christ is discovered to us the judgment to come, by the sentence of which the everlasting state of all the children of men will be finally and irreversibly determined. Men have their day now, Felix hath his; but God's day is coming, when everyone shall give account of himself to God, the Judge of all. Paul reasoned concerning this; that is, he showed what reason we have to believe that there is a judgment to come, and what reason we have, in consideration thereof, to be religious ...

3. What impressions Paul's discourse made upon this great but wicked man: Felix *trembled*, ἔμφοβος γενόμενος—*being put into a fright*, or made a *terror to himself, a magor-missabib*, as Pashur, Jer. 20:3, 4.[4] Paul never trembled before him, but he

---

4. Jeremiah 20:1-4, When Pashhur the priest, the son of Immer, who was chief officer in the house of the Lord, heard Jeremiah prophesying these things, Pashhur had Jeremiah the prophet beaten and put him in the stocks that were at the upper Benjamin Gate, which was by the house of the Lord. On the next day, when Pashhur released Jeremiah from the stocks, Jeremiah said to him, "Pashhur is not the name the Lord has called you, but rather Magor-missabib. For thus says the Lord, 'Behold, I am going to make you a terror to yourself and to all your friends; and while your eyes look on, they will fall by the sword of their enemies. So I will give over all Judah to the hand of the king of Babylon, and he will carry them away as exiles to Babylon and will slay them with the sword.'"

was made to tremble before Paul. "If this be so, as Paul says, what will become of me in another world? If the unrighteous and intemperate will be condemned in the judgment to come, I am undone, for ever undone, unless I lead a new course of life." We do not find that Drusilla trembled, though she was equally guilty, for she was a Jewess, and depended upon the ceremonial law, which she adhered to the observance of, to justify her; but Felix for the present could fasten upon nothing to pacify his conscience, and therefore trembled. See here, (1.) The power of the word of God, when it comes with commission; it is searching, it is startling, it can strike a terror into the heart of the most proud and daring sinner, by *setting his sins in order before him*, and showing him *the terrors of the Lord*. (2.) The workings of natural conscience; when it is startled and awakened, it fills the soul with horror and amazement at its own deformity and danger. Those that are themselves *the terror of the mighty in the land of the living* have hereby been made a terror to themselves. A prospect of the judgment to come is enough to make the stoutest heart to tremble, as when it comes indeed it will make *the mighty men and the chief captains* to call in vain *to rocks and mountains to shelter them*.

4. How Felix struggled to get clear of these impressions, and to shake off the terror of his convictions; he did by them as he did by Paul's prosecutors (v. 25), he deferred them; he said, Go thy way for this time, when I have a convenient season I will call for thee. (1.) He trembled and that was all. Paul's trembling (ch. 9:6), and the jailer's (ch. 16:29), ended in their conversion, but this of Felix did not. Many are startled by the word of God who are not effectually changed by it. Many are in fear of the consequences of sin, and yet continue in love and league with sin. (2.) He did not fight against his convictions, nor fly in the face of the word or of the preacher of it, to be revenged on them for making his conscience fly in his face; he did not say to

Paul, as Amaziah to the prophet, Forbear, why shouldst thou be smitten? He did not threaten him with a closer confinement, or with death, for touching him (as John Baptist did Herod) in the sore place. But, (3.) He artfully shifted off his convictions by putting off the prosecution of them to another time. He has nothing to object against what Paul has said; it is weighty and worth considering. But, like a sorry debtor, he begs a day; Paul has spent himself, and has tired him and his lady, and therefore, "*Go thy way for this time*—break off here, business calls me away; but *when I have a convenient season*, and have nothing else to do, *I will call for thee*, and hear what thou hast further to say." Note, [1.] Many lose all the benefit of their convictions for want of striking while the iron is hot. If Felix, now that he trembled, had but asked, as Paul and the jailer did when they trembled, What shall I do? He might have been brought to the faith of Christ, and have been a *Felix* indeed, *happy* forever; but, by dropping his convictions now, he lost them forever, and himself with them. [2.] In the affairs of our souls, delays are dangerous; nothing is of more fatal consequence than men's putting off their conversion from time to time. They will repent, and turn to God, but not yet; the matter is adjourned to some more convenient season, when such a business or affair is compassed, when they are so much older; and then convictions cool and wear off, good purposes prove to no purpose, and they are more hardened than ever in their evil way. Felix put off this matter to a more convenient season, but we do not find that this more convenient season ever came; for the devil cozens us of all our time by cozening us of the present time. The present season is, without doubt, the most convenient season. *Behold, now is the accepted time. Today if you will hear his voice.* [5]

This is where evangelism begins. It starts with the work of the

---

5. Henry, *Commentary on the Whole Bible*, 6:313-316.

Holy Spirit in conviction of sin. God brought similar conviction, shame, and fear into the lives of Adam and Eve. After the fall, "the Lord God called to the man, and said to him, 'Where are you?'" (Gen. 3:9). Adam responded, "I heard the sound of You in the garden, and I was afraid because I was naked; so I hid myself" (Gen. 3:10). Fear gripped our first parents. Shame gripped our first parents. God said, "Who told you that you were naked?"(Gen. 3:11). There was no shame prior to the fall. "The man and his wife were both naked and were not ashamed" (Gen. 2:25). Because Matthew Henry lays before us a typical Puritan view regarding sin and conviction of sin, I again quote Henry at length.

> We have here the arraignment of these deserters before the righteous Judge of heaven and earth, who, though he is not tied to observe formalities, yet proceeds against them with all possible fairness, that he may be justified when he speaks. Observe here,
>
> I. The startling question with which God pursued Adam and arrested him: *Where art thou?* ... It is rather an upbraiding question, in order to his conviction and humiliation: *Where art thou?* Not, In what place? But, In what condition? "Is this all thou hast gotten by eating forbidden fruit? Thou that wouldest vie with me, dost thou now fly from me?" Note, 1. Those who by sin have gone astray from God should seriously consider where they are; they are afar off from all good, in the midst of their enemies, in bondage to Satan, and in the high road to utter ruin. This enquiry after Adam may be looked upon as a gracious pursuit, in kindness to him, and in order to his recovery. If God had not called to him, to reclaim him, his condition would have been as desperate as that of fallen angels; this lost sheep would have wandered endlessly, if the good Shepherd had not sought after him, to bring him back, and, in order to that, reminded him where he was, where he should not be, and where he could not be either happy or easy. Note, 2. If sinners

will but consider where they are, they will not rest till they return to God.

II. The trembling answer which Adam gave to this question: *I heard thy voice in the garden, and I was afraid*, v. 10. He does not own his guilt, and yet in effect confesses it by owning his shame and fear; but it is the common fault and folly of those that have done an ill thing, when they are questioned about it, to acknowledge no more than what is so manifest that they cannot deny it. Adam was afraid, because he was naked; not only unarmed, and therefore afraid to contend with God, but unclothed, and therefore afraid so much as to appear before him. We have reason to be afraid of approaching to God if we be not clothed and fenced with the righteousness of Christ, for nothing but this will be armour of proof and cover the shame of our nakedness. Let us therefore put on the Lord Jesus Christ, and then draw near with humble boldness ...

Observe, I. How their confession was extorted from them. God put it to the man: *Who told thee that thou wast naked?* v. 11. "How camest thou to be sensible of thy nakedness as thy shame?" *Hast thou eaten of the forbidden tree?* Note, Though God knows all our sins, yet he will know them from us, and requires from us an ingenuous confession of them; not that he may be informed, but that we may be humbled. In this examination, God reminds him of the command he had given him: "I commanded thee not to eat of it, I thy Maker, I thy Master, I thy benefactor; I commanded thee to the contrary." Sin appears most plain and most sinful in the glass of the commandment, therefore God here sets it before Adam; and in it we should see our faces ...[6]

Matthew Henry continues the theme of fear and shame in his comments upon Genesis 3:22. The text reads, "Then the Lord God

---

6. Ibid., 1:27-28.

said, 'Behold, the man has become like one of Us, knowing good and evil; and now, he might stretch out his hand, and take also from the tree of life, and eat, and live forever.'" Henry observes,

> Sentence being passed upon the offenders, we have here execution, in part, done upon them immediately. Observe here,
>
> I. How they were justly disgraced and shamed before God and the holy angels, by the ironical upbraiding of them with the issue of their enterprise: "*Behold, the man has become as one of us, to know good and evil!* A goodly god he makes! Does he not? See what he has got, what preferments, what advantages, by eating forbidden fruit!" This was said to awaken and humble them, and to bring them to a sense of their sin and folly, and to repentance for it, that, seeing themselves thus wretchedly deceived by following the devil's counsel, they might henceforth pursue the happiness God should offer in the way he should prescribe. God thus *fills their faces with shame, that they may seek his name*, Ps. 83:16. He puts them to this confusion, in order to their conversion. True penitents will thus upbraid themselves: "What fruit have I now by sin? Rom. 6:21. Have I gained what I foolishly promised myself in a sinful way? No, no, it never proved what it pretended to, but the contrary."[7]

We will look at the subject of conviction and providence in Chapter 11 along with the fact that conviction engenders a proper fear of God.

---

7. Ibid., 1:34-35.

11

THE CONVICTION OF SIN: PROVIDENCE AND THE FEAR OF GOD

Pursue them with Your tempest and terrify them with Your storm. Fill their faces with dishonor, That they may seek Your name, O Lord. ~Ps. 83:15-16

IN STUDYING "CONVICTION OF SIN AND THE WORD OF GOD" we looked at Adam and Eve in the Garden of Eden. God convicted Adam and Eve of their sin. I quoted Matthew Henry's explanation.

> God thus *fills their faces with shame, that they may seek his name,* Ps. 83:16. He puts them to this confusion, in order to their conversion. True penitents will thus upbraid themselves: "What fruit have I now by sin? Rom. 6:21. Have I gained what I foolishly promised myself in a sinful way? No, no, it never proved what it pretended to, but the contrary."[1]

Note Matthew Henry's use of Psalm 83. In addition to direct proclamation of His Word, Providence also works to bring men and women under conviction. David's prayer in Psalm 83:13-18 is astounding. He prays God will bring the forces of the created order to bear against the enemies of Israel. He prays the enemies of Israel will therefore sense deep shame, humiliation and terror before God.

O my God, make them like the whirling dust;
Like chaff before the wind.

---

1. Ibid.

> Like fire that burns the forest,
> And like a flame that sets the mountains on fire,
> So pursue them with Thy tempest,
> And terrify them with Thy storm.
> Fill their faces with dishonor,
> That they may seek Thy name, O LORD.
> Let them be ashamed and dismayed forever;
> And let them be humiliated and perish,
> That they may know that Thou alone, whose name is the LORD,
> Are the Most High over all the earth.

Early in the history of Israel, God promised His people, "I will send My terror ahead of you, and throw into confusion all the people among whom you come, and I will make all your enemies turn their backs to you" (Exod. 27:27). It would therefore seem perfectly appropriate to pray that God would engender fear in the hearts of unbelieving men and women who stand before His face and when they come in contact with His church. How would God answer such a prayer? He might act directly, through Providence, upon men and women in such situations that they have no recourse but to call out to Him.

God displays the might of His judgmental power in earthquakes, floods, tornadoes and hurricanes. We are fond of saying, "It rained." Who or what is this "it"? The Biblical perspective is that God controls the rain. Men and women ought to "listen" to these acts of God. Jonah 1:4-5 presents a good example. "The Lord hurled a great wind on the sea and there was a great storm on the sea so that the ship was about to break up. Then the sailors became afraid and every man cried to his god, and they threw the cargo which was in the ship into the sea to lighten it for them."

> The ship's crew were alarmed by this mighty tempest, but Jonah only, the person concerned, was unconcerned, v. 5. The mariners were affected with their danger, though it was not

with them that God has this controversy. 1. They were afraid; though, their business leading them to be very much conversant with dangers of this kind, they used to make light of them, yet now the oldest and stoutest of them began to tremble, being apprehensive that there was something more than ordinary in this tempest, so suddenly did it rise, so strongly did it rage. Note, God can strike a terror upon the most daring, and make even great men and chief captains call for shelter from rocks and mountains. 2. They cried every man unto his god; this was the effect of their fear. Many will not be brought to prayer till they are frightened to it; he that would learn to pray, let him go to sea. Lord, in trouble they have visited thee. Every man of them prayed; they were not some praying and others reviling, but every man engaged; as the danger was general, so was the address to heaven; there was not one praying for them all, but every one for himself. They cried every man to his god, the god of his country or city, or his own tutelar deity; it is a testimony against atheism that every man had a god, and had the belief of a God; but it is an instance of the folly of paganism that they had gods many, every man the god he had a fancy for, whereas there can be but one God, there needs to be no more. But, though they had lost that dictate of the light of nature that there is but one God, they still were governed by that direction of the law of nature that God is to be prayed to (*Should not a people seek unto their God?* Isa. 8:19), and that he is especially to be prayed to when we are in distress and danger. Call upon me in the time of trouble. Is any afflicted? Is any frightened? Let him pray ... [2]

In a similar vein, Hugh Martin says the mariners were overcome with fear by the Providence of God.

Sailors are not speedily alarmed. They are proverbially brave and bold. But when even the crew themselves on this occasion,

---

2. Henry, *Commentary on the Whole Bible*, 4:1280-1281.

were alarmed, we gather that the tempest was unusually terrific. God, indeed, employed no miracle raising this storm; but having a special purpose to serve by it, He stamped upon it a special terror, that His power and will might be the more readily recognized as engaged in it. When we provoke a controversy with God, and constrain Him to send after us a prosecutor or pursuer, He can easily confer on His agent some mark of majesty or terror,—some insignia of special power, some resistless tone or token, whereby we may be baffled in attempting to hide from ourselves the source of his commission ...

The mariners "cried every man unto his god." Their heathenism here displayed itself in their worship of many gods, every man praying to his own god: while the amount of religion natural to the human mind comes to light in these poor heathen men. For there is in the bosom of every man by nature the conviction that there is a God; that there are at least superior beings, if not One Supreme. There is wrought into the inmost frame of our minds a conviction that we are dependent creatures; not our own masters, not gods unto ourselves. The consciousness of sin—and sin is just an attempt to be gods unto ourselves is itself sufficient to testify to us of a God. Were our effort to be independent a calm, simple, strengthening thing, the proof might fail. But no man can consider his own feelings without being convinced that the attempt to be his own lord and master, to do just as he pleases, to be in subjection to no lord over his inmost will, to walk in the light of his own eyes—the attempt, in short, to be his own ruler or his own god, is really a revolt against the deepest convictions in his soul; that it carries with it anything but rest, calmness, strength, and satisfaction; that, on the contrary, it has in it all the marks of a struggle, of an unsuccessful struggle; that he remains still restless, unsatisfied, struggling—struggling still in vain. The stronger his will is, the more is he doomed to feel that he cannot assert its supremacy;

and circumstances outwardly conspire to aid the inward conviction. There is a power controlling all things, and not to be controlled by us. The will of man must break or bend; it cannot possibly reign supreme. The very restlessness—the very impatience of restraint or contradiction—which men so often exhibit against the allotments of Providence, is a confession that they feel themselves in the grasp of a power mightier than their own. Whether we bend in submission, meek and patient, or resist and defy, we are alike owning a superior power. We are constituted so as that we cannot help doing so. A knowledge, a feeling, an intuitive belief in a God, is one of the deepest principles created in our nature, and never extinguished.

Nor is it merely a superior power that we are by nature so profoundly convinced of, but a living and personal Being; and this profound conviction manifests itself in calling upon Him, as one who can exercise His power voluntarily, or refrain from exercising it. This knowledge of a God may be unattended to by multitudes, whether of heathens or of nominal Christians. For the most part, it lies buried under worldly security. Sensual indulgence seems to drive it farther and farther back into a region of concealment and slumber. The prosecution of worldly interests as the chief good tends more and more to impair its testimony. But it is never dislodged. Men may "not like to retain God in their knowledge"; but the knowledge of a God abides within them still. Seasons of danger and terror call it forth to view; and the sudden prayer of alarm is the proof that even the most profane and profligate carry in their bosom the evidence of their righteous condemnation; when, not liking to retain God in their knowledge, they are "given over to a reprobate mind" for being unfaithful to the knowledge conferred upon them from the first (Rom. 1:28). [3]

---

3. Hugh Martin, *A Commentary on Jonah* (Carlisle, PA: Banner of Truth, 1978), 83-85.

War is also a providential work of God that engenders fear. Professor John Murray sets out several points regarding war, particularly World War II. Here are three of them.

> 1. *This war is an evil consequent upon sin.* It is one of the logical issues of sin. "From whence come wars and fightings among you? Come they not hence, even of your lusts that war in your members?" (Jas. 4:1) ...
>
> 2. *This war is divine retribution for sin.* We may think lightly of sin, we may be indifferent to it. But not so God. Sin is the contradiction of his glory, the contradiction of that law that is the reflex of his holy nature ...
>
> 3. *This war is the divine call to repentance.* "When thy judgments are in the earth, the inhabitants of the earth will learn righteousness" (Isa. 26:9) ...
>
> *Our minds are very liable in these times to be blinded by a certain kind of panic.*[4] We quite properly desire and set our minds upon the preservation of our national liberties and integrity and, in order to that end, upon the defeat of those enemies that are arrayed against us. But in preoccupation with that end we are too prone to that panic that blinds our vision of the kingdom of God and his righteousness. I would not set up a false antithesis. But we should remember that no temporal catastrophe can be as bad as the strengthening of the bands of godlessness. I am not saying that it is necessary for us to undergo ultimate defeat in order to learn righteousness. May God forbid that this should be the case. But it would be better for us to suffer the humiliation of defeat, if thereby we should learn righteousness, than to be crowned with sweeping military victory if thereby we are to be confirmed in the ways of ungodliness. "Seek ye first the kingdom of God, and his righteousness" (Matt. 6:33). "The kingdom of God is not meat and drink; but righteousness, and

---

4. Italics added.

peace, and joy in the Holy Ghost" (Rom. 14:17). Let us ever remember the sovereign prerogatives of God's kingdom and even in the pursuance of a life-and-death military conflict let us learn to think even then in terms of the kingdom of him who is the "King eternal, immortal, invisible, the only God" (1 Tim. 1:17). "If my people, which are called by my name, shall humble themselves, and pray, and seek my face, and turn from their wicked ways; then will I hear from heaven, and will forgive their sin, and will heal their land" (2 Chron. 7:14). [5]

We notice in each of the cases or circumstances cited, there is a certain attendant fear. I said above, fear is a characteristic of conviction. Fear fell upon Adam. "I heard the sound of You in the garden, and I was afraid because I was naked; so I hid myself'" (Gen. 3:10). "Felix became frightened" (Acts 24:25). The Philippian jailer was terrified by the earthquake and open jail. "When the jailer awoke and saw the prison doors opened, he drew his sword and was about to kill himself, supposing that the prisoners had escaped" (Acts 16:27). Sensing his just condemnation, the thief on the cross knew the fear of God (Luke 23:40). Christ struck complacent Paul to the ground. "And he trembling and astonished said, Lord, what wilt thou have me to do?" (Acts 9:6, KJV).

This is the fear of the Lord that is truly the beginning of knowledge and the beginning of wisdom (Prov. 1:7 and 9:10). We fear fear most of all. Fear is evil and unwanted. Yet the Psalmist exclaims, "The fear of the Lord is clean, enduring forever" (Ps. 19:9). He therefore exhorts, "Come, you children, listen to me; I will teach you the fear of the Lord" (Ps. 34:11). Moses instructed the children of Israel to teach the fear of the Lord.

> Assemble the people, the men and the women and children and the alien who is in your town, so that they may hear and learn and fear the Lord your God, and be careful to observe all

---

5. John Murray, *Collected Writings of John Murray, The Claims of Truth* (Carlisle, PA: Banner of Truth, 1976), 347-352.

the words of this law. Their children, who have not known, will hear and learn to fear the Lord your God, as long as you live on the land which you are about to cross the Jordan to possess (Deut. 31:12-13).

Fear is a strong motivator. As a result, Jonathan Edwards and other Puritan preachers were unashamed to view the natural fears of men and women, enhanced by the work of the Holy Spirit, the acts of God possibly preparing fallen hearts to receive the gospel. When God convicts men and women of their sins, they are awakened to their peril before God. John Gerstner describes such awakening and conviction.

> The first thing that happens to a person who is unconverted as we said when we began on Friday evening, we're born into this world dead on arrival, unconverted, quite incapable of converting ourselves—what brings us alive, usually, in the first instance, is what the Puritans use to call awakening. You have all heard of the Great Awakening, around 1740, roughly to about '42 or '43, the principle figure in which was George Whitefield. Jonathan Edwards was the central figure in New England but it was the British evangelist, George Whitefield who was especially blessed of God in actual conversion of individuals. Now when you hear about or read about the Great Awakening you have to realize that does not mean the Great Revival. What awakening means is this. The person who is in the pew and basically persuaded of Christianity but, nevertheless, not converted, and he is living in imminent danger so that if he falls over in his pew dead of a heart attack he goes immediately to hell. The first thing that happens to him, usually, if he is converted, is to be made aware of his peril. He knows it in a certain academic sense. It's preached from to the pulpit and at the same time it comes home to him emotionally. What was in his head, as a sort detached externalistic concept, suddenly is felt in the depth of his being. "Dear me, if I die now I would

go to hell. I'm under the wrath of God." He knew that. His pastor had told him faithfully all along that unless a person is converted he is going to perish. But suddenly he feels it; he is alarmed. He's scared. And indeed he ought to be.

Now that's the first step, usually, in a genuine conversion. I keep saying usually because God is sovereign. And while the process he normally follows is the process I'm briefly describing this evening, He sometimes snatches persons out of the kingdom of darkness into the kingdom of God's dear Son with the most minimal introduction to the rudiments of the gospel. That is not the way it usually happens but rather a person is, first of all, made aware in deep experience of the horror of his peril and the necessity of something happening quickly. He is alarmed is fundamentally what is meant by awakening. There's no love for Christ here, you understand. He just knows that Christ is not his Savior. Christ is going to be his judge. He is in great peril. He takes no comfort in the Name of Jesus. He's frightened by it because he doesn't come to Jesus as a Savior and he is aware that if Jesus isn't his Savior, Jesus is going to be his judge at the last day. So instead of being comforted by the precious Name of Jesus, every thought of which fills the Saint with joy, he is alarmed and awakened.[6]

Fear arising from the work of the Holy Spirit is a good thing. It is not evil or bad. In most circumstances, when a person is afraid, we put our arms around them and try to comfort them. "Everything will be all right," we say. Everything will not be all right. If this person is an unbeliever and is under conviction, we are guilty of quenching the work of the Spirit with our false consolation. We ought to tell men and women the root reason for their fear. We ought to pray the Holy Spirit will work true conviction in their hearts.

---

6. John H. Gerstner, *Reformed Evangelism* (Sterling, KS: The Sterling Pulpit, 1996), 3-4.

Jonathan Edwards and other Puritan preachers understood the benefits of this Spirit engendered fear.

> "Natural men cannot see anything of God's loveliness, his amiable and glorious grace, or any thing, which should attract their love; but they may see his terrible greatness to excite their terror ... A wicked man, while a wicked man, is capable of hearing the thunders, and seeing the devouring fire of Mt. Sinai; that is, he is capable to being made sensible of that terrible majesty and greatness of God, which was discovered at the giving of the law." In an early sermon on Heb. 9:12 [Edwards] informed Northampton: "The consideration of hell commonly is the first thing that rouses sleeping sinners. By this means their sins are set in order before them. And their conscience stares them in the face, and they begin to see their need of a priest and sacrifice" (cf. the sermon on Hos. 5:15). Most wicked men who have heard of hell have internal uneasiness (Prov. 29:25). On the other hand, a principal means of being lost is thinking there will be no punishment (Gen. 3:4).

> Many of Edwards' sermons illustrate his use of this doctrine in evangelistic preaching. The sermon on Jude 13, is an example. "The wicked in another world shall eternally be overwhelmed with the most dismal and perfect gloominess of mind." This theme is followed by a searching application after which the preacher has his people asking, What shall we do? His answer is, Be born again. The sermon on Matt. 23:33 on the rationality of eternal punishment follows the same procedure. In the application Edwards shows the necessity of the new birth. Unlike most modem evangelists, who would either let the matter rest once they had advised men to be born again or would assure them, in Arminian fashion, that they would be born again if they would believe, Edwards tells his hearers to repair to God if, peradventure, he may give them the gift of the new birth. This evangelist does not believe that faith is a potentiality of

corrupt natures. Until God gives the disposition to believe men remain unbelieving. There is, therefore, nothing that they can do to produce regeneration ...

On other occasions, Edwards does not proceed from the fear of hell to the topic of the new birth. Rather, he sometimes dilates on the necessity of fleeing the wrath that is to come. Of course there is only one successful end in fleeing and that is being born again. But in some sermons the preacher is intent merely on having his people flee. No doubt they understood what was involved in this fleeing and why they were advised to do it.[7]

Conviction by the Holy Spirit engendering fear is therefore salutary. It is God's preparation for salvation. I emphasize it is God's preparation. Many people malign the Puritans for their evangelistic doctrine. For many, the very word preparation smacks of Arminian theology. Beyond doubt, human beings do not prepare themselves to meet Christ. God prepares them. Conviction evidenced by a healthy fear of the consequences of sin is God's preparation. Thomas Hooker, a preparationist of the first order, defines preparation for us.

And in this great work of preparation, the Lord works these three things. First, he stops the soul from going any longer into sin. Secondly, he wearies the soul with the burden of sin. Thirdly, by hatred the soul is brought to go away from those carnal lusts and corruptions, with a secret dislike of those sins which he has been wearied withall.[8]

Many congregations regularly put this same theme on their lips in song with the familiar words of John Newton. The first two stanzas of his famous hymn, "Amazing Grace," read as follows.

---

7. John H. Gerstner, *Jonathan Edwards, Evangelist* (Morgan, PA: Soli Deo Gloria, 1995), 28-29.

8. Thomas Hooker, *The souls preparation for Christ, or A treatise of contrition wherein is discovered how God breaks the heart and wounds the soul in the conversion of a sinner to himself* (Ames, IA: International Outreach, 1994), 190.

Amazing grace-how sweet the sound
That saved a wretch like me!
I once was lost but now am found
Was blind, but now I see.

'Twas grace that taught my heart to fear,
And grace my fear I relieved;
How precious did that grace appear
The hour I first believed.[9]

By the grace of God, the wretched sinner learns to fear and then learns the remedy to this proper fear in Jesus Christ. While the fear may not be welcome, the sinner learns its importance and calls the grace of God precious. Newton's hymn lays the Puritan perspective before us. The genius of God's work of conviction is to impel men and women to seek His face.

---

9. Orthodox Presbyterian Church, *Trinity Hymnal* (Philadelphia: Great Commission Publications, 1961), 402, italics added.

12

CONVICTION: GOD'S MEANS TO PROMOTE SEEKING

O my God, make them like the whirling dust, like chaff before the wind. Like fire that burns the forest and like a flame that sets the mountains on fire, so pursue them with Your tempest and terrify them with Your storm. Fill their faces with dishonor, that they may seek Your name, O Lord. Let them be ashamed and dismayed forever, and let them be humiliated and perish, that they may know that You alone, whose name is the Lord, are the Most High over all the earth.
~ Ps. 83:13-18

1. INTRODUCTION

The genius of Gods work of conviction, engendering fear, is to impel men and women to seek His face. In the beginning, God created men and women for this purpose. Paul is quite clear on this point. J. A. Alexander concurs. Acts 17:26-27 is a "further statement of the end for which this one race was created and established on the earth."[1]

> He made from one man every nation of mankind to live on all the face of the earth, having determined their appointed times and the boundaries of their habitation, *that they would seek God, if perhaps they might grope for Him and find Him, though He is not far from each one of us* (italics added).

---

1. Alexander, *Acts of the Apostles*, 2:156.

Sin not only clouds the issue but disinclines sinners to follow any of God's commands or purposes. The standard criticism of the notion of seeking the Lord is the word of Paul in Romans 3:11 where he quotes Psalm 14, "There is none who understands, there is none who seeks for God." Beyond doubt, no one seeks for God without God taking the initiative. Sinners are disinclined to seek the God they despise or insist does not exist. God must act first. He acts in bringing conviction of sin upon fallen rebels. He engenders fear of the consequences of sin. Response to the Divine initiative is inevitable. Men and women either seek God or, as Felix, they seek to avoid God. In either case, we presuppose the Divine initiative.

Again, consider Psalm 83:15-16. David prays, "So pursue them with Your tempest, and terrify them with Your storm. Fill their faces with dishonor, *that they may seek Your name, O LORD*" (italics added). God engenders fear and shame to induce sinners to seek His face for salvation. From the Puritan perspective, conviction has the virtue of awakening men and women to their peril before God. Because fear is a powerful motivator, this fear may induce the sinner to take appropriate action. The inspired Word of God says the proper response of unbelievers to the convicting work of God is to seek His face. Matthew Henry makes the point well in commenting on Psalm 83.

> He [David] prays here that God, having filled their hearts with terror, would thereby fill their faces with shame, that they might be ashamed of their enmity to the people of God (Isa. 26:11), ashamed of their folly in acting both against Omnipotence itself and their own true interest. They did what they could to put God's people to shame, but the shame will at length return upon themselves. Now, 1. The beginning of this shame might be a means of their conversion: "Let them be broken and baffled in their attempts, *that they may seek thy name, O Lord!* Let them be put to a stand, that they may have both leisure and reason to pause a little, and consider who it is that they are fighting against and what an unequal match they are

for him, and may therefore humble and submit themselves and desire conditions of peace. Let them be made to fear thy name, and perhaps that will bring them to seek thy name."[2]

Spurgeon frequently speaks of seeking God in response to fear and raises the same subject in his exposition of the Psalms. For example, Psalm 107:4-9 reads,

> They wandered in the wilderness in a desert region; they did not find a way to an inhabited city. They were hungry and thirsty; their soul fainted within them. Then they cried out to the Lord in their trouble; He delivered them out of their distresses. He led them also by a straight way, to go to an inhabited city. Let them give thanks to the Lord for His lovingkindness, and for His wonders to the sons of men! For He has satisfied the thirsty soul, and the hungry soul He has filled with what is good.

Here are a few of Spurgeon's comments. Note that Spurgeon speaks of awakened sinners under distress of soul and their efforts after salvation. Their consciences are awakened. Thus they seek the Lord. This is a process issuing in divine results.

> 4. "They wandered in the wilderness." ... They were lost in the worst possible place, even as a sinner is lost in sin; they wandered up and down in vain searches and researches as a sinner does when awakened and sees his lost estate ... Men when under distress of soul find nothing to rest upon, no comfort and no peace; their efforts after [in search of] salvation are many, weary, and disappointing, and the dread solitude of their hearts fills them with dire distress.

> 5. *"Hungry and thirsty their soul fainted within them."* ... Such is the condition of an awakened conscience before it knows the Lord Jesus; it is full of unsatisfied cravings, painful needs and fears ...

---

2. Henry, *Commentary on the Whole Bible*, 3:556.

8. *"Oh that men would praise the LORD for His goodness."* ... [H]e puts forth his wisdom, power, and love to perform marvels on behalf of those who seek him ...

9. *"For he satisfieth the longing soul."* ... The spiritual sense is, however, the more rich in instruction. The Lord sets us longing and then completely satisfies us. That longing leads us into solitude, separation, thirst, faintness and self-despair, and all these conduct us to prayer, faith, divine guidance, satisfying of the soul's thirst, and rest: the good hand of the Lord is to be seen in the whole process and in the divine results.³

God sets men and women to a seeking of Him through His convicting work. Calvin reflects this in a typical prayer offered at the end of one of his expositions.

[L]et us prostrate ourselves before the face of our good God, acknowledging our innumerable sins, by which we continually provoke his heavy wrath, and indignation against us. Beseeching him that it would please him *to make us feel our sins and iniquities*, more than ever-to-fore we have done, *to the end that we might seek for such remedies* as he hath ordained for us *in exercising ourselves about the reading of his holy word, and the daily Preaching* thereof which he hath granted to us.⁴

Why does Calvin pray that we might feel our sins more than ever before? The answer is simple. Only then will we be constrained to seek the face of God for the remedy so much needed. And we will do so using the means of grace.

Paul quotes Psalm 32:1-2 to explain justification, right standing with God. In verses 3-5 David gives us his own experience in coming to right standing with God. It was through the excruciating pain of conviction.

---

3. Charles H. Spurgeon, *A Treasury of David* (Newark, DE: Cornerstone, n.d.), 2:115-117.
4. John Calvin, *Sermons on Psalm 119* (Audubon: NJ, Old Paths, 1996), 43, italics added.

> When I kept silent about my sin, my body wasted away
> Through my groaning all day long.
> For day and night Your hand was heavy upon me;
> My vitality was drained away as with the fever heat of summer. Selah.
> I acknowledged my sin to You, and my iniquity I did not hide;
> I said, "I will confess my transgressions to the Lord";
> And You forgave the guilt of my sin.

Calvin says, "If we are not drawn by forcible means, we will never hasten to seek reconciliation with God so earnestly as we ought."[5] Spurgeon comments on verse 3. "None knows the pangs of conviction but those who have endured them."[6] He then adds, "No doubt the case of David has led thousands to *seek the Lord* with hopeful courage who, without such an instance to cheer them, might have died in despair."[7] Conviction brings fear that promotes seeking.

2. CONVICTION: A HUMAN REACTION TO DIVINE INITIATIVE

What is this conviction of sin, which ought to set men and women to seeking God? We need to be clear as to the nature of this convicting work of the Holy Spirit.

> Convictions are human reactions to the working of the divine Spirit ... This work of the divine Spirit is an augmenting of the workings of men's own spirits or minds .... For though men have lost the moral image of God since the fall, ... they still have natural conscience ... The Spirit of God sets in to assist conscience.[8]

Dr. John H. Gerstner explains further,

> In the *Divine and Natural Light* sermon [by Jonathan Edwards]

---

5. John Calvin, *Commentary on the Book of Psalms* (Grand Rapids: Baker, 1979), 1:528, italics added.
6. Spurgeon, *A Treasury of David*, 1:91.
7. Ibid., 92, italics added.
8. John H. Gerstner, *The Rational Biblical Theology of Jonathan Edwards* (Orlando: Ligonier, 1993), 3:22-23.

we have an even clearer discussion of the difference between natural conscience and the Spirit of God in the work of convicting sinners.

> Conscience is a principle natural to men; and the work that it doth naturally, or of itself, is to give an apprehension of right and wrong, and suggest to the mind the relation that there is between right and wrong and a retribution. The Spirit of God, in those convictions, which unregenerate men sometimes have, assists conscience to do this work in a further degree than it would do if they were left to themselves. He helps it against those things that tend to stupefy it, and obstruct its exercise. But in the renewing and sanctifying work of the Holy Ghost, those things are wrought in the soul that are above nature, and of which there is nothing of the like kind in the soul by nature; and they are caused to exist in the soul habitually, and according to such a stated constitution or law that lays such a foundation for the exercises in a continued course, as is called a principle of nature. Not only are remaining principles assisted to do their work more freely and fully, but those principles are restored that were utterly destroyed by the fall; and the mind thenceforward habitually exerts those acts that the dominion of sin had made it as wholly destitute of as a dead body is of vital acts.

So we see that this work of convicting is basically a natural work. It is the effect of the conscience of man merely augmented by the work of the Holy Spirit. It is the work of the Spirit on the unchanged nature of fallen man; it is not a change within man. It differs in degree but not in kind from the unaided work of conscience. While Edwards makes this the beginning of the process that may lead to salvation, it is apparent that this, in itself, is not saving activity. Men are not able to be saved without this work, but they could have this work of the Spirit all their lives without ever being saved.[9]

In his discussion of effectual calling, A. A. Hodge discusses the common operations of the Spirit, lending credence to Gerstner and Edwards.

> Common grace preceding regeneration makes a superficial moral impression upon character and action but is generally resisted ... "Common grace" is the restraining and persuading influence of the Holy Spirit acting only through the truth revealed in the gospel, or through the natural light of reason and of conscience, heightening the natural moral effect of such truth upon the understanding, conscience, and heart. It involves no change of heart, but simply the enhancement of the natural powers of the truth, a restraint of the evil passions, and an increase of the natural emotions in view of sin, duty, and self-interest.
>
> That God does so operate upon the hearts of the unregenerate is proved, 1st from Scripture, Gen. vi. 3; Acts vii. 51; Heb. x. 29.[10]

3. CONVICTION: A HUMAN REACTION TO DIVINE INITIATIVE CAPABLE OF RESISTANCE

The texts adduced by Hodge indicate men and women may resist and quench the convicting work of the Holy Spirit. They may throw off or cover their fears. The angelic Stephen upbraided the Jewish council, "You men who are stiff-necked and uncircumcised in heart and ears are always resisting the Holy Spirit; you are doing just as your fathers did" (Acts 7:51). Hebrews 10:29 has similar import. "How much severer punishment do you think he will deserve who has trampled under foot the Son of God, and has regarded as unclean the blood of the covenant by which he was sanctified, and has insulted the Spirit of

---

9. Ibid., 23-24.
10. A. A. Hodge, *Outlines of Theology* (Grand Rapids: Zondervan, 1976), 448-449.

grace?" If conviction is a stirring of *natural abilities* by the Spirit and a heightening of the *natural ability* of the conscience, convictions may wane and be lost. Individuals may resist this particular work of the Spirit and quench the fire of conviction. Such was the case with Felix.

In Genesis 6:3 God warns, "My Spirit shall not strive with man forever, because he also is flesh; nevertheless his days shall be one hundred and twenty years." God's Spirit strives with men and women in the work of conviction as a first step in breaking down their hostility toward God. In Genesis 6, believers and unbelievers intermarry. Jack Scott identifies the intent behind these marriages. "The sin then is the intermarriage of God's children with Satan's children, the attempt to erase the enmity that God has established."[11] As is typical with fallen creatures, they move in the wrong direction, they oppose Gods commands. In conviction, God's Spirit strives to show sinners this is the case. Marriage with unbelievers is the wrong way to remove God introduced enmity. Sinners are obdurate. Matthew Henry therefore urges us to see

> God's resolution not always to strive with man by his Spirit. The Spirit then strove by Noah's preaching (1 Pt. 3:19, 20) and by inward checks, but it was in vain with the most of men; therefore, says God, He shall not always strive. Note,
>
> 1. The blessed Spirit strives with sinners, by the convictions and admonitions of conscience, to turn them from sin to God.
>
> 2. If the Spirit be resisted, quenched, and striven against, though he strive long, he will not strive always, Hos. 4:17.
>
> 3. Those are ripening apace for ruin whom the Spirit of grace has left off striving with.[12]

The word translated *strive* in Genesis 6:3 means *to abide, to min-*

---

11. Jack B. Scott, *God's Plan Unfolded* (Clinton, MS: Author, n.d.), 18.
12. Henry, *Commentary on the Whole Bible*, 1:51-52.

ister judgment, to plead the cause, to vindicate.[13] The Spirit pleads the cause of God. After a time, God will no longer abide with evil. He will judge and vindicate His great Name. Striving with evil men will cease. Keil and Delitzsch translate the verse, "My Spirit shall not rule in men forever."[14] The Jewish commentator, Maurice Simon, renders the text, "My spirit shall not abide in man for ever."[15] Calvin says,

> I interpret the words simply to mean, that the Lord, as if wearied by the obstinate perverseness of the world, denounces that vengeance as present, which had hitherto been deferred. For as long as the Lord suspends judgment, he, in a certain sense, strives with men, especially either by threats, or by examples of gentle chastisement, he invites them to repentance. In this way he had striven already, some centuries, with the world, which, nevertheless was becoming worse. And now, as if wearied out, he declares that he has no mind to contend any longer.[16]

4. CONCLUSION

We therefore have the Biblical position that the striving of the Spirit in conviction, in raising the natural abilities of conscience and heightening the sinner's sense of danger because of sin, may be resisted and quenched. "It is the work of the Spirit on the unchanged nature of fallen man; it is not a change within the man."[17]

We therefore make three important observations. *First*, convictions and awakenings are works of the grace of God common to the lot of fallen humanity. They are works of grace sovereignly dispensed by God as he wills (John 3:8). *Second*, those experiencing such convic-

---

13. Francis Brown, S. R. Driver, Charles A. Briggs, *A Hebrew and English Lexicon of the Old Testament* (New York: Oxford University Press, 1962), 192.
14. C. F. Keil and F. Delitzsch, *Commentary on the Old Testament, The Pentateuch*, trans. James Martin (Grand Rapids: Eerdmans, 1981), 1: 134.
15. Maurice Simon, *The Soncino Chumash*, ed. A. Cohen (Jerusalem: Soncino, 1993), 25.
16. John Calvin, *Commentaries on the First Book of Moses*, trans. John King (Grand Rapids: Baker, 1979), 1:241.
17. Gerstner, *Jonathan Edwards, Evangelist*, 42.

tions and awakenings are not necessarily regenerate.[18] Again, Felix is a prime example. Two other examples are Pharaoh and King Saul. After the plague of hail devastated Egypt, "Pharaoh sent for Moses and Aaron, and said to them, 'I have sinned this time; the Lord is the righteous one, and I and my people are the wicked ones'" (Exod. 9:27). And after the subsequent plague of locust, Exodus 10:16 explains, "Pharaoh hurriedly called for Moses and Aaron, and he said, 'I have sinned against the Lord your God and against you. Now therefore, please forgive my sin only this once, and make supplication to the Lord your God, that He would only remove this death from me.'"

The plagues were designed to engender great fear in the heart of Pharaoh. Moses is straightforward with Pharaoh. "But as for you and your servants, I know that you do not yet fear the Lord God" (Exod. 9:30). There may have been temporary temporal fear but there was certainly no real reverence for God within the heart of Pharaoh.

The same was true for King Saul. After failing to destroy the Amalikites and being severely upbraided by Samuel, Saul confesses, "I have sinned" (1 Sam. 15:24, 30). Saul genuinely fears the loss of the kingdom. Later, on two occasions, while Saul is seeking to kill David and David spares his life, Saul is convicted and constrained to confess his sin. We find the first incident, quoted below, in 1 Samuel 24:8-17. The second is in 1 Samuel 26:17-21.

> Now afterward David arose and went out of the cave and called after Saul, saying, "My lord the king!" And when Saul looked behind him, David bowed with his face to the ground and prostrated himself. David said to Saul, "Why do you listen to the words of men, saying, 'Behold, David seeks to harm you'? Behold, this day your eyes have seen that the Lord had given you today into my hand in the cave, and some said to kill you, but my eye had pity on you; and I said, 'I will not stretch out my hand against my lord, for he is the Lord's anointed.'

---

18. Appendix C diagrams an extended order of salvation and shows the place of conviction in God's work of bringing sinners to Himself.

> Now, my father, see! Indeed, see the edge of your robe in my hand! For in that I cut off the edge of your robe and did not kill you, know and perceive that there is no evil or rebellion in my hands, and I have not sinned against you, though you are lying in wait for my life to take it. May the Lord judge between you and me, and may the Lord avenge me on you; but my hand shall not be against you. As the proverb of the ancients says, 'Out of the wicked comes forth wickedness'; but my hand shall not be against you. After whom has the king of Israel come out? Whom are you pursuing? A dead dog, a single flea? The Lord therefore be judge and decide between you and me; and may He see and plead my cause and deliver me from your hand." When David had finished speaking these words to Saul, Saul said, "Is this your voice, my son David?" Then Saul lifted up his voice and wept. He said to David, "You are more righteous than I; for you have dealt well with me, while I have dealt wickedly with you."

Third, while conviction of sin is a work of grace common to the unregenerate, it is indispensable to conversion and is the first step in the work of God in bringing lost sinners to Himself. Conviction, awakening, is the first step in God's work in breaking down hostility toward Himself. Although conviction in itself is not a sign of regeneration, when God effectually calls men and women to himself, conviction of sin is part of the process, the first part of the process. Understanding the nature of conviction of sin and the awakening of the conscience is indispensible to the work of evangelism.

We have a vital point of contact with unbelievers, their suppressed knowledge of God as Creator, Lawgiver, and Judge, and their consciences (Rom. 1:18-20, 2:14-15). We know the work of the Holy Spirit to convict "concerning sin and righteousness and judgment" (John 16:8). We know our responsibility to define sin as violation of the Ten Commandments (1 John 3:4). We must declare the penalty for sin is death (Ezek. 18:4, 20; Rom. 6:23). We must lovingly show men and women that Christ died to pay the penalty for sin (1 Pet. 2:24), that He was raised from the dead (1 Cor. 15:3-4), and that they need to be born again by the power of resurrection life (John 3:3; 1 Pet. 1:3). We must urge men and women to turn from their sin in repentance and turn to God through faith in Jesus Christ (John 3:16, 14:6; Acts 3:19, 16:31, 20:28) in order to receive God's gift of eternal life (John 17:3; Rom. 6:23). We must lay out the necessity to confess Christ as Lord (Rom. 10:9).

We must pray for the work of the Spirit in our lives and in the lives of those to whom we speak to bring conviction, regeneration, repentance, and faith (1 John 5:14). We must realize that God's work is changing lives (Acts 16:14), that God is sovereign (Rom. 9:18), and that He works as He wills (John 3:8). We must remember that the faith in Christ of true converts does "not rest on the wisdom of men, but on the power of God" (1 Cor. 2:5). Therefore, we must be wise and not resist the work of the Spirit thinking that conviction of sin is a necessary indication of regeneration (Acts 24:25). We also must not interpose some form of decision that awakened sinners are not necessarily prepared to make (1 Cor. 1:20-21). We must trust God to do and complete the work He does so well (Prov. 3:5, Phil. 1:6).

Appendix A: Tract

YOU CANNOT ESCAPE FROM GOD

Permission is granted by the author to reproduce hard copy of "You Cannot Escape from God" as it appears in this appendix.

A. You were created by God and you are therefore responsible to Him.

"And God created man in His own image, in the image of God He created him; male and female He created them" (Genesis 1:27).

"Since the creation of the world His invisible attributes, His eternal power and divine nature, have been clearly seen, being understood through what has been made, so that they are without excuse" (Romans 1:20).

B. You often break God's law and you are a sinner.

"*Sin is the transgression of the law*" (1 John 3:4, KJV).

"*To one who knows the right thing to do, and does not do it, to him it is sin*" (James 4:17).

"*There is no difference: for all have sinned, and come short of the glory of God*" (Romans 3:22-23, KJV).

C. You will be judged and you face eternal punishment for your sin.

"It is appointed for men to die once, and after this comes judgment" (Hebrews 9:27).

"Depart from me, accursed ones, in to the eternal fire which has been prepared for the devil and his angels" (Matthew 25:41).

The alternative...

A. Forgiveness of sin and freedom from guilt are obtained through repentance of sin and faith in the Lord Jesus Christ.

"While we were still helpless, at the right time Christ died for the ungodly" (Romans 5:6).

"Repent therefore and return, that your sins may be wiped away" (Acts 3:19).

"Believe in the Lord Jesus, and you shall be saved" (Acts 16:31)

B. The gift of eternal life and access to heaven are obtained through faith in the Lord Jesus Christ.

"The gift of God is eternal life through Jesus Christ our Lord" (Romans 6:23, KJV).

"And this is eternal life, that they may know Thee the only true God, and Jesus Christ whom Thou hast sent" (John 17:3).

"Come, you who are blessed of My Father, inherit the kingdom prepared for you from the foundation of the world" (Matthew 25:34)

C. The Lord Jesus Christ Freely offers Himself to you saying:

"Come to Me, all who are weary and heavy-laden, and I will give you rest" (Matthew 11:28).

"The one who comes to Me I will certainly not cast out" (John 6:37).

"If you confess with your mouth Jesus as Lord, and believe in your heart that God raised Him from the dead, you shall be saved" (Romans 10:9)

A PRAYER
For Those Sincerely Desiring to Come to Christ

Dear God, I see that you are my creator and that I have sinned against you. I have broken your law and I am a sinner. I repent of my sin. Please forgive me. I believe that Christ died on the cross to pay the penalty for my sins. I trust in Christ alone as my savior from sin. I confess Christ as my Lord. Give me strength to lead a new life for Him. In his name I pray, Amen.

This tract was prepared to help you both understand the Gospel and present it to others. For more help or other copies of this tract write: Dennis Prutow, Evangelist, Westminster Evangelistic Ministries, P.O. Box 303, Sterling, Kansas 67579. Scripture quotations are from the New American Standard Bible, © The Lockman Foundation, 1960, 1962, 1963, 1968, 1971, 1972, 1973, 1975, 1977.

COPYRIGHT 1982 by Dennis J. Prutow

APPENDIX B 241

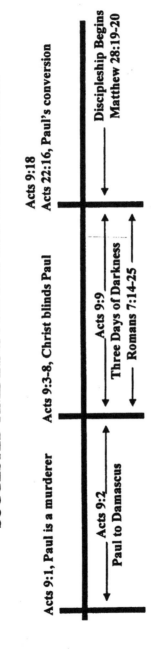

GOD'S MEANS OF DRAWING SINNERS TO HIMSE[LF]

I. We must preach and teach: (1) Depravity (2) The Law (3) The Gospel

II. We must exhort awakened sinners to, "Seek the Lord while He may be found" ([)

———————————————— WSC Q&[A]

III. We must trust God's use of means to produce each of the following:

Common Operations of the Spirit, WCF 10:4

	Hostility Genesis 3:15	Conviction of Sin	Illumination
Paul's Experience	Acts 9:1	Acts 9:9 Romans 7:9	Romans 7:22
	Only Removed By God Ephesians 2:14-15	John 16:8 Genesis 6:3 Psalm 83:13-16 Eph 5:11 Romans 7:9 Luke 23:39-43 1 Sam 26:21[1] Acts 24:24-25[1]	2 Cor 4:6 Romans 7:22 Hebrews 6:4[2] Matt 13:20-21[2]

[1] An Example of conviction without regeneration or conversion.
[2] An Example of illumination without regeneration or conversion.
[3] An example of only apparent regeneration. Compare 1 Corinthians 13:1-3.

APPENDIX C   243

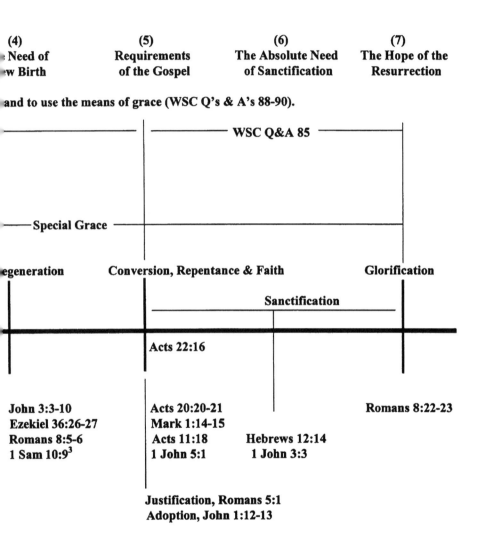

(4)	(5)	(6)	(7)
Need of w Birth	Requirements of the Gospel	The Absolute Need of Sanctification	The Hope of the Resurrection

and to use the means of grace (WSC Q's & A's 88-90).

WSC Q&A 85

——— Special Grace ———

egeneration   Conversion, Repentance & Faith   Glorification

Sanctification

Acts 22:16

John 3:3-10	Acts 20:20-21		Romans 8:22-23
Ezekiel 36:26-27	Mark 1:14-15		
Romans 8:5-6	Acts 11:18	Hebrews 12:14	
1 Sam 10:9[3]	1 John 5:1	1 John 3:3	

Justification, Romans 5:1
Adoption, John 1:12-13

BIBLIOGRAPHY

Adams, Jay E. *Trust and Obey*. Phillipsburg: Presbyterian and Reformed, 1978.

Alexander, Joseph Addison. *Acts of the Apostles*. Carlisle: Banner of Truth, 1980.

Bavink, Herman. *The Doctrine of God*. Translated by William Hendricksen. Edinburg: Banner of Truth, 1977.

Brown, Francis, S. R. Driver, Charles A. Briggs. *A Hebrew and English Lexicon of the Old Testament*. New York: Oxford University Press, 1962.

Calvin, John. *Commentaries on the First Book of Moses*. Translated by John King. Grand Rapids: Baker, 1979.

_____. *Commentary on the Book of Psalms*. Translated by William Pringle. Grand Rapids: Baker, 1979.

_____. *Institutes of the Christian Religion*. Translated by Ford Lewis Battles. Edited by John T. McNeill. Philadelphia: Westminster Press, 1960.

_____. *Sermons on Psalm 119*. Audubon: NJ, Old Paths, 1996.

Colson, Charles. *Kingdoms in Conflict*. Grand Rapids, MI: Zondervan, 1987.

Elwell, Walter A. *Evangelical Dictionary of Theology*. Grand Rapids: Baker, 1984.

Frame, John M. *Apologetics to the Glory of God*. Phillipsburg, NJ: P & R, 1994.

Gerstner, John H. *Jonathan Edwards, Evangelist*. Morgan, PA: Soli Deo Gloria, 1995.

_____. *Reformed Evangelism*. Sterling, KS: The Sterling Pulpit, 1996.

_____. *The Rational Biblical Theology of Jonathan Edwards*. Orlando: Ligonier, 1993.

Hendriksen, William. *Exposition of the Gospel According to John*. Grand Rapids: Baker, 1972.

_____. *Exposition of the Gospel According to Matthew*. Grand Rapids: Baker, 1973.

Henry, Matthew. *Matthew Henry's Commentary on the Whole Bible*. Grand Rapids: Fleming H. Revell, 1985

Hodge, Archibald A. *Outlines of Theology*. Grand Rapids: Zondervan, 1976.

Hooker, Thomas. *The Soul's Preparation for Christ or A Treatise on Contrition wherein is discovered how God breaks the heart, and wounds the Soul, in the conversion of a Sinner to Himself*. Ames, IA: International Outreach, 1994.

Keil, C. F. and F. Delitzsch. *Commentary on the Old Testament, The Pentateuch*. Translated by James Martin. Grand Rapids: Eerdmans, 1981.

Kittel, Gerhard, Editor. *Theological Dictionary of the New Testament*. Translated by Geoffrey W. Bromiley. Grand Rapids: Eerdmans, 1966.

Kuyper, Abraham. *Sacred Theology*. Wilmington: Associated Publishers and Authors, n.d.

Martin, Hugh. *A Commentary on Jonah*. Carlisle, PA: Banner of Truth, 1978.

Moo, Douglas J. *The Epistle to the Romans*. Grand Rapids: Eerdmans, 1996.

Morris, Leon. *The Gospel According to John*. Grand Rapids: Eerdmans, 1973.

Murray, John. *Collected Writings of John Murray, The Claims of Truth*. Carlisle, PA: Banner of Truth, 1976.

_____. *The Epistle to the Romans*. Grand Rapids: Eerdmans, 1965.

Orthodox Presbyterian Church. *Trinity Hymnal*. Philadelphia: Committee on Christian Education, 1961.

Robertson, A. T. *Word Pictures of the New Testament*. Nashville: Broadman, 1964.

Simon, Maurice. *The Soncino Chumash*. Translated by A. Cohen. Jerusalem: Soncino, 1993.

Scott, Jack B. *God's Plan Unfolded*. Clinton, MS: Author, n.d.

Spurgeon, Charles H. *A Treasury of David*. Newark, DE: Cornerstone, n.d.

Van Til, Cornelius. *Apologetics*. Philadelphia: Westminster Theological Seminary, n.d.

_____. *The Defense of the Faith*. Philadelphia: Presbyterian and Reformed, 1972.

Whitefield, George. *George Whitefield's Sermons*, Volume I. New Ipswitch, NH: Pietan Publications, 1991.

Index of Persons

Aaron, brother of Moses 230
Adam, first man 22, 69-70, 206-208, 209
Agrippa, king 164-165
Ananias 191-193
Andrew, the disciple 105
Apostles of Jesus 110-113
Artists 17
Barnabas, companion of Paul 18-19, 116-117
Bavinck, Herman 4-5
Blackburne, Gladys 84-85
Blind man 107-108
Calvin, John 4, 224, 229
Colson, Charles 84
Daniel 143-144
David, king 222-225, 230-231
Disciples of Jesus 108-110
Dispensationalists xi
Edwards, Jonathan 177, 216, 218-219, 225-226
Ethiopian eunuch 86
Eve 22
Felix, governor of Judah 26-27, 201-206, 228, 230
Gerstner, John 216-217, 225-227
Hebrews, writer of the Epistle to the 29-30
Henry, Matthew 199-200, 202, 206-208, 209, 222-223, 228-229
Hodge, A. A. 227
Hooker, Thomas 219
Jeff, the atheist 123-124
Jesus Christ 48-50, 70, 167-170, 237, 238, 239
    Active obedience 67-68
    Death 48
    Example 104-108
    Lorship 145-146
    Resurrection 37, 152
    Righteousness 71
    Second coming 29-30
John, the Baptist 52-53, 54
Jonah, the prophet 210-213
Keil and Delitzsch 229
Luther, Martin 121
Lydia, of Thyatira 62-63, 86-87
Martin, Hugh 211-213
Matthew (Levi), the disciple 81, 106
McCurry, Chips 84-85
Mormon missionaries 166
Moses 215-216, 230
Moses, parents of 142
Mother-in-law of Peter, the apostle 106
Murray, John 118
Newton, John 195, 219-220
Paul, the apostle ....
    4, 7, 13, 18-19, 31-32, 34-37, 87-88, 116-124, 153-155, 164-169, 185-195, 201-206, 241, 242-243
Peter, the apostle .... xiii, 44, 53, 54, 55, 105, 137-142, 144
Pharisees 52-53, 187
Pharoah of Egypt 230
Philip, the deacon 86
Philippine jailor 87-88
Puritans 216, 218-219, 222
Referees 173-175
Sadducees 52-53
Saul, king 230-231
Shadrach, Meschach, and Abednego 142-143
Silas, the evangelist 87-88
Simon, Maurice 229

Spurgeon, Charles Haddon.......... 99, 223-224
Stephen, the deacon...................... 227
Stillborn believers 97
Synagogue official......................... 107
Thessalonians 56
Van Til, Cornelius................... 4, 5, 6-7

Whitefield, George......................... 99, 193-194, 216
Woman at the well 82
Woman with the hemorhage of blood 107
Zaccheus, the inquirer.............. 82-83
Zimmer, Norma............................ 162

Index of Scripture Verses

Genesis
1:27 .... 6, 234
2:15-16 69
2:25 206
3:4 218
3:9 206
3:10 .... 206, 215
3:11 206
3:15 242
3:22 208
4:6 157
6:3 .... 227, 228 (2x), 242

Exodus
9:27 230
9:30 230
10:16 230
20:8 25
20:14 24
27:27 210

Leviticus
18:5 .... 68 (2x), 69 (4x), 70

Deuteronomy
31:12-13 215-216

1 Samuel
10:9 243
15:24 230
15:30 230
24:8-17 230-231
26:17-21 230-231
26:21 242

2 Chronicles
7:14 215
14:2-4 .... 178, 179

Psalms
14 178
19:9 215
24:3 71
24:4 71
32:1-2 224
32:3-5 224
34:11 215
45 190
45:3-5 188-189
51:17 200
83 222-223
83:13-16 .... 179, 242
83:13-18 .... 209-210, 221
83:15-16 .... 209, 222
83:16 .... 208, 209
107:4-9 223
110:1-3 190
110:2-3 199

Proverbs
1:7 215
3:5 232
9:10 215
15:1 157
29:25 218

Ecclesiastes
12:13 39

Isaiah
8:12-13 146
8:12-14 146
8:13 158
8:19 211
26:9 214
26:11 222
42:8 158

53 .... 86 (2x)
55:6 .... 177 (2x), 181, 183, 242-243
55:11 27

Jeremiah
20:1-4 204
20:3-4 204
31:31-33 121
31:33 23

Ezekiel
18:4 .... 67, 231
18:20 231
36:26-27 243

Daniel
3:13-18 143
6:1-5 143-144

Hosea
4:17 228
5:15 218
6:7 69

Joel
2:13 200
3:14 130

Jonah
1:4-5 210-211
1:5 210

Habakkuk
2:4 68

MalachI
2:14 74

Matthew
1:21 67
3:1-2 .... 54, 163
3:7-8 52
4:12-13 105
4:17 163
4:18-19 105
4:23 104
5:10-12 139
5:23-24 48-49

6:5 .... 92, 94
6:5-6 89
6:6 92
6:7 92
6:23 189
6:33 214
7:7 182
7:21-23 71
7:22-23 145
8:5-7 106
8:14-15 106
9 106-107
9:1 106
9:9 .... 81, 106, 108
9:10 106
9:18-19 107
9:20-22 107
9:23-26 107
9:25 .... 103, 104 (2x)
9:27 .... 107 (2x)
9:28-29 108
9:35 .... 129, 132
9:35-36 xiii
9:35-38 104
9:36 .... 9, 129, 130
9:36-37 .... 130, 137
9:38 130
10 108
10:1 108
10:5 108
10:7 109
10:11-14 108-109
10:12 109
10:14 109
11:15 63
11:28 .... 8, 43, 45, 99, 181-182, 239
13:20-21 242
13:36-43 130
15:8 145
18:15 .... 197, 198
23:33 218
25:31-33 133
25:34 .... 71, 72, 77, 238
25:41 .... 6, 67, 236
25:43 8
26:28 75
26:69-70 140
26:71-72 140

Index of Scripture Verses

26:73-74 141
26:73-75 142
27:46 49
28:19-20 .... 88, 241

Mark
1:4 .... 54 (2x)
1:14 56-57
1:14-15 ..... 54, 163, 243
1:15 56
1:17 79

Luke
5:29 106
11:13 93
13:24 180
19:1-10 82
19:5 83
19:6 83
19:9 83
23:39-43 242
23:40 215

John
1:12-13 ...... 59, 62, 243
2:41 95
2:42 95
3:3-10 243
3:3 232
3:8 .... 87, 229, 232
3:16 .... 153, 232
4:1-2 88
4:1-42 82
4:25 82
4:26 82
4:28-29 82
4:39 82
6:37 239
6:44 .... 56, 62
8:44 133
10:24-25 133
10:27 133-134
14:1 141
14:6 .... 72, 232
14:27 141
16:8 .... 25, 29, 30, 57 (2x), 91, 182, 197 (2x), 201, 231, 242
17:3 .... 8, 73, 76, 77, 232, 238

Acts
1:18-21 116
1:19 122
2:14-15 .... 122, 148
2:23 48
2:37 .... 197, 199 (2x)
2:37-38 .... 53, 163
2:40 44
3:15 162
3:19 .... 7, 47, 51, 54 (2x), 65, 163, 232, 237
5:28-29 144
5:42 .... 110, 115
6:23 238
7:22 242
7:51 .... 227 (2x)
7:54 199
8:1 112
8:4 112
8:35-36 86
9:1 .... 241, 242
9:1-2 187
9:1-19 185-186
9:2 241
9:3-8 .... 187-188, 241
9:4 188
9:5 .... 188 (2x)
9:6 .... 188, 205, 215
9:9 .... 241, 242
9:10-19 191-192
9:13-14 192
9:15 192
9:18 241
10:9 239
11:18 .... 55, 242
11:19 .... 55, 112
11:20-21 112-113
14:8-18 18-19
14:12-13 116
14:14 19
14:14-15 116
14:15 119
14:17 .... 19, 124
16:14 .... 93, 232
16:14-15 .... 62, 86
16:27 215
16:28-33 87-88
16:29 205

16:30	63
16:31	7, 56, 62, 63, 65, 232, 237
17:2	87
17:22	31-34
17:24-28	178-179
17:26-27	221
17:28	173
17:32	37
18:5	87
20:18-21	111
20:20-21	51, 163-164, 243
20:21	53, 56
20:28	232
20:31	111
22:3	187
22:9	188
22:13	193
22:14-15	192
22:16	192, 241
24:10	154
24:10-15	153
24:15	162
24:24-25	242
24:25	31, 215, 232
25:24-25	201, 202
25:25	204
26	170
26:1	164
26:1-8	154
26:1-18	164
26:2-3	165
26:4-5	165
26:6	169
26:6-7	154
26:6-8	169
26:8	154
26:9-11	166, 187, 189
26:12	167
26:12-18	167
26:13-15	167-168
26:8	169
26:16-18	168
26:19-20	164
28:23	57

Romans

1	118, 124
1:16	50, 94
1:18	17, 23, 123
1:18-19	4, 15
1:18-20	231
1:20	6, 15, 234
1:21-25	44
1:22-25	116
1:25	73, 115
1:28	213
2	118, 124
2:14	23
2:14-15	4, 21, 119, 124, 231
2:15	23, 121
3:11	178, 222
3:19-20	199
3:22-23	6, 235
3:23	69
5:1	243
5:1-5	58
5:2	13
5:5	58, 75
5:6	7, 47, 48, 50, 65, 167, 237
5:8	75, 167
5:8-10	50
5:12	69
5:18	69
5:19	90
6:1-2	55
6:6	44, 55
6:21	208, 209
6:22-23	231, 232
6:25	8, 67 (2x), 72 (2x), 77
7	194
7:7	27, 191
7:9	187, 189, 190, 191 (2x), 200, 201, 242 (2x)
7:12	26
7:13-14	26
7:14-15	194 (5x), 195
7:14-25	241
7:22	242
8:1-2	194
8:5-6	243
8:7	120-121
8:7-8	55
8:18	58
8:21	58
8:22-23	243
9:8	232

9:22-24 90
10:9 .... 8, 146, 193, 232
10:13 193
11:5 90
12:1-2 162
14:17 215

1 Corinthians
1:20-21 232
2:5 232
9:27 27
12:3 8
15:1-4 152-153
15:3-4 232
15:45 69
15:55 162

2 Corinthians
4:6 242
5:11 58
5:20 48
5:21 71
7:9-10 52
13:5 155

Galatians
2:2 83
2:20 .... 75, 181
3:10-14 68
4:4 .... 48, 70
4:4-5 70
4:8-9 73
5:23 157

Ephesians
1 64
1:1-21 155
1:13-14 75
1:14 .... 59, 162
2:1 44
2:4-5 93
2:8 61
2:8-9 157
2:12 156-157
2:14-15 242
5:6 203
5:7-13 198
5:11 .... 197, 242

5:32 74-75

Philippians
1:6 232
4:3-6 201
4:13 113

Colossians
1:13 45
1:19-20 50
1:27 155

1 Thessalonians
1:9 53-54

2 Thessalonians
1:9 49

1 Timothy
1:17 215
5:20 197

2 Timothy
1:12 172
4:2 197

Titus
1:9 197
1:13 197
2:12 203
2:15 197

Hebrews
4:12 53
4:15 .... 48, 68, 70
6:4 242
6:16 33
7:26 70
8:10 23
9:12 218
9:27 .... 6, 29, 123, 236
9:27-28 67
10:7 67
10:29 .... 227 (2x)
11:1 .... 57 (2x), 58, 59
11:23 142
11:27 142
12:14 243

James
2:19 181
4:1 214
4:17 .... 6, 235

1 Peter
1:3 .... 61, 87, 155
1:3-5 152
1:8-9 57
1:13 .... 152, 232
1:23 168
1:23-25 168
2:24 232
3:4 157
3:13 .... 137, 139, 144, 164
3:14 .... 27-28, 138, 139, 141
3:14-15 .... xiv, 137, 144, 145, 148, 149, 159, 161
3:14-16 137
3:15 .... xiv, 149, 150 (2x), 152, 154, 155, 159
3:15-16 161
3:19-20 228

2 Peter
1:20-21 60

1 John
1:6 55
3:3 243
3:4 .... 6, 24, 231, 235
4:7 .... 61 (2x)
4:10 49
5:1 .... 61, 243
5:14 232
5:14-15 90

Jude
13 218
15 197

Revelation
3:19 197
6:2 199
13:8 48

INDEX OF SUBJECTS

Absolutes 174-176
Active obedience of Jesus Christ 67-68
Adultery 24
Always ready 156-157
Amazing Grace (hymn) 219-220
Antioch 113
Arminianism 218, 219
Army 171, 172, 182
Assurance of faith 182
Athens 34-37
Bad news 6-7
Baptism 88, 95
Basketball 173-176
Bible 60, 168
Bible club xii
Bible knowledge 150-151
Blindness, spiritual 187-188
Born again 59-60, 61
Boy Scouts 166
Capernaum 105-108, 111
Cities and towns 103-113
Common grace 227, 229, 231, 242
Conscience 23-24, 122-125
Conversion 44-45, 55, 185-195
"Convict" (verb) 197
Conviction of sin 197-208, 209-220, 221-232
Conviction of truth 57-58
Creation 118-119, 210-211, 234
Creator 34-35, 116-119, 124-125, 234
Darkness, Spiritual 189-191
Day of judgment 74, 75-76
Discontent 27
Distressed people 130-131
Door-to-door calling ..... xiii, 115, 148
Downcast people 131

Election of grace 90-91
Ephesus 111-112
Eternal life 73-76, 238
Evangelistic campaign 97-98
Evangelistic tract .... xii-xiii, 233-240
Faith 51, 56-61, 68-69, 72-73, 237, 238
Faith and works 68
Fear in evangelism .... xiii-xiv, 137-148, 157-158
Fear of God 209-220
Forgiveness of sin 54-56, 237
Four Spiritual Laws 180
Fourth Commandment 25
Free offer 239
Gentiles 90
Gentleness 157-158
God 15-18, 22, 56, 209-220
God-centered 162
Good news 7-9, 65
Grace of God 56
Great Awakening 177, 216-217
Great Commission 88
Harvest 130-135
Healing 106
Heaven 238
Helpless unbelievers 47-48
Holy Spirit 9, 25, 30, 31, 59, 62, 75, 93, 178, 198, 242
Hope 58-59, 149-159, 163-164
House-to-house calling 103-113, 115, 148
Idolatry 36
Image of God 22
Jerusalem 110
Jews 90
Joy 163

Judge 175-176
Judgment 27, 29-30,
  36, 49, 74, 91-92, 236
Justice 175-176
Justification 71-72
Kingdom of God 214-215
Knowledge of God 4-5,
  15-19, 50, 116-125, 231-232
Known by God 74-76
Law of God 21-28, 119-122, 235
Limited atonement 180-181
Lord's Supper 75
Lordship of Christ 145-146
Lying 140, 142
Lystra 18-19
Man as responsible to God 17-20
Man-centered 162
Marketing 79-89
Marriage 74-75
Mars Hill 178-179
Maze Prison (Northern Ireland) ......
  84-85
Means of grace 242-243
Mercy 45
Messiah 190-191
Moral law 26
Morality 175-176
Natural man 5
Neighbors 3
New birth 61
Ordo salutis 61
Panic 214-215
Pentecost 53
Persecution 112, 138
Perseverance of the saints 182
Philosophers 34-37
Point of contact 4-7, 24-25,
  115-119
Polytheism 210-213
Prayer 89-95, 240
Preaching 242
Preparation for conversion ....
  218-219
Preparation for evangelism ....
  150-159
Prepared responses 151
Propitiation 49
Providence of God 209-220

Public confession 95
Punishment, Eternal 236
Receiving Christ 58-60
Reconcilation 48-56
Reformed Presbyterian Theological
  Seminary xi
Regeneration 60, 181, 218-219
Repentance 52-56,
  181-182, 214, 237
Resurrection of Jesus Christ ....
  37, 152
Righteousness 71-72, 91
Rules 173-176
Sailors 210-213
Salesmanship 62
Salvation 43-45
Sanctification of Christ as Lord ....
  144-148
Sangre de Christo Seminary xi
Second Commandment 36
Second Coming of Christ 29-30
Seed of religion 4
Seeking evangelism 177, 242-243
Self-control 26-27
Sheep without a shepherd ....
  131-132, 134-135
Sin 52, 73, 116-124, 179,
  198-208, 214-220, 221-232, 235
Slaves to sin 73
Sorrow for sin 52
Sovereignty of God 63-65
Storms at sea 210-213
Substitutionary atonement 48
Suffering 137-148
"Talking with a Stranger"
  (Conversation) 125-127
Teaching 242
Ten Commandments 24, 120-122
Tenth Commandment 27
Testimony, Personal 162-172
Thieves 22
Tracts 134-135
Trembling 203-204
Troubled mind in witnessing ....
  141-144
Two minute defense 164-170
Unconditional election 180
Vacation Bible school 96-97

Index of Subjects

Vacuum clearner 80, 96
War 214-215
West Point Military Academy 171
Westminster Confession of Faith .. xi
   Section 10.4 242
Westminster Larger Catechism xi
Westminster Shorter Catechism ... xi
   Question 1 162
   Question 14 198
   Question 31 242

Question 33 71-72
Question 38 163
Question 77 140
Question 85 243
Questions 88-90 243
Question 100 89
World War Two 214-215
You Cannot Escape from God (tract)
   xii-xiii, 3, 7, 13, 14, 233-240